CHRISTIAN THOUGHT
TO THE REFORMATION

BY

HERBERT B. WORKMAN, M.A., D.LITT.

AUTHOR OF
'PERSECUTION IN THE EARLY CHURCH'; 'THE DAWN
OF THE REFORMATION'; 'THE LETTERS
OF JOHN HUS,' ETC.

DUCKWORTH
3 HENRIETTA STREET, LONDON, W.C.

First Published . . . 1911
Second Impression. . . 1935
Third Impression . . . 1947

PRINTED IN GREAT BRITAIN BY
THOMAS NELSON AND SONS LTD
PARKSIDE WORKS EDINBURGH

PREFACE

THE limits of the present volume have been fixed in accordance with the general plan of the series. The writer therefore is not responsible for the effort to compress so vast a field into so small a compass. The difficulties of the task have proved almost insuperable. On the one side was the danger of so emphasising detail as to make the book a pocket dictionary of names and opinions; on the other hand, generalisation without considerable foundation of fact is valueless when not dangerous. The writer has sought the mean—with what success it must be for his critics to judge. Passing by much that is of the highest importance, he has attempted to point out the main movements of Christian Thought from the close of the Apostolic Age to the dawn of the Reformation. For the detailed contents of such thought search must be made in the many familiar handbooks of theology or philosophy; here the writer's object has been to draw attention to the changes and developments due to the action and reaction upon theology, not only of the current philosophy and science, but also to some extent of the general environment, the influence of which is oftentimes unduly neglected.

The writer believes firmly in the evolutionary standpoint as alone explanatory of the history of the Christian Church as the expression of the will of the Holy Spirit. He admits, therefore, the principle of development as not only an historic fact, but as part of the work of God. True Christianity is not to be found by going back to some ill-defined period of antiquity, the beliefs and practices of which it is now almost impossible to reconstruct, but by the incorporation into itself of the ever-enlarging knowledge, the ever-expanding horizons of life. It is the glory of Christianity that this can be done. She shows her universality and her eternal truth by her ability to interpret in terms of her faith the thought and knowledge not only of the first, but of the twelfth and of the twentieth centuries; only when the Church of any generation is tempted to regard her interpretation of her Lord as final and complete does that Church demonstrate her limitations of outlook, her weakness of faith. No generation, not even in the first century, is sufficiently big to be able to take in all the facets of the one Divine Life. Jesus Christ, the same yesterday, to-day, and for ever, is for us, as for the author of the *Epistle to the Hebrews*, not the claim for a stereotyped creed unable to assimilate or advance, but the proclamation that in the conception of Christ as the eternal Logos, and in the ever-repeated return to the historic Jesus, will be found the one solution by every generation of the problems that confront, of the troubles that harass.

Such a view of development or evolution may well be called biological. It is evolution exhibited in a living organism, affected by and sensitive to the changes in the

environment in which its life is placed. As such it is to
be distinguished from logical development in which the
premises and deductive processes are exclusively studied.
Unfortunately in theology the logical methods have too
often been allowed to monopolise attention, with the
result that theology has been divorced from history and
actual life. Logical development is a simple process;
the tracing of biological evolution needs the accurate
measurement of many complex factors; above all, the
perpetual insistence on life itself as the key to the whole.

Limits of space have driven the writer, much against
his will and usual practice, to exclude all references to
the original sources. Nor has it been possible, in a work
covering so vast a period in so small a compass, to
acknowledge the full measure of indebtedness, or to
indicate the authority or reasons upon which certain
opinions have been formed. To the same cause must
be attributed a necessary, though unwelcome, positiveness
of expression as regards some matters that in a larger
work would demand discussion and justification. The
bibliography at the close, which it would have been easy
to make as large as the text itself, has been constructed
with a view to the requirements of the busy pastor or
general reader.

Manuals of theology and philosophy abound. Surveys
of the development of Christian Thought—apart from the
great works of Harnack, Loofs, and Seeberg—are somewhat rare. The best known, probably, is Dr. Allen's
excellent *Continuity of Christian Thought*, the scale of
which, however, is even more restricted than in the

present work. A niche, therefore, may be found for the following attempt, in spite of many imperfections of knowledge and execution of which no critic can be more conscious than the author himself.

It may be well to point out that quotations from sources reasonably contemporary with the writer or event in question are enclosed within '....'; quotations from modern writers in the usual "....".

WESTMINSTER,
March 1911.

CONTENTS

CHAPTER I

CHAPTER II

CHAPTER III

CHAPTER IV

CHAPTER V

CHAPTER VI

CHAPTER VII

CHAPTER VIII

CHAPTER IX

CHAPTER I

THE JEWISH FACTORS

Argument

I

OVER the Cross of the Saviour the inscription was written in three languages, Hebrew, Greek, Latin; a threefold appeal to the great races, which by their organisation and thought influenced and moulded the infant Church. Christ was born amid the clash of East and West; historical Christianity is the product of many movements with intense differences, local and racial. From the Jew, the Greek, and the Roman the new faith received elements, differing according to the genius of the different races, yet all of value in building up the City of God. For the Jew, the Greek, and the Roman on entering the Church did not lose their racial idiosyncrasies or abandon their distinctive tempers and modes of thought. The Jew came to the New Testament through the Old; the Greek, even if he entered the Church through the synagogue, yet brought with him his philosophy; while the Roman construed all in terms of his polity.

For our present purpose the direct contribution of the Jew is relatively slight, even if we understand by the Jew the larger Eastern world of which he formed, especially in Alexandria, the mediator and interpreter to the West. The Apostles, it is true, were Jews. The monotheism of Christianity was Jewish and not Greek; its doctrine of the Messiah wholly Jewish. The superstructure of Christian doctrine was built upon Jewish foundations, and can only be construed through the Judaism of Palestine or of the Dispersion. The root ideas of the Gospel were planted deep in Old Testament soil. For the Gentile Christian as for the Jew the older Scriptures were canonical, authentic,

and inspired; at one time, in fact, his only Bible. But
with the accomplishment of this their historic purpose, the
further direct influence of the Jew upon Christian thought
after the Apostolic Age became comparatively insignificant.
The new conceptions of religion could receive little but
hostility from Jewish conservatism. Even in Jewish
Christian circles (the so-called Nazarenes) little was added
with growing years to their first crude ideas of the Messiah.
What is absent is more noteworthy than what is present.
Nothing is more remarkable than the poverty of the
Christology of such a representative Jewish writer as St.
James. Sublime as are his ethics, his Christian teaching,
as distinct from what Micah would have written, is but
slight. In the Jewish writers who came after St. James,
with their stunted Christianity, e.g. the Christian inter-
polations in the *Testaments of the Twelve Patriarchs*, we miss
altogether the great Pauline or Johannine conceptions. We
find instead the anticipation of the teaching of Arius, that
Christ is no more than a creature of God. The difficulty
which the Jewish mind seems always to have discerned
in the doctrine of a crucified Messiah found its expression
in the docetism of Cerinthus (A.D. 90), who taught that the
Christ who descended upon Jesus at His baptism forsook
Him before His passion. But the Jewish consciousness,
even when nominally Christian, was generally unable to
interpret Christ.

Another and more rigid section of the Jewish Christians,
known as Ebionites, has left us an extensive but obscure
literature. The chief of these, known as the pseudo-
Clementine *Recognitions* and *Homilies* (both probably independent abridgments of a lost work called the *Circuits
of St. Peter*) display at times a remarkable animosity to
St. Paul, and absolutely ignore any idea of Atonement.[1]
Christ, however, as the eternal interpreter of the Law by

---

[1] It is difficult to understand Harnack's (*H.D.* i. 311 ff.) contention that the
Clementine literature is 'Catholic,' or at most syncretistic (i. 314 *n.*).

His successive incarnations in perfect men, culminating in His incarnation in Jesus, delivers men from the attraction of the earth-spirit. Whether the Jewish Christians would ever have advanced beyond these crude and undisciplined notions it is now impossible to say. For the Jewish Christian Church, the earliest form of Christianity, almost ceased to exist with the close of the second century. Jewish Christians lingered on, it is true, here and there, especially in Pella and Kochaba, and still survive, it would appear, in Mesopotamia in a hopelessly corrupt condition.[1] Their history, for the most part a blank, is that of a rudimentary organ in the Church, a perpetual warning of the atrophy which awaits blindness to the signs of a new age.

We have spoken of the comparatively slight influence, as it seems to us, of the Jew upon Christian thought after the Apostolic Age. Probably if we knew more we should see that this influence was greater than we think. Later Judaism, the Judaism of the Apocalypses and of Alexandria, and early Christianity, especially in its non-Pauline types, were so closely connected and were differentiated so gradually that they must have exercised considerable influence one upon the other. Unfortunately the century which followed the death of St. Paul is a silent century that has left us but " fragments of fragments " of its history. Annalists had slight place in a community that lived in expectation of the sudden coming of the Lord. Of such literature as existed we have now only a few torn leaves. Only here and there is the curtain lifted upon those memorable days. Only very imperfectly do we yet understand the process by which a young, proscribed creed, transplanted from the land of its birth to the abodes of men of alien thought and of alien institutions, in the teeth of relentless edicts, without as yet settled doctrines, a settled canon—apart from the Old Testament—or settled organi-

[1] *Encyc. Brit.*[9], s.v. Mandaeans.

sation, became a homogeneous force which the Roman
Empire could not overthrow, and with which the culture
of the world was bound to come to terms. But in the
process Christianity and Judaism drifted fatally apart ;
not unnaturally when we remember that Pauline doctrine
really negatives all that is most characteristic in Mosaism.

II

In three directions the Jew influenced, though chiefly
in a negative way, the development of Christian thought,
especially in the second century. An intense hostility to
everything Jewish, combined with the acceptance of the
Jewish Scriptures as canonical and inspired, is one of the
marks of much early Christian literature, most strongly
emphasised, perhaps, in orthodox writings, in the *Epistle
of Barnabas*. In this work, probably written in the second
century, and long regarded as of apostolic authority, the
writer claims that all Jewish ceremonies are of the devil.
Confronted with the difficulty what to make in this case
of the Old Testament, he and his school boldly twisted
it into an allegorical or spiritual narrative. Others went
further, and maintained that the Old Testament from cover
to cover had nothing to do with the Jews, who were but ' a
synagogue of Satan.'

Another sect of extremists, under the lead of Marcion
(c. 150)—an " old-world Count Tolstoy " [1]—pushed to an
extreme the doctrines of *Barnabas*, and repudiated both
Judaism and the Old Testament, though careful to acknowledge its historicity. The drift of Marcion's thought is
shown by the title of his chief work, *Antitheses*, or ' Con-
trasts.' To such lengths did Marcion carry his hostility
that he makes Christ descend into hell and release the
heathen, even Sodomites and Egyptians, while passing
by the great Jewish saints. A man of deep and genuine

[1] T. M. Lindsay, *Church and Ministry*, p. 219.

piety, he believed that he had discovered the secret of St. Paul, that the Gospel was essentially a revelation of grace, love, and redemption which had nothing in common with the external restraints and legal conditions of the Old Testament. He forgot that St. Paul had sought to deduce his special doctrines from the Old Testament itself. In Marcion we find the exact opposite of the Ebionite and pseudo-Clementine writings of the Jewish Christian Church. These last had discerned in Christianity little else than a continuation of Judaism, a Mosaism purified and enlarged. Marcion refused to allow any association or link whatever. He will have nothing to do with progressive manifestation and disciplinary delays. As usual, the extremes met. The one denied the possibility of development in religious thought ; the other so exaggerated the new elements at the expense of the old as to leave no room for development at all. The Church was founded upon a cataclysm, and left unrelated to history.

From this heresy, organised by Marcion into a regular system which lasted until the sixth century, the Church was saved, not so much by the logic of its leaders—for many of the positions into which they were driven seem more than questionable—as by its sense of historic spiritual continuity, that ' rock ' upon which so much that is more valuable than logic is founded. Men realised that it was better to throw a bridge between the Church and the past than, with Marcion of Pontus, to leave Christianity without historic (*i.e.* Jewish) foundations and supports. The Apologists especially, in their attempt to win the cultured Gentiles, felt the necessity of dating back the Christian religion to the beginning of the human race ; while the average Christian clung firmly to the Jewish foundations as the one effective barrier against that complete Hellenisation of Christianity the results of which he fancied he had already seen in Gnosticism. Even Tertullian, much as he detested Judaism, dreaded even more ' the Pontic

mouse who nibbled away the Gospels,' with whom ' all
things happened on the sudden.'

One result of this reaction against Marcion was to fasten
upon the Church a heritage of Old Testament legalism,
which in many directions cramped the larger spirit of the
Church. The new wine, in spite of the warning of Jesus,
was poured into old bottles. Another result was the
triumph of the allegorical method. The Church henceforth frankly accepted the Old Testament, but the difficulty of its interpretation still remained ; nor was this
lessened by the rigid view of inspiration which the early
Christians inherited from Judaism. There was much in
the Old Testament that was unintelligible to Greek converts, much that seemed contradictory to their new faith,
some things that jarred upon their moral consciousness.
The modern explanation by historical and ethical development was unknown ; yet some solution must be discovered.
Refuge from these difficulties was found in the adoption
of allegory as the true key for the unlocking of the Bible
treasures, a method nowhere more firmly carried out than
by the unknown author of the *Epistle to the Hebrews*.

For the origin of the allegorical method many different
sources may be claimed with equal truth. In reality the
method completely met diverse different needs of the age.
We have seen its adoption by the writer of *Barnabas*
because of the intense hatred of sections of the Early
Church to everything Jewish. Strange to say, the method
was itself Jewish, or rather rabbinic ; though Philo, the
leader of the Jewish allegorical school of Alexandria, speaks
of it as the method of the Greek mysteries. Philo was
right. For centuries the Greek philosophers had used the
method as a means of protecting their sacred poems and
myths from the critics, and the system had been completed by the Stoics, especially Heraclitus and Cornutus.
By the writers of this school the varying theories of ethics,
physics, and metaphysics alike are made to find their

support and proof in Homer, whose verses were the Bible of the Greek race. By this means also reconciliation was found between the new world of ideas and the old Homeric world from which men were slipping away. When, therefore, in the third century of the Christian Church, the influence of Philo was aided by that of Hellenic culture, by the need for overthrowing Marcionism, and by the fashionable syncretism, the result was inevitable. By orthodox and unorthodox, Gnostics and Apologists, the simplest words and incidents both of the Old and New Testament received most daring interpretations. The one hundred and fifty-three fishes caught in the Sea of Galilee were resolved, to give an example, into the square of the Apostles and the square of the Trinity. The books of the prophets especially suffered ; their every sentence was wrested into a prediction ; their moral ' forthtelling ' was lost in the emphasis of ' foreknowledge.' The method became universal. In dealing with the heathen myths the Apologists will have none of it, though they fall back upon it for the defence of Christianity. Gnostics fled to it for the advancement of their own views, and turned the *Nunc dimittis* of Simeon into a thanksgiving of the Demiurge to the Infinite Depth. Even Celsus and Porphyry, in spite of their bitter attacks upon the Christian exegesis, in the interpretation of their own religion became allegorists themselves.

When the work of the Gnostics, Apologists, and Alexandrians had resulted in the expression of Christianity in terms of Hellenic thought, the allegorical method became even more supreme. In part this was due to the curious fact that the Greeks, who of all others have done most by their literature for the intellectual advancement of the race, always looked on the written word with some suspicion.[1] Writing, said Socrates in the *Phaedrus*, can do no more than remind the reader of something which he knows

---

[1] See Butcher, " The Written and the Spoken Word," in *Some Aspects of the Greek Genius.*

already. Knowledge is not the outcome of books, but of illumination ; into the mystery of learning few can penetrate. We may note in passing, as a matter of some importance, that this illumination, or power of allegorical interpretation, was regarded as having been handed down from the Apostles through a succession not of bishops but of teachers.[1]

By many modern writers the allegorical method is regarded as the peculiar mark of mysticism and orthodoxy. This is one of the curious reversals of opinion of which history contains so many. In reality, as we have seen, the allegorical method grew out of a tendency to rationalism ; it was primarily an attempt to explain away for Greek readers the difficulties of the Scriptures (e.g. the story of the Fall), by getting rid of their literal or historical significance. As rationalistic the method received condemnation at the hands of certain early writers, whose zeal was scarcely in proportion to their knowledge.

In spite of all its radical unsoundness, when viewed from the standpoint of a more scientific age, this much may be said for the allegorical method, that it attained a true goal. The allegorist rightly felt that the Bible was a treasure held in trust for the human race. The value of the Bible does not lie in its historical or scientific detail, but in its spiritual, universal content; all else is immaterial, local, and temporal. But spiritual content cannot exist unless there is the capacity of eternal self-adjustment. That this cannot be attained by slavish homage to the letter was the constant testimony of the allegorical method. Though the road by which allegorism travelled was one that we should not care to tread to-day, the conclusion reached was really one with that of modern criticism. The spiritual was made all in all, and the letter, in many cases, a veil that hid it ; to-day we regard the letter not as a veil, but as the vehicle of the spiritual, of little value in itself save in so far as it bears

[1] Bigg, *Christian Platonists*, i. 57.

witness to eternal truth. The allegorical method in its search for the spiritual did not take sufficiently wide sweeps; it laboured under the delusion that every separate verse of Scripture, nay, every separate word, was profitable, instead of discerning the spiritual in the sum-total of the messages or the movement.

The after history of this allegorical method may here be summarised.[1] Made into a system by Origen, of whom we are expressly told that he had studied the works of the Stoic Cornutus, it was the chief but least valuable part of his teaching which survived the condemnation of his positions. Henceforth it dominated the Church, though not without opposition from the school of Antioch, especially from Theodore of Mopsuestia (†429). While pleading for greater fidelity to the grammatical, literal, and historical sense, for the allegorical significance Theodore attempted to substitute the ' typical,' ofttimes, it is true, falling into the very ' allegory ' from which escape was sought. By means of the *Instituta Regularia* of Junilius Africanus (c. 550), the ' typical ' school obtained an entrance into the West, and is not extinct in certain quarters even to-day. But, compared with the allegorists, the ' typical ' school had little influence ; partly because of the critical freedom with which Theodore had dealt with the doubtful books both of the Old and New Testament; to a greater degree because of the association of the school with Nestorianism. Further developed by Jerome and Augustine, the ' allegorical ' method became the one acknowledged principle of exegesis of the Middle Ages, reaching its most interesting expression in Bernard of Clairvaux's *Sermons on the Canticles*. By most medieval writers Scripture was given a fourfold interpretation, literal or historical, tropological, allegorical, and analogical. Thomas Aquinas carefully distinguished the historical signification from ' the

---

[1] For allegory, see Geffcken in Hastings' *Dictionary of Religion and Ethics*, vol. i. ; Hatch, *Influence of Greek Ideas*, chap. iii.

spiritual sense founded upon it.' This distinction prevailed until long after the Reformation began a more
critical exegesis.

III

A second direction in which we may trace the impulse
of Judaism was in the influence of its eschatological or
apocalyptic literature. Christianity had its historical
origin at the very centre of what we may describe as the
apocalyptic period (300 B.C.-200 A.D.). Among the Jews
apocalypses of all sorts had flourished exceedingly since
the time of Antiochus Epiphanes, and were regarded as
possessing almost canonical authority. They were, in
reality, the continuation under a grosser form of the yearning for that mysterious new order which Hebrew prophets
had first dimly seen, and then changed into a national
expectation, and which Jesus had proclaimed as fulfilled
in the 'Kingdom of Heaven.' These writings were naturally
received by the Christians as part of their heritage from
Judaism, and, where necessary (as in the case of the chaotic
wilderness of the *Sibylline Oracles*), adapted to Christian
needs by means of Christian alterations or additions.
Among the elements of this apocalyptic literature we may
discern, as in the second part of the *Apocalypse of St. John*,
an intense hatred of the Roman Empire, and a tendency to
bury the simple eschatological teaching of Jesus beneath a
mass of allegory. Nevertheless, in spite of millenarian
exaggeration or sensuous imagery, we may recognise the
service done to Christian thought by this apocalyptic
literature in the sustained emphasis laid upon eschatological hope, the ' athanasia ' through Jesus Christ.[1] In
times of persecution, as we see from the *Acts of Perpetua*,
the *Acts of Marianus and James*, and other similar human
documents, it was to these delineations of the blessedness

---

[1] *Didache*, ix. 10.

of the triumphant that the tortured turned.[1] As an integral part of this eschatological hope, we find at a very early date the identification of Jesus with the Son of Man who was to appear in judgment, though apocalyptic literature never rose to the great conception that ' the Father hath given authority to the Son to execute judgment, *because* He is the Son of Man.' The human sympathy of the judgment was generally lost in the fiery details with which the apocalypses abounded, which became part of the stock of Christian thinking.

Of this current literature another outcome was the strength of chiliastic conceptions ; a transfiguration of the ancient hopes of Israel, begun by the Jews, taken over by the Church, and then enlarged and refined by being linked on with the Lord. A belief in the immediate coming of Christ was common in the Early Church, and soon passed into the idea that this would begin the reign of the Saviour and His saints for a thousand years at Jerusalem. The Church, in the second century especially, was largely influenced by parousian conceptions. The Christian watchword was still, as in apostolic days, *Maran Atha*, " the Lord is at hand." The wandering ' prophets ' (an order in the Church which died out with Montanism) made this theme in special, as Celsus complains, the basis of their sermons, and gloried—at least that was the impression produced upon the heathen—in the retribution so speedily to come upon the world. By many writers, *e.g.* in the *Epistle of Barnabas* and the *Shepherd* of Hermas, as well as by Papias and Justin, we find the millenarian idea strongly developed, while Tertullian and Irenaeus give evidence of the same belief. To these conceptions, the basis of which was the literal interpretation of certain passages in the *Apocalypse* and other similar writings, a blow was given by the introduction of the allegorical method in Alexandrian theology. In the third century,

---

[1] Workman, *Persecution in the Early Church*, p. 321 ff.

partly through the influence of the treatise of Dionysius
of Alexandria, *On the Promises*, partly through the more
friendly relations between the Church and the Empire,
partly through the discredit of the prophets and the failure
of Montanism, partly through the greater influence of
Greek thought, chiliastic conceptions became generally
discounted, especially in the East. A century later they
were regarded as heretical.

But the importance of these chiliastic conceptions,
especially in the second century, must not be forgotten
because of their later discredit. By these beliefs men were
supported through a great crisis in the world's history.
In a society rapidly hastening to dissolution the Church
was enabled to hold fast to the conviction that God was
leading all things to an issue in which righteousness and
love should be fully vindicated. " Because Christianity
was thus," as Professor Burkitt aptly puts it, " organised
for a time of catastrophe," [1] when the crash came Christianity alone of the institutions of the world survived the
catastrophe.

In chiliastic conceptions we recognise also a fundamental
truth ; though in the issue of events it took a different
form from men's first expectations. Chiliasm proclaims
that for the Christian, as for the Jew of old, there is a
divine interpretation of human history. History is not
limited to any one ' aeon.' The optimism of this view,
both for the individual and for society, though concealed
by much allegorical verbiage, is apparent when contrasted
with the pessimism of the great Stoic thinker, Marcus
Aurelius. Chiliasm, whatever its faults, has no despair
of the spiritual possibilities of human nature. With its
proclamation of ' aeons of aeons,' it refuses to narrow its
vision by circles premature. With Marcus Aurelius renunciation becomes a hopeless concentration upon present
duty, for whose sake all else must be put aside. It is

[1] Prof. Burkitt, in *Cambridge Biblical Essays*, p. 207.

magnificent, in some respects the most magnificent flight
of the unaided human soul. None the less, it is not so much
spiritual vision as despair. The City of God, or realised
Kingdom of Heaven, that organised ideal in which lay
the strongest appeal of the new religion, by its very nature
utterly subversive of the established order as it then
existed, had little meaning for the absoluteness of Stoic
individualism. The ultimate value of this chiliastic hope
as a factor in thought and progress is too often overlooked,
because in the first enthusiasm of this larger vision the
early Christians, as Schweitzer claims, may perhaps have
had a tendency to forget the common duties of this life.
The claims of the old ' world ' that was ' passing away with
the fashion thereof,' and of the new world that men ' greeted
from afar,' were not always easy to adjust, and in their
adjustment (*Interimsethik*) both in thought and life, the
Christians of the second century were not always successful.

But the apocalyptic literature did more than hold out
to the Church a new world to redress the balance of the old.
This voluminous literature has rightly been called " tracts
for hard times." It was a literature produced by a sense
of antagonism to the world-power ; it bears on its pages
the marks of the blood and fire with which the world-
power sought to crush out the infant Church. When in the
third and fourth centuries the Church conquered the State,
apocalyptic literature lost its main motive. The parousia
was pushed into the dim distance ; the world-power was
beneath the foot of the saint. Apocalyptic literature
became discredited and, as far as possible, forgotten. The
fragments that survive, like some fossil remains, bear
witness to a state of life and feeling long since extinct.

Yet in one particular the motives of apocalyptic literature survived its discredit. For the antagonism of the
Church to the world-force rested on a conviction that the
Church was also an empire that lay parallel to, outside
of, possibly in antagonism to, the Roman dominion. In

their writings Christians professed that ' nothing was more
alien to them than politics ' ; in reality, from the standpoint of a Roman governor, they were intense politicians
of a most dangerous type. In their constant persecutions
the basis of condemnation by the magistrates was not the
theological views of the Christians—for these the Roman
magistrates cared little or nothing—but their supreme
loyalty to a law and to a throne outside the Roman law and
throne. The Christians were not anxious to run counter
to the law and customs of the Empire ; they were, in fact,
almost unanimous in upholding them. But if at any time
such law and customs came into conflict with the will of
God, as interpreted by themselves and by their standards,
they must obey God rather than man. By the Roman
executive such a doctrine could not be regarded as otherwise than revolutionary, for their whole political theory,
civil and religious, was built up on the absolutism of Caesar,
and demanded complete submission of life and will from
all subjects. Even the great politician maxim of Jesus :
" Render unto Caesar the things that are Caesar's, and unto
God the things that are God's," became treasonable in a
State that made little difference between Caesar and God.
The results of such antagonism were seen in the three
centuries of persecution through which the Church was
called to pass, in reality three centuries of struggle between
the incompatible claims of Caesar and Christ.[1] And when
the era of persecution had passed away, the consciousness
of the Church as an empire in possible antagonism and
opposition to the world-state still survived. Of this we
shall see the full fruition in the rise of the medieval papacy
and the growth of Canon Law.

In another direction also we note the influence of this
apocalyptic literature, and of the spirit which gave rise to
it. The tendency to develop angelology, and the continuance in the Christian Church of the popular belief

[1] On all this see Workman, *op. cit.* chaps. ii. and iv.

in demons, powerfully influenced Christian thought for
centuries after the apocalyptic literature to which it owed
its strength had been forgotten. But for the apocalyptic
literature, or rather but for the outlook on life of which
it was the expression, it is possible that the Church might
have been delivered from the current naturalistic religion.
As it was, the Church renamed the old fears and super-
stitions to mark adoption, and put these back in their old
place sealed with her sign, consecrated to her service. For
a thousand years we find the effects not only in Christian
life, but also in Christian thought.

The strength of the popular belief cannot be exaggerated.
From the Emperor on the throne to the meanest slave men
trembled at the awful powers of the unknown, and trembled
the more because of their loss of religious faith. They
peopled the heaven and earth with a host of demons—
'daemons' the philosophers vainly called them—and
believed with all their hearts in the alliance of magicians
and sorcerers with the hordes of the black one. Dreams
and omens haunted high and low alike.

In their belief in demons and other supernatural agencies
the Christians, as the Jews before them, were not before
their age, save in their grasp of the supremacy of one benign
Father of good, their conviction that they had been met
and overcome by the Saviour. Between the Christian
doctrine of angels and devils and the heathen doctrine of
demons there are so many coincidences that we must assume
their close historical connection. For the Church when it
laid its hold on the soul of the common man left him his
ghosts. Behind every idol statue, however beautiful, the
followers of Jesus discerned the grinning face of a fiend.
Not only were the demons the source of idolatry, through
them also the natural light which would have led the
philosophers to the truth had been turned into darkness.
The devil and his angels were thus terrible realities, whose
evil machinations, as Origen tells us, were only thwarted

by the ceaseless vigilance of the attendant spirits of good.
As in the romance of *Enoch*, archangels and demons
struggled for the soul and body, nor was the struggle
one-sided. For the demons, in the words of Cassian of
Marseilles, 'fill the atmosphere which extends between earth
and heaven.' In the demons, on the contrary, Plutarch
finds the chain which unites the world to the throne of
God ; they are the mediators between God and man, the
representatives of Providence. Owing to their speed they
are almost omniscient, and thus ' attain credit for causing
that which they announce.' They give oracles, prophecies,
and revelations ; they cause or cure diseases ; they work
miracles. The result of all this was the production of a
state of thought, once universal, now so discredited that
we find it difficult to understand its former hold. Magical
and semi-magical beliefs invaded the Church. For the
Christian, as for the pagan, the miraculous was so common,
so natural, that it ceased to be miraculous ; it formed part
of the ordinary machinery of the universe. Cyprian in his
De Lapsis tells us stories of the supernatural power of the
consecrated elements worthy of a place in that storehouse
of medieval marvels Caesarius of Heisterbach's *Dialogus
Miraculorum*. St. Augustine solemnly asserts that in his
own diocese of Hippo there had occurred in the space of
two years no less than seventy-two miracles, among them
five cases of restoration to life. But illustrations of this
belief in the miraculous are almost co-extensive with the
literature of the early and medieval Church.

IV

Of the positive ideas in Christian thought which may be
traced to Jewish philosophical sources, the most important
is the doctrine of the Logos, or Reason of God immanent in
the creation which He fosters and sustains. The name and
the thought, it is true, are fully developed in the Stoic and

Platonic philosophies, possibly also in the pre-Philonic
Jewish literature. Nevertheless, it is probable that their
entrance into Christianity should be attributed to the
influence of the Alexandrian Jew, Philo [1] (b. B.C. 20). The
object of Philo was to reconcile religion, *i.e.* Mosaism, with
philosophy, *i.e.* Platonism. In so doing he contributed
to the schools of Alexandria a general stock of hazy
and unsystematised ideas, which by different channels
passed into current Christian and Hellenic thought. His
most lasting contribution was the change of the half-
personified ' Wisdom ' of early Jewish Alexandrian writers,
e.g. the author of *Proverbs* viii., into the Logos. The result
was remarkable. " Philo's Logos reflects light from count-
less facets. It is one of those creative phrases which mark
an epoch in the development of thought." " God holds
a place in all systems subsequent to Philo such as He had
never held in those prior to Him." [2] From Philo the idea
passed to the author of the Fourth Gospel, though worked
out in a very different way ; while Justin, Clement, and
Origen all show their indebtedness to the Jewish thinker,
whose system anticipates much that is found in later
Neoplatonism.

According to Philo the Logos is the ' Idea of ideas ' ; the
' ideas ' or content of the mind of God being identified, in
a characteristic Jewish manner, with the angels. From
this the transition is easy to the conception of the Logos
as the wisdom of God expressing itself in act, and as therefore the agent in creation. Philo goes so far as to call this
Logos ' a second God,' a ' divine Angel.' " He is the
eternal image of the Father, and we, who are not yet fit to
be called sons of God, may call ourselves His sons." [3]

The Christian doctrine of the Logos of necessity differed
from that of Philo, if only because it had reference to a
realised Incarnation. Philo, on the contrary, had left no

[1] Bigg, *op. cit.* p. 15.   [2] Fairbairn, *Christ in Modern Theology*, p. 65.
[3] Inge, *Christian Mysticism*, p. 85.

room for an Incarnation. With the Christians, moreover,
the conception of the Logos was developed so as to meet
Gnostic heresy, especially its docetism. Hence causation
is a mark rather of exaltation than of inferiority; the
revealed Creator is the ' glory ' of God. With the Gnostic
the divine Energy is degraded as it approaches the sphere
of material existence. Yet " In one remarkable point
the ideal of Christianity was in danger of falling below
that of Philo. For there was a tendency in less philosophical minds to distinguish between the unspoken and the
spoken Word, to conceive of the Divine Reason or Logos
as at first immanent in the mind of the Father, then
assuming hypostasis for the purpose of Creation." [1] The
effect of this was seen later in the doctrine that the Son
is the ' thought ' of the Father, who is Himself trans-
cendental and absolute, who cannot be known, but only
approached by Vision or Ecstasy.[2]

[1] Bigg, *op. cit.* pp. 60-65. Bigg points out, *op. cit.* pp. 203-4, that the
doctrine of the Logos in the Stoics, though earlier than Philo, must be passed
by, as with the Stoics the Logos is really the First Cause.
[2] *Infra*, pp. 52, 200 f. There is an excellent chapter on the theology of
Philo in E. Caird's *Evolution of Theology in the Greek Philosophers*, vol. ii.
c. 21.

CHAPTER II

THE INFLUENCE OF HELLAS

Argument

I

FROM the Jewish influences which moulded Christian thought we pass to the Hellenic. As forces " Hebraism and Hellenism stand out distinct, the one in all the intensity of its religious life, the other in the wealth and diversity of its secular gifts and graces, and in the depth of its philosophic insight.

> "Thus the sharp contrasts of the sculptor's plan
> 　Showed the two primal paths our race has trod ;—
> Hellas the nurse of man complete as man,
> 　Judaea pregnant with 'the living God.'"[1]

Hellas was necessary to Judaea, if Christianity was to receive its fulness of meaning, if the Messiah of Nazareth was ever to become the Christ of the world instead of the possession of a single people. There is a school of theologians the chief representatives of which, though from different reasons, are Harnack and Ritschl, which constantly deplores what it calls the " Hellenising of the primitive faith." The developments which Christianity received from its contact with the Greek world are treated as if they were doubtful growths, oftentimes of a fungus order, from which the Church would be well to free itself by a " return to Jesus." Such a conception seems to us to be wrong. Greek philosophy had a divine function in the world as well as Mosaic law. The story of the Church, in its truest sense, is the record of the education of the human race in all things that belong to the spirit. It is essentially, therefore, the story of a development of the

[1] S. H. Butcher, *Harvard Lectures*, p. 42.

C

whole " in Jesus Christ "—the full import of this Pauline
phrase can never be exhausted. As we turn its pages we
see the unfolding of the relation of every age to the one
Centre of all ages, the assimilation by the one Life of all
true thought and life. To us, therefore, ' Hellenisation '
was a necessary factor in the growth of the Church, and
part of the work of the Holy Spirit. " The construction of
Christianity through the media of the older philosophies
and religions was a necessary prelude to its construction
by a spirit and through a consciousness of its own creation.
The absolute ideal had, in order to be intelligible, to use
constituted and familiar vehicles, but only that it might
win the opportunity of fashioning vehicles worthier of its
nature and fitter for its end." [1] The story of Hellenisation
is not the story of degeneration, but the study of the conditions under which the Spirit worked, and of the continuity of the life of which He has ever been, under different
forms and in diverse manners, the Lord and Giver. " The
partial Hellenising and Latinising of Christian thought and
terminology, which began soon after the end of the Apostolic Age, may not have been without danger to the Faith,
but few will now doubt that valuable results have followed.
If we owe to these processes certain accretions which do
not harmonise with primitive simplicity, on the other hand
they enriched the Christian society with much that appealed to the thought and imagination of the centuries
through which it had to pass ; nor would any thoughtful
believer at the present day willingly abandon the best
heirlooms that the Church has received from the Greek
East or the Latin West." [2]

The Hellenic spirit, though of greater importance than
the Jewish in the development as opposed to the birth of
Christian thought, was later in producing any real influence.
The preparatory work of the Hebrew religion had first to

[1] Fairbairn, *Christ in Modern Theology*, p. 62.
[2] H. B. Swete in *Cambridge Theological Essays*, p. 10.

be consolidated. In the New Testament, though written
in Greek, specifically Hellenic ideas, as distinct from
Jewish ideas in Hellenic dress, have little place, even in
the teaching of St. Paul, or in the prologue to the Fourth
Gospel. The consciousness of universalism, upon the
Greek character of which stress has often been laid, might
with equal right claim to have been Roman, the opposition
of the two empires of Christ and of Caesar. As such it was
recognised by Roman governors as the political ground of
persecution. But with the gradual submergence of the
Jewish Christians, and the weakening authority of their
apocalyptic literature, Greece came to her own. Justin
Martyr tells us that only in his own day had the Gentiles
in the Church begun to outnumber the Jews. It is not
surprising, therefore, that with Justin Martyr we begin the
triumph of Hellenic culture, and the modification of the
primitive simplicity of Christianity. The word " theology " itself, first found in Justin, seems to have been
borrowed by him from the Stoics. Slowly, unconsciously,
but surely, Greek moral ideas and ideals penetrated Christian thought, in the same way as the Judaism of the
Dispersion had been altered, even before the coming of the
Messiah, by the Hellenism with which it was surrounded.

The influence of Hellenic thought upon Christianity was
increased by the growing religious seriousness of the Graeco-
Roman world. The advent of Christianity coincided with a
great spiritual fermentation in the heathen world,[1] which
showed itself not merely in the rapid spread of the newer
cults, the worship of Isis, of Mithra, and the like, but in the
revival of belief in the older faiths and forms ; in a renewed
study of the Platonic philosophy ; in the rush of smiths
and carpenters to join the ranks of the Cynic friars ; above
all in the growth throughout Europe of a social conscience.
We see this awakened conscience in the guilds and charities,

---

[1] On this see Dill, *Roman Society from Nero to Marcus Aurelius*, bk. iii.
chap. iii. and bk. iv.

the constant efforts to extend and endow education, to found orphanages and hospitals, to emancipate women, and to rescue the slave from the unlimited power of his lord, which form the nobler features of the legislation of the Antonines. At the root of this larger ethical ideal there lay an increase of spirituality. Repentance, expiation, immortality, the belief that man can enter into union with God, became potent factors in the better life of the times. That this upward movement of thought and creed, of which on the one side Mithraism, on the other the teachings of Epictetus, were the best expressions, undoubtedly helped the ultimate triumph of Christianity seems to us a certainty ; nay, who shall say that this upward movement as not the work of the Spirit fulfilling Himself in diverse ? But the first effects were curiously mixed. Christ and the revived paganism both repelled and racted each other ; their mutual influence is as certain as is the fierceness of the conflict into which they plunged.

One result of this spiritual uplifting of paganism thus coinciding with the rise of the Church was syncretism, both philosophic and practical, or that tendency to find unity and identity amidst the multitudinous details of polytheism, the most familiar example of which is the identification of the gods of Greece and Rome. In the second and third centuries syncretism especially manifested itself in the popular faiths, *e.g.* the worship of the Great Mother, of Isis, or of Mithra, in a willingness to assimilate the best elements in any cult, Christianity included. It was this that gave to these religions their strength. Their aim was the union of all gods and all myths in a vast synthesis. They were willing not only to live and let live, but to take up and make part of themselves whatever features of religion seemed especially popular or serviceable.

Equally remarkable was the tendency to syncretism on the part of the philosophic sects. Of this syncretism the

noblest expression was Neoplatonism, the most curious the
Life of Apollonius, a third-century philosophico-religious
romance, founded on a certain substratum of fact, composed by the sophist Philostratus at the command of
Julia Domna (†217), the wife of Septimius Severus. In
this apotheosis of the dying paganism the story of Jesus
is re-edited, and improved so as to suit heathen notions.[1]
The effect of this syncretism was undoubtedly in the long
run the bringing Christianity and current thought into
closer touch. Christianity, it is true, especially in its
earlier and purer days, refused any compromise with other
faiths. ' Et ipse pileatus, Christianus est '—' That man
with the Mithraic cap is a Christian,' said a priest of Mithra
to St. Augustine, who started back in horror from this
attempt to identify his faith with this ' devils' imitation.'
But all men were not so uncompromising in their convictions as St. Augustine. The most potent approximations
between rival faiths and opinions are generally sub-
conscious, and marked with open professions of hostility.
So with Christianity and the revived paganism, with its
ally in Greek thought. The two influenced each other
more profoundly than we should gather from the opposing
arguments between the Fathers and Celsus and Porphyry.

II

At the outset of our treatment it were well to remember
the capital defects of Greek thought, for these, as we shall
see, constantly appear in the influence of Hellenism upon
Christianity. One source of error was the general incapacity to distinguish illustration from argument. Ana-
logy unverified by experiment, daring leaps from the known
to the unknown, and then back again from the guesses thus

[1] It is right to point out that many modern critics attach more independence and historicity to the narrative. See Hastings, *E.R.E.* i. 610-611.

deemed to be knowledge to the known, were construed as if equivalent to reasoned demonstration. Another danger was the tendency to mere abstractions; philosophers seemed to think the greater the abstraction, the greater the truth. In the abstractions of geometry the Greeks had made remarkable progress, and reached definite, certain conclusions. They supposed that the abstractions of metaphysics could be traced in the same way. In consequence they identified abstractions with realities, and names with things. Too often, as Jowett puts it, " they were mastered by their ideas, and not masters of them." For the most part also the ancients were " helpless against the influence of any word which had an equivocal or double sense";[1] while they suffered much from the tyranny of numbers, in which they were disposed to find the secret of the universe. Add a rude science, totally unacquainted with the slower but surer path of the modern inductive philosophy. The result is seen in such extraordinary phantasies as the *aeons* of the Gnostics, or the speculations of Origen on the sun, moon, and stars; are they animated and rational; shall they finally be brought into the great unity where God shall be all in all ?

One characteristic of Greek thought which had a remarkable influence upon Christianity—though whether for good or bad may be deemed a moot point—is its tendency to insist upon definition, even of the undefinable. Hence the inclination to over-subtlety, always one of the vices to which the Greek intellect was prone, most disastrous of all when applied to spiritual phenomena. We shall see the effects in the controversies with respect to the Person of Christ. Approved definitions came to be regarded as synonymous with the faith; slight differences as legitimate ground for excommunication. Inferences from definitions were treated as if they were the realities of experience.

[1] Jowett, *Dialogues of Plato*, iii. 559-567.

A more important defect of Greek thought has been well set forth by Dr. Fairbairn : "The philosophies that had owed their being to the Greek genius were made in the image of Greek man, but even he had too narrow a humanity behind and around as well as within him to be just to man universal, and so his systems had feeling enough for the Hellenic individual and state, but not for mankind collective and historical. They were too appreciative of the philosophers who ought to govern to be just to the manhood which needed government. They started outside religion, and became religious only by force of reason, and in its terms. Their theistic conception was metaphysical rather than ethical, never even in its ethics transcending metaphysics, ever remaining an object of contemplation or thought, never becoming an object of worship and conscience." [1] The effect of this upon the development of Christian theology will be abundantly illustrated in these pages.

But the defects of Greek thought were small in comparison with the services Hellas rendered, both to civilisation and Christian theology. To the Greeks we owe the discovery of the sovereign efficacy of reason. In the words of Euripides, they deemed him alone ' happy who has learned to search into causes.' Hence the conception of law, both in the physical and moral worlds, became firmly fixed in the Greek mind. From this it further resulted that the Greek philosopher was always thinking of the world as a rational whole, and he compelled the theologian to do the same. In spite of the premature generalisations into which his crude science led him, this conception of unity was of inestimable value in the training of mankind. Without this conception of unity Theology as a science would have had little chance of development. In Ethics, also, for man to feel habitually that he is part of the order of the universe is one of the highest motives of which he

[1] Fairbairn, *op. cit.* p. 64.

is capable. When the Greek set before himself as the paramount end the perfection of his whole nature— ' nothing human alien to him '—he introduced into the Church a conception which, in the long run, was destined to be destructive of many early ideas. Monasticism, to give but one example, was not able to survive the renaissance in the fifteenth century of the Greek spirit.

When Greek thought first came into touch with Christianity it had assumed a form that might lead to sympathy and understanding. The ancient schools had worked themselves out. In their despair of truth from any one school, men were now less inclined to form dogmatic systems than to select and combine. Moreover, the craving was not so much for bold speculations, such as we find in the prime of Greek thought, as for some basis of moral life, some inner law which should bring order into the chaos of desires. Ancient philosophy had in a sense died away into theology. The Stoic proclaimed, though in different words, that " the kingdom of heaven is within " ; while Epictetus insisted that logic must be subordinated to moral reformation. The Stoic's religion of " ethical Calvinism," as we may describe it, had no yearning, it is true, either for prayer, or for all that to the Christian is contained in the idea of a future life—that opportunity for completing the incomplete, for making life's crooked straight. In this, as in its intense individualism, Stoicism is a religion of despair. The Stoics " made solitude in the heart and called it peace." [1] But the Stoic proclaimed that man was free to break away from his cruel servitude to passion, through the strength of the rational or divine element in his soul, and that obedience to this law of reason and of nature, ' living harmoniously,' will infallibly lead to the highest good, the freedom which makes him a fellow-citizen of the gods. Moreover, this law of conduct is only part of natural religion, the movement of the world as one

[1] T. R. Glover, *The Conflict of Religions in early Roman Empire*, p. 67.

polity under the ' Spermaticos Logos ' or governing intelligence. So the good man will realise that he is of necessity a citizen in the universal commonwealth, and cannot, therefore, ' live to himself.' In Stoicism also, to mention another point of contact, the conception of God as cold, impersonal Law is always giving way to the thought of a God of providence, ' who is not far from any one of us.'

We must not overlook the influence of what has been called the Platonic Trinity. In the *Timaeus* of Plato we have the three conceptions of God : the Ideas or permanent realities which remain unchanged amid all changes, and the World-Spirit, this last being formed according to the pattern of the Ideas, which again are subordinate to God, though possessing an independent eternal existence. Though Plato himself never attempted to harmonise this triad, the unknown author or authors of the so-called *Epistles of Plato* speaks of them as Three Gods. Shortly before the time of Clement of Alexandria, the Platonist philosopher, Numenius, a Syrian of Apamea, conceived of these Ideas, which possessed a substantive existence outside the Divine Mind, as gathered into one, the divine Arch-Idea. Of his trinity the first is thus Mind, simple, changeless, good, and wise ; the second is the Creator ; the third is the World-Spirit. But how much of this conception of a trinity was derived from Jewish or Christian sources, to what extent this philosophic conception made more easy the adoption of Christian dogma, it is impossible to say.

On the other hand, there was an approach to Christian monotheism. In a recent work Dr. E. Caird has shown the stages by which Greek thought advanced from the belief in many deities to the acknowledgment of a divine unity.[1] Pure monotheism was reached by few ; the majority took refuge in *henotheism*, or the belief in the substantial identity of all the deities worshipped by the vulgar under distinct names ; really an intermediate stage between

[1] E. Caird, *Evolution of Theology in Greek Philosophers.*

polytheism, or the assertion of the absolute existence of the diverse deities, and monotheism, or the proclamation that God is one. Henotheism, through lack of any real repugnance to the current forms of idolatry, preserved in a confused way the personality of the different deities, and so, in spite of its leanings to monotheism, in its practical outcome sided with paganism. The moral value of henotheism was thus slight. Nevertheless, when Celsus insists that all men really worship the same God, whether called ' Jehovah, Jah, or Lord,' we see forces at work which rendered more easy the triumph of a monotheistic faith.

There was one curious influence of the Greek world upon the theology, or rather the language of theology, of the Church, the effect of which was felt until modern times. We refer to the free use of the idea of ' deification ' by the Fathers of both East and West to express the highest state of spiritual experience, when man " is lost in God." The term seems first to have arisen in the Mysteries ; ' deification ' was the idea of salvation that they taught. From the Mysteries the idea passed into Christian thought, with, however, a significance of its own. " If we try to analyse the concept of θεός thus loosely and widely used we find that the predominant idea was that exemption from the doom of death was the prerogative of a Divine Being, and that therefore the gift of immortality is itself a deification." [1] The idea of the deification of man was more than the corollary of the belief in the incarnation of God. It was the expression of the eschatological hope in which Christianity was nurtured, the correspondence in the mind and soul of the individual to the vision of the City of God as an established polity among men.

Before we enter upon our more detailed examination the reader would do well to note that the great touchstone of the Christian Faith, as distinct from philosophical

---

[1] See Inge, *Christian Mysticism*, App. C., for detailed investigation, or Harnack, *H.D.*, Index, s.v. ' deification.'

speculations, will always be found in a real theory of the Atonement, and a piercing and profound sense of sin which cannot be explained away into a shallow, feeble, and vague abstraction or negation. The optimism of Greek philosophy never really grappled with the problem of evil or understood its dire significance. In consequence, to the Greek the Cross was ever ' foolishness,' and Greek thought is constantly making desperate efforts to explain it away. To Celsus the Cross was one of the gravest objections to Christianity. In the *Life of Apollonius* the details of the Crucifixion are changed into a mysterious translation to heaven. But, whatever other compromise might be made with current speculation, the Cross was too vital to be surrendered. In the philosophic syncretisms of the second and third centuries the Cross—and its consequent doctrine of the reality of sin—remains the one great dividing line between faith and unbelief, between a reformed heathenism and Christianity. To many Greeks the conception of an Incarnation was not difficult, though Celsus will have none of it. But the great idea of the *Kenosis* involved in the Incarnation, the root idea which links the life of the Redeemer to His death and which constitutes His life the profoundest revelation of Divine Love, was altogether alien. It is by its fidelity to these great principles that we must discern between Greek and Christian thought, and also determine the consistency of Christian thinkers with their basic ideas. Modernisation or assimilation, whether in the second or twentieth century, if faithful to these, is not to be dreaded ; but, if faithless, the ship is at sea, far from the shore she has left, far from the shore for which she is making.

III

The first effect of the contact of Christianity with Hellenism was somewhat disastrous for the Church. The meeting of the two streams led to a welter, in the whirl-

pools of which many were lost. For two centuries the
history of the Church is the history of its struggle with
heretical beliefs. The student of these heresies, as he
turns over the pages of their ' refutations ' by Irenaeus or
Hippolytus, is bewildered by their number, amazed by
their extravagance. A classification or enumeration lies
outside our purpose ; it must suffice that we point out
their main drifts. We may observe that such heresies
were inevitable ; they were the necessary result of the
growing thought of the age as to the meaning and content
of the Christian idea. Only slowly and by sad experience
could the Church discover what were the real limits of
thought in its application to faith, or what opinions were
incompatible with the primitive deposit. Many of these
heresies were the results of a praiseworthy but premature
attempt to set up the Christian faith in complete and
systematic form in all its relations to the world around.
By the subtle discussions issuing in clearer views to which
these heresies gave rise they really rendered no small
service to theological science.

Of these heresies the most conspicuous group was
Gnosticism, the basis of which was an eclectic philosophy
of religion chiefly Hellenic in character, though in union
with many Oriental elements, cosmical speculations, and
mystic theosophy similar to what we find in Hinduism.
Gnosticism, unfortunately, is almost wholly known to us
from its opponents, who have made the most of its fantastic speculations, obscuring thereby its real significance.
Gnosticism, on its theoretical side—for its ascetic principles and its ritual system do not here concern us—was
an attempt to transform Christianity into a philosophy of
history, and a revealed system of ethical cosmology. The
second century, the flourishing period of Gnostic sects,
was pre-eminently noted for its syncretism, the desire to
fuse together the diverse myths, philosophies, religions,
and mysteries of the civilised world. In Gnosticism this

tendency tried to find lodgment in the Church itself. It is typical of Gnosticism, and of its lack of any true idea of the historical development of the faith, that in one of its schools the image of Jesus was placed side by side with those of Pythagoras, Plato, and Aristotle.

If the earlier Gnostic developments were Judaic in character, they soon became secondary to the Hellenic. Through Greece, also, the religions of Persia and India, with their systems of incarnations and emanations, made their contributions. The problems of Gnosticism were, in the main, two : the first philosophical—the nature of the Absolute, and the method whereby the Absolute can be the creator of matter ; the second ethical—the origin of evil. The first of these was predominantly Hellenic ; " the ideas of Plato seen through the fog of an Egyptian or Syrian mind." [1] In the second we trace the Oriental elements, for the religious thought of the East was always deeply imbued with the sense of evil. Gnosticism, which Dorner has happily called " the Pelagianism of the intellect," sought an answer to these questions by its claim to a deeper insight or knowledge (γνῶσις) than the *Pistis* or faith of the ordinary Christian. It was essentially an esoteric Christianity, which differed widely in its tenets according to its local habitation—Alexandria, Syria, Asia Minor, or Rome—and the degree of admixture of East and West. Of the Syrian Gnosis, the leader was Saturninus, who flourished in the reign of Hadrian. Allied with him were the Ophites, Naassenes, Peratae, and others, who seem to have mixed their Christianity with snake-worship. In Alexandria the Gnostics looked up to Basilides and Valentinus (fl. 140), whose eclectic system is the best known of all, as, in fact, it was the most widely diffused. With Basilides the leading thought is the continuity of the religious development of the world ; between Christianity and the other religions he recognises little or no break or

[1] Bigg, *Christian Platonists*, p. 27.

distinction. In Roman Gnosticism the leader was Marcion, with whose tenets in their antagonism to Judaism we have already dealt. But the Gnostic elements in Marcion's teaching—chief of which were the opposition between the good God of love, first revealed in Jesus, and the creator of the world, and the docetism which such a view logically demanded as to the humanity of Jesus—were not, on the whole, of great importance for Marcion's system.

Amid all the diversities of Gnostic creed we may discern certain fundamental agreements. The treatise which more than any other powerfully affected the religious thought of the second century was the *Timaeus* of Plato. In this we find the Deity, in spite of His essential goodness, withdrawn from the world into a distant heaven, aloof altogether from creation, because of the evil which matter necessarily brings.[1] In a similar manner the Gnostic, in common with the majority of Greek thinkers, in his dualistic opposition between matter and spirit, identified matter with evil. Hence he refused to recognise in the supreme God the creator of the world. To explain creation he was driven to take refuge either in a lower being called the Demiurge, or, with Valentinus, in a bewildering phantasy of ' *aeons*,' the lists of which, with their ' orders ' and 'pairs,' their uncouth jargon and fantastic progenies, are for most people the great difficulty in taking Gnosticism seriously. Their endless successions of emanations span the gulf between the absolute and the universe. Of necessity, therefore, the body of Christ was not real flesh and blood ; the Incarnation and the death on the Cross were conceived of as ' docetic.' The ' tabernacling ' of the Word as ' flesh ' was one of the illusions of life, certainly not ' the glory ' of God. For the Gnostic, also, redemption is a wider and therefore less personal problem than the sin of the individual. Human sin becomes one feature only of ' the sin of the world,' the mystery of pain, death,

[1] See Jowett, *Plato*, iii. pp. 596, 613; *Timaeus*, p. 30 ff.

and decay in all their forms. As the responsibility for the
world is thrown back upon the Demiurge, the tendency
of Gnosticism was towards the denial of free will. In this
we see the beginnings in Christian thought of an endless
debate.

Gnosticism stands hopelessly condemned by its follies—
for by no other name can we dignify these metaphysics of
wonderland—as well as by its attempt to introduce into
Christianity what Dorner rightly calls "the intolerable
distinction of an esoteric and exoteric truth." It is too
late to seek to reverse the verdict of the Church. Nevertheless certain points should be pleaded in mitigation of
sentence. Deeply as they misunderstood St. Paul, the
Gnostics, especially if Marcion be included, stand out
almost alone in the first two centuries in their effort to
understand the great Apostle at all. In Gnosticism, also,
we have the beginnings of the critical spirit, premature and
imperfect, as all such beginnings must necessarily be, but of
value as pointing the Church to the need of a more reasoned
theology. For instance, it is to the Gnostics we owe the
importation of such words as οὐσία, ὑπόστασις,[1] and
ὁμοούσιος; while the need of meeting their wild conceptions
led to the development of the doctrine of the Logos. In
Gnosticism we find the first attempts to answer many of
the questions which still occupy the attention of Christian
thinkers, *e.g.* the real meaning of the sufferings of Christ,
when we consider His Deity rather than His humanity.
Again, in Gnosticism we have the first crude representations
of the ideas of transubstantiation, of purgatory, and of
prayers for the dead. Disastrous as we may deem the
development of these ideas to have been, the historian
cannot do otherwise than recognise their importance.

Gnosticism, in fact, sprang from the very same source
as medieval Scholasticism, the desire to reduce to logical
unity all the phenomena of religion and life. But the

---

[1] Its use in *Hebrews* i. 3 is of uncertain date.

sense of authority which saved Scholasticism was altogether absent from the more restless inquirers of the second
century. Yet by the dangers to which they bore witness
the Gnostics contributed to the growth of that authority,
the outcome of which was the Catholic Church. Moreover,
Gnosticism, in spite of its docetism, in spite also of its
tendency to look upon history as " only the fluctuating
outward expression of intellectual and moral ideas," [1]
bore a witness of its own to the fact of Christ. The evidence
of these early heretics to the hold of Jesus upon cultivated
minds in the early years of the second century has not
always, we think, been sufficiently appreciated by Christian
Apologists. The very fecundity of their systems shows
how profound an impression Jesus Christ had made on the
world. Even their Christology, as Dorner has pointed
out, bore witness to a great truth.[2] The Ebionites and
other Jewish Christians had allowed to Christ little more
than a glorified humanity ; Valentinus laid stress upon
His pre-existence. For the Gnostics " Christ's coming was
the epoch of a great extrication. The sparks of divine
nature in all susceptible souls were to be gathered to
Christ as their true centre, and to the upper world as their
true home." [3] " In their wildest flights we see how the
Gnostics realised, as the earlier followers of the Messiah
had failed to do, that not merely mankind, but the whole
cosmos, seen and unseen, had been affected by the Incarnation." [4]

Gnosticism, when defeated in the Church, took refuge
underground. For a thousand years we find it living a
subterranean existence, ever and anon coming to the surface in some new heresy, the roots of which lie deep in the
older Gnosticism, or rather in the religions older even than
Gnosticism to which Gnosticism was so largely indebted.

[1] Ottley, *Incarnation*, i. p. 178.
[2] Dorner, *op. cit.* bk. i. p. 252.
[3] Rainy, *Ancient Catholic Church*, p. 105, and Harnack, *H.D.* i. p. 253 (1).
[4] Foakes-Jackson in *Cambridge Theological Essays*, p. 484.

In the third century it appears in the formidable movement known as Manichaeism, so called from Mani (b. 215), the founder of the sect. As might be expected from its head-quarters being in Babylon, the doctrines of the sect were in the main akin to the old Babylonian nature-religion, modified by Persian Dualism, with some admixture, especially in the West, of the Gnostic Christianity of Basilides and Marcion. Owing partly to their minute and strict asceticism and their rigid morality, partly also to the great number " of the cultured who sought for a rational and yet to some extent Christian religion, and who had exalted free inquiry, especially as regards the Old Testament, into a battle-flag," [1] Manichaeism obtained considerable influence in Christian circles, especially in North Africa, and at one time succeeded even in capturing Augustine.

Manichaeism in African Christianity was finally crushed out by the persecution of the Vandals. Elsewhere the Gnostic-Manichaean movement still survived. Of few heresies can the continuity of existence under different names be more clearly traced. In the Eastern Church we find these heretics reappearing as Paulicians from one of their two leaders, Paul and John of Samosata. After repeated persecutions the Paulicians were driven to the mountains of Armenia, whence they carried on their struggle with the orthodox Empire. Efforts to exterminate them were fruitless, while if left in the East they would prove dangerous allies of the Saracens. So in 973 John Zimisces tried the experiment of toleration, and trans-ported a great colony to Thrace, thus introducing their doctrine into Europe. Judged by its results, no step was more disastrous. They multiplied rapidly, and by means of the Crusades, more also through their restless propa-ganda, in the twelfth century they spread everywhere in the West. Under the various names of Bogomils, Bulgarians,

[1] Harnack, *H.D.* iii. p. 334.

D

or Bougres—a name innocent and national in origin, odious in application—Patarins, Albigensians, and Cathari, we may discern a heresy almost as united and widespread as the Catholic faith.

The Cathari or ' Puritans ' owed their name to their high morality. There was, in fact, nothing in the Joyless Manichaean creed to attract the sensual. Their tenets were the familiar positions of Gnosticism. As their ideal of spiritual growth lay in the destruction of the flesh, the propagation of life in any form was the work of the devil. So they refused to eat meat, eggs, milk—everything, in fact, which resulted from the sexual passion, with the exception of fish, for which their rude science suggested a different origin. Their fasts were endless : three days in each week, three periods of forty days in each year. Their strict vegetarianism had, however, other roots than their hatred of generation. We have records of Cathari who chose death rather than kill a fowl ; to them it was the spirit of a fallen brother passing through another probation. But their tenderness was confined to animals. They tortured themselves by swallowing pounded glass or poisonous potions, while suicide was held up as the crowning virtue of the ' perfected.'

We are not writing the history of heresy, but of Christian thought. We need not, therefore, inquire into the causes chiefly to be found in the corruption of the Church, which led this extravagant hybrid of purity and falsehood to threaten for a while the very existence of Christianity. Nor need we detail the steps by which this age-long heresy was finally crushed in the thirteenth century by the crusade of Innocent III. against the Albigensians, most of all by St. Francis pointing out the more excellent way of sunshine and love. But one reflection upon this remarkable heresy is very pertinent to our purpose.

We notice the Manichaean doctrine, emphasised by the Cathari, of a twofold morality, a higher standard for the

small body of the ' Elect ' or ' perfected,' a lower for the
general mass. Orthodox Christianity reproduced, almost
unchallenged, the same distinction ; it formed, in fact, the
fundamental feature of its ethical systems, the chief factor
in its organisation. It is not without significance that
Monasticism and Manichaeism—including in this title
the long heresy from the Gnostics to the Cathari—rose
and perished together. Both recognised and understood
" the imperious desire for immolation which lies in the
depth of every soul." [1]   Both took as their foundation the
conception of a double ideal—the higher reserved for the
' spiritual ' or ' religious '—instead of a single ideal of life,
attainable by all. For a thousand years the effect of this
distinction was apparent in forms of thought and ideals of
life too obvious to need enumeration.

IV

In the long struggle between Gnosticism and the faith
of Jesus the theological student will discern more than
the manifestation of difference. He will detect the growth
of points of contact between a regenerated Hellenism and
Christianity. It was inevitable, therefore, that attempts
should be made to bring about a closer understanding.
The Church no longer boasted that ' not many wise men
after the flesh ' were called ; nor could Celsus complain
with justice that Christianity was confined to the ' ignorant,
unintelligent, and uneducated.'   Hence, as Origen tells us,
' When men, not only the labouring and serving classes,
but also many from the cultured classes of Greece, came
to see something honourable in Christianity . . . scholars
endeavoured to penetrate deeper into the truth of Christianity.'   To this we owe the rise of " Apologies," or
philosophic defences of Christianity for the sake of out-
siders.

[1] Sabatier, *St. Francis* (Eng. Tr.), p. 73.

The Apologists, generally speaking, are chiefly concerned with a defence of Christianity against the charges brought against it by political opponents. They appeal against the prevailing intolerance, misunderstanding, and persecution. But in seeking to change the attitude of the government they are driven to present Christianity in terms that could be understood—on the lines, that is, of natural theology and of the older schools of thought. Hence the emphasis by the Apologists of the doctrine of the Logos and its relations to the cosmos, and the attempt in diverse ways to date back Christianity as an actual fact in the world to the time before the beginning of history. To Justin Martyr, for instance, in his *Apology*, written about 150, the Incarnation is but the final and complete manifestation of the Logos, the presence of which in the world he recognises wherever there has been goodness or wisdom. Christianity is no break in continuity, no light that comes *per saltum*, but the fulfilment in Christ Jesus of all reason, religion, and prediction. Justin identifies Christ with the Divine Wisdom manifested, though sporadically, in all ages and among all peoples. He is the teacher of Socrates as well as of Abraham ; of Orpheus and of Moses. ' We have been taught,' he writes, ' that Christ is the first-born of God, and we have declared that He is the Word of whom every race of men were partakers. Those who have lived with reason (μετὰ λόγου) are Christians, even though they have been thought Atheists, as among the Greeks Socrates and Heraclitus, and men like them.' But the ' teacher whom the Christians followed ' was ' reason itself ; it was visible and appeared bodily in Him.'

For Gentile idolatry the Apologists have nothing but scorn ; though at the same time they point to the eternal elements in Gentile philosophy and Gentile religion. Pre-Christian philosophies, save the Epicurean, though sadly marred by the rule of ' demons,' could thus claim kinship with Christianity by reason of ' the seed of the Logos '

implanted in them.   No doubt this acknowledgment of
identity of content is purchased sometimes by a lack of
the due emphasis on the special and significant doctrines
of Christianity, the doctrines of the Trinity, of sin, of the
Atonement, of natural immortality, and the like.   Justin,
for instance, at times seems to echo Plato rather than Paul.
But "Apologies" never reveal the deeper man ; the author
is always thinking of his opponent.   Yet the ultimate
effect of the Apologist was to lift Christianity from being
the religion of a sect founded upon enthusiasm into a
world-religion that appealed to the universal conscience
and reason.   Minucius Felix, the last of the group, reminds
us of our own Bishop Butler, when he claims that every
man who possesses reason and speech will find Christian
truth in his own constitution, and in the rational order of
the world.

The close approach of Christianity and Greek philosophy
is nowhere better seen than in two writers who at first sight
appear to demonstrate the opposite.   The Apologist Tatian's
Oratio ad Graecos is a violent polemic against all Greek
philosophers ; Celsus, on the contrary, is equally violent
against Christianity.   But while Tatian, and Clement after
him, maintained that the philosophers have borrowed from
and distorted the teaching of Moses and the prophets,
Celsus similarly derives the teachings of Jesus from the
philosophers.   Both alike, though with different stress,
would approve the memorable sentence ascribed by
Clement to the Neoplatonist Numenius : ' What is Plato
but Moses speaking in the language of Athens ? '   Such
charges of plagiarism were common, and witness to growing sympathy.

Or, again, we may note the similarity in certain points
of all the schools of thought of the second and third centuries, whether called Gnostic, Christian, or Neoplatonic.
All alike fall back upon an abstract notion of God as the
transcendent Absolute.   All need a mediator between this

Absolute and the world, and, according to their outlook, find the bridge over the chasm, in the Logos, a system of 'aeons,' of ' powers ' (Philo), or of ' demons.' Further, as all of them, not excepting the orthodox, tend to find the secret of evil in matter—some make the two one—all lay emphasis upon self-discipline and renunciation as the secret of the higher vision.

In their belief in the relation of Christianity to reason Apologists and Gnostics are one. But while the Gnostics sought to transform Christianity into a religion after their own heart, the Apologists were loyal to the traditional Christianity, except in so far as their silence on certain matters may be deemed disloyalty. The Apologists were conservative ; they accepted the historical elements of Christianity, and tried to make them intelligible. To Theophilus, for instance, the first chapters of *Genesis* contain the sum of all Christian knowledge ; while all the Apologists look upon the Old Testament as the full revelation of truth, completely identical with the teaching of Jesus. The Gnostics, on the contrary, dealt with the materials so as best to fit them in with certain *a priori* philosophical speculations. To the one Christianity was a complete revelation which brought assurance in proportion as it was pondered ; to the other it was part of a process which led by diverse ways to the Absolute.

One difference between the Apologists and the Greek philosophers is conspicuous and vital. When Celsus sneered at Christianity as fit only for fullers and bakers, he expressed the exclusiveness of all Hellenism. Stoicism, for instance, for all its ideals of moral freedom, left the mass of mankind hopelessly grovelling in filth and darkness. The steep upward road is only for the few. But the Apologists share the universalism of the Gospel in their claim that Christianity can be grasped by all, and can lift even women and uneducated men into saints and sages.

If we turn to the positive contents of the Apologists we

note the development, especially in Justin, of a Platonic
rather than a Johannine conception of the Logos as the
organ of divine revelation.   Many of the activities in
human history which a more developed theology attributed
to the agency of the Holy Spirit, Justin attributes to the
Logos, who is not only the creative reason of God, but
His revealing Word ever hovering between God and the
world.   Thus both in the Apologists and Alexandrians
there is little real place for the Holy Spirit, in spite of their
orthodox tribute to His claims.[1]   In one aspect the Logos
is the thought of the world within the mind of the ' increate '
God, which the act of creation—a voluntary energy, not,
as with the Gnostics, a physical necessity—projects from
God, thus giving to the Logos a separate hypostasis.   From
this begetting arises the subordination of the Logos, and
the realisation in creation of the idea of the world.   The
exaggerated emphasis which all the Apologists lay upon
the monotheistic explanation of the world as the chief part
of Christian doctrine was as much due to the pressure of
Greek thought as to the conflict with surrounding polytheism.   In all early Christian writers, as in the official
creeds, the doctrine of God as creator is the first and most
important article of the Christian faith.

As regards the Atonement, the Apologists say little or
nothing, whatever may have been their personal views.
Here again we see the influence of Hellenism.   In the
teaching of the schools it is always ' gnosis ' as such that leads
to salvation.   So with the Apologists.   It is as the divine
teacher that Christ brings ' salvation,' and faith is the conviction of the truth of His teaching.   ' Salvation ' is the
consequent gift of eternal life ; for most of the Apologists
—in this departing from Plato—argue against the conception of the natural immortality of the soul.   The
neglect by the Apologists of the essential factor of sin

[1] Bigg, *O.P.A.* p. 171, thinks differently.   But I am not convinced by his
argument.

is due to their looking upon sin as the result of bondage to the ' demons ' ; from which bondage man can be delivered by the exercise of his own will. In this last the Apologists will have no parley with Stoic fatalism, as represented, for instance, by Marcus Aurelius.

v

Clement of Alexandria and Origen have often been classi-fied with the Apologists. But this is scarcely to do justice to these great scholars and true saints. The Apologists were on the defensive ; Clement and Origen had a far larger design. They were the first of a succession of writers, learned in all the wisdom of Greece, and enthusiastic for its philosophy, but yet loyal to the teaching of Christ, who tried to incorporate into the new faith all that was best in the culture of the Hellenic world, especially in the Platonic and Stoic philosophers. ' The way of truth,' Clement said, ' is one. But into it as into a perennial river streams flow from all sides.'

The permanent value of their work will be differently judged according to the student's bias towards the Platonic or Aristotelian philosophy, or his belief in the greater value of an institutional Church. But of the greatness of their attempt there can be no question. To give an historical parallel : Clement and Origen attempted, with a wonderful measure of success, to do for the Christianity of the third century what Thomas Aquinas and the great Schoolmen accomplished for the medieval Church, what Erasmus and the Humanists of the Renaissance failed to do for the Church of the Reformation, what many of the deepest thinkers and most loyal Christians of to-day see must be done for the Church of the twentieth century. Owing to the success of the reactionaries at Trent and elsewhere, the modern world of thought lies outside the Church rather than within ; at best on parallel lines ; rarely under its

influence ; never under its control. The success of
Clement and Aquinas thus seems the greater by contrast
with the disastrous failure at the Reformation, and by
the ever-growing necessity, in the world of thought to-day,
for a new reconciliation of Christianity and culture.   In
many respects, especially if we remember the times in
which it was done, the work of Clement is the boldest
undertaking of the sort in the history of the Church.
" There is no one whose vision of what the faith of Jesus
Christ was intended to do for mankind was so full or so
true." [1]

The boldness of Clement is seen in his refusal to surrender the title ' Gnostic ' to the heretics.   He claims that
the perfect Christian must be a ' Gnostic,' for ' gnosis '
is the purification of the ruling faculty of the soul.   The
' achievements of the Gnostic faculty ' are ' to know what
is right, to do what is right, and to help others to do it.'
But the difference between the school of Clement and
Origen and the Gnostics must not be overlooked.   Their
aims were similar, almost identical—to bring Christianity
into touch with the thought of the times ; to combine
in one creed the immanence and transcendence of God,
definite Christian conditions, and a free outlook upon the
experience of the world.   But their methods were opposite.
The attempt of the Gnostics was premature.   Christianity
and Greek philosophy were not yet in sufficient sympathy.
In consequence the Gnostics dealt with the materials of the
Christian faith with a destructive freedom which witnessed
to the uncertain nature of Christian tradition and dogma.
But between their effort and that of Clement, largely in
consequence of the Gnostic heresies themselves, Christian
tradition had become sacred, Christian Scriptures and
dogma more definite.   To this tradition and dogma
Clement and his school were thoroughly loyal, though
anxious to present both in philosophic form.   The Gnostics

[1] Hort, *Ante-Nicene Fathers*, p. 93.

had allowed their philosophy to overmaster their faith ; Clement and Origen made it subservient. With the latter, as with Anselm of Aosta, faith is the foundation, knowledge the superstructure. Faith is the summary knowledge of urgent truths, knowledge a sure demonstration of what has been received through faith. Knowledge not based on faith is neither stable nor effective ; though, on the other hand, 'nothing is to be believed which is unworthy of God,' that is, which is contrary to reason.

Though Clement [1] may have been by birth as well as by training an Athenian, it is his connection with the Christian catechetical school at Alexandria, founded a few years previously by Pantaenus, that gives him his special claim. No place could have been for Clement a more suitable sphere of work. Alexandria, the second city in the world, was the meeting-place of East and West. It was the home of three great tendencies, which then, as now, were potent in shaping the thoughts of men : Egyptian symbolism with its esoteric beliefs and ancient priesthood, Jewish monotheism, and Greek science, philosophy and culture. Among its restless crowds, and in its famous university, all that was plausible in speculation, and much that was foolish, found disciples and expositors. In a city of so many religions thought was free. No dominant creed or ritual hindered the most critical inquiry ; while the spectacle of the many altars led the thoughtful to inquire as to the one 'unknown God' whom all alike 'ignorantly worshipped.' The value, amid such surroundings, of the Christian school was incalculable. Its method was determined by the varied needs of the people—catechumens or candidates for orders,—to whom it appealed, as well as by the non-ecclesiastical character of its organisation. In the higher classes, after the discipline of mathematics and sciences, the Greek systems of philosophy, save only the 'godless Epicureans,' and the Old Testament

[1] Born about 150. He was still living in 211, but not in 216.

Scriptures were studied side by side as propaedeutic to
higher knowledge. The final destruction of this school in
the fourth century, in the struggle between Theophilus of
Alexandria and the Egyptian monks, was one of the
many disasters which led to the ruin of the Egyptian
Church.

In his pre-Christian days Clement had investigated not
only Judaism, but the creeds of paganism. To the influence of the 'mysteries' we may trace his manifest
tendency to treat Christianity as itself a 'mystery,' [1] the
initiation into a higher 'gnosis.' His learning, diffuse
and uncritical, was as vague and unsystematic as his
philosophy; altogether in keeping in its 'studied disorder' with the title which he gave to one of his most
important works, *Stromateis*, or *Clothes-bags of Gnostic
Notes on the True Philosophy*. But his sympathies are
wide and generous. He refuses to speak harshly even of
those 'orthodoxasts' who would reduce Christianity to
'faith only, bare faith,' who claim 'that philosophy comes
of evil, and was introduced into life for the ruin of men.'
But while he thus fights the battle of education within the
Church, he differs from many Christian thinkers, both in
ancient and modern times, by his insistence, especially
in his practical work called the *Pedagogue* or '*Tutor*,'
upon Christian life and experience in all their fulness as
the great corrective of all theories, and the outcome of all
true 'gnosis.' He maintains that purity is the condition
of insight : 'conduct follows knowledge as surely as the
shadow the body.' With Origen, too, conduct is all important ; with all his abstract thinking he is ever showing
us the effect of action. In fact, with both Origen and
Clement, 'Faith means Belief determining Action and
leading up through Obedience to Love.' [2]

[1] See on this Inge, *Christian Mysticism*, App. B.
[2] Bigg, *C.P.A.* p. 209 *n.* As an illustration we note that Pantaenus, their
master, in his old age had set off as a missionary to India.

Clement boldly asserts the unity of all knowledge in Christ. ' Just as every family goes back to the creator, so does the teaching of all good things go back to the Lord ' ; in whom alone we find the ' sovereign unassailable Faith,' and from whom comes the inevitable impulse of the human mind to philosophy. But all such philosophy is only ' the preliminary training towards the perfection that comes by Christ.' For the Greeks who lived ' before the advent of the Lord, philosophy was necessary for righteousness ' ; ' Philosophy was the " schoolmaster " for the Greek world, as the Law was for the Hebrews, " to bring them to Christ " ' ; for the Greeks ' it was a sort of Covenant of their own,' communicated to them possibly by angelic mediation ; though necessary no longer, ' it is still profitable for piety.' Thus the whole story of the world—cosmology, psychology, and ethics alike—is centred in the benevolent action of the Logos, whose Incarnation is the final manifestation of truth and goodness ; for whose Advent the world has been prepared by trial and discipline.

Clement's pupil and successor, Origen (Origenes Adamantius), who died at Tyre in 253, broken with his sufferings in the Decian persecution, completed—so far, that is, as such a movement can ever be said to be completed—the work that Clement had begun. There is no need to go over the theories of Origen in detail, for the chief features of his teaching are identical with those of Clement. But, as is natural with a successor, the theories are more completely thought out, there is greater reserve over doubtful points, while the outlines of the whole are more clearly, sometimes more narrowly, presented, always, too, without signs of haste or heat. With more discrimination than Clement, he introduced everything worth knowing into the sphere of theology, completely welding together Christianity and the culture and science of the age. That in this respect " orthodox theology of all creeds has never advanced beyond

the circle mapped out by his mind " [1] is a wonderful
testimony to his success.

With greater clearness and more exegetical skill than
Clement, Origen sets out the assumption that there is an
esoteric form of Christianity, ' mystical economies made
known by Holy Scripture,' which, however, must be
handled with due ' reserve.' The deciphering of this
' pneumatic ' or ' spiritual Christianity ' is the task of
theology, necessary indeed if the Bible is to be commended
to the Greek mind. All Scripture has in reality a threefold sense, a pneumatic, psychic, and ' somatic,' correspond-
ing to the elements of body, soul, and spirit which we find
in the cosmos. The simple man is edified by means of the
' flesh ' of the Bible, the more advanced by means of its
' soul,' while for the perfected there is its pneumatic interpretation. The somatic or historical sense, the lowest
rungs in the ladder, must first be ascertained before we can
climb to the higher. In some passages, it is true, the literal
sense is absurd and impossible, as in the story of the Fall.
Such ' stumbling-blocks ' have been deliberately introduced
that we may not be drawn away from the spiritual ' by the
obvious.' By stripping off ' the covering ' of history we
pass to the psychic or moral sense. In *Joshua*, for instance,
the kings are really the ' names of vices.' The final stage
in this " Biblical Alchemy," as Dr. Bigg calls it, is the
pneumatic sense. He who has attained this has become
inwardly united with God's Logos, and from this union
obtains all that he requires.

In this connection one matter of historical importance
must not be overlooked. For the ' spiritual Church ' there
is an ' eternal Gospel,' related to the written one as the
letter is to the law, as the shadow to the substance. This
eternal Gospel is the full revelation of God's highest inten-

[1] Harnack, *H.D.* ii. p. 334. Cf. Westcott, *History of Religious Thought
in the West*, pp. 243, 252 ; Pfleiderer, *Philosophy and Development of Religion*, ii. p. 280

tions, and is hidden in the Holy Scripture, waiting for interpretation by the 'mystic sense.' The later development of this doctrine in the Middle Ages by Joachim di Fiori and the Spiritual Franciscans can thus be traced back to Origen.

As regards the will, Clement is definite and clear. He refuses to have anything to do with the fatalistic tendencies of Gnosticism and Pantheism. With him will is an essential feature in human nature, and as such is always free. The will can reject the light ; hence the value of the discipline by means of which the unbelieving will is led to surrender to the light. The decision from moment to moment rests with us, but not the end. But Origen, while he claims that freedom is the mark of the created spirit, in reality denies freedom, or rather makes it to be but temporal. For in its ultimate analysis evil is ' unreal,' ' non-existent,' certainly not ' eternal '—in the assertion of this lies Origen's optimism or heresy—inasmuch as it is the work of ourselves and not of God. In the end, therefore, the spirit must return to that which is good ; freedom is merely the appearance under which we see the necessity of the created spirit developing itself in time on the lines of its indestructible spirituality. For souls not purified before death Origen and Clement provide the cleansing flames of purgatory. ' Even Peter and Paul must come into that fire,' and pass from sphere to sphere, ever gaining increase of illumination and strength. But the gross conceptions of a later age are altogether lacking, for the purifying fire consists in the torments of conscience, and is kindled by the sinner himself. ' The soul, when it has collected unto itself an abundance of sins, glows into punishment and bursts into penal fire.' For some spirits, as compared with their pre-existent condition, the present life is a prison-house of correction, though for others it may be a place of relief. But the eschatology of the Alexandrians, in spite of constant appeals to texts of Scripture, is largely Platonic,

one chief source being the *Gorgias*.[1]   Nevertheless, in
Origen's doctrine of purgatory the churches of the East
and West find the germs of much later teaching, in the
main identical, though the Greeks, it is true, have no word
for purgatory.[2]   The refusal of both the Greek and Latin
Churches to admit Origen's contention, that purgatory
admits of repentance or probation, would appear to be
their chief difference from the Alexandrian Father.

As regards the Eucharist, the Alexandrians held a spiritual real Presence of Christ, of which the bread and the wine
were symbols.   The theory now called Transubstantiation
was alien to their genius ; necessarily so, for, as Dr. Bigg
rightly points out, " Transubstantiation rests upon Aristotelian or Stoic Realism, and is diametrically opposed to
Platonism." [3]

The chief defect of the Alexandrian position is the defi-
ciency, so characteristically Greek, in the idea of the divine
holiness.   From this follows the absence of any adequate
doctrine of sin.   There is no sufficient explanation of the
moral and spiritual condition in which the mass of mankind, as distinct from the few enlightened philosophers,
find themselves.   Origen compares evil to the ' chips and
similar rubbish which a carpenter leaves in executing the
plan of a building,' while his optimistic doctrine of its
' unreality ' lands him in universalism.   For any further
explanation of evil he falls back upon his conception of
pre-existence.   Creation is eternal ; the ' spirits ' that
sinned in a higher world have become ' souls ' in this lower
scene of discipline.   He fails to see that this explanation
but pushes the problem one step farther back.   In consequence, he only deals slightly with the Atonement, while
redemption is presented in terms of illumination or escape
rather than grace.   The way of light is not the way of the

---

[1] Bigg, *C.P.A.* pp. 112, 113 *n.* 4, 229-230; Jowett, *Plato*, ii. p. 297 ff.
[2] Bigg, *C.P.A.* pp. 295 *n.*, 298 *n.*
[3] *Ibid.* p. 219 *n.*   Cf. *infra*, p. 236 f.

Cross—'to know Christ crucified,' writes Origen, 'is the knowledge of babes'—but 'the turning inwardly to one-self, restoring one's own nature, and thus practising righteousness.' Owing to their fundamental premise of the unchangeableness of the Absolute, forgiveness is always a difficult notion for the Alexandrians, and is by them, as a rule, associated with the 'washing' of Baptism. We ascend to God through contemplation rather than by reconciliation; in fact, we might say that to the illuminated, 'pneumatic,' or 'Gnostic' Christian the Saviour is of little importance save as a teacher. He is 'the light that lighteth every man that cometh into the world.'

Origen's doctrine of Atonement is further limited by the prevalent notion of the tyranny of the demons. While he acknowledges that all sins require expiation, and even attributes to the death of Christ a vicarious significance, he yet fatally warped Soteriology for a thousand years by his conception of the Atonement as a ransom paid to the devil, who was, however, cheated of his price by the Resurrection, this last a detail first found among the Gnostic Basilidians.

This doctrine of Origen—with whom, however, it is not original, for it is found in Irenaeus—was taken up and developed by Gregory of Nyssa (332-395). Gregory's emphasis on the 'deceit,' 'fraud, and surprise' with which the devil was thus cheated of his prey accentuates the worst features in Origen's theory, and is a curious commentary on the ethical conceptions of his age. Gregory Nazianzen (330-389), it is true, indignantly asks : 'To whom was this ransom paid, and for what cause ? If to the devil, fie upon the shameful thought.' But closer examination shows that he substitutes for the deception of the devil by God self-deception in the Evil One, 'inasmuch as he was taken in by God's assumption of our nature.' Even Augustine, in spite of his lifting the doctrine of the Atonement to a higher plane by the stress that he laid upon sin,

and by his noble conception of reconciliation by a mediator,
in spite also of his manifest desire to avoid any antagonism
in the relations of Father and Son, commits himself to this
repulsive theory, and calls the Cross a ' mouse-trap.' The
claims of the devil to an equivalent he regards as most
just, though forfeited by his inflicting death upon One
who was sinless. Finally, Gregory the Great completed
this vulgarisation by speaking of the devil as captured on
the hook of the Incarnation by the ' bait ' of the body of
Christ.

That a theory with such huckstering conceptions of
God could be accepted by the Church for nearly a thousand
years as the explanation, if only in part, of the Cross, must
always seem extraordinary to the modern mind. Nevertheless, with but few protests it endured until overthrown
by Anselm. Neither Irenaeus, nor Origen, nor any of the
Fathers seem to have been conscious of the " residuary
dualism," a legacy of Gnosticism, which underlay the belief.[1]
In Athanasius's profound *De Incarnatione*, Satan, it is true,
retires into the background. The keynote is the goodness
of God. The Apologists had insisted on the *teaching* of
Christ as the real revelation of the Godhead. Athanasius,
with truer insight, lays the stress upon His Person. His
main thesis is the thought of redemption. The ' coming
of the Logos in the flesh ' is ' the ransom and salvation of
all creation,' the destruction of the principle of corruption
which held man captive. The Incarnation, whereby the
creative Logos became our perfect representative before
God, thus becomes the Atonement, for the Cross is but
part of the Incarnation, the complete purpose of which
is to ' deify ' human nature. As such its ' achievements
are of such purpose and kind that if one should wish to
enumerate them he may be compared to men who gaze at
the expanse of the sea and wish to count its waves.' But
the theory of Athanasius, with its superficial resemblance

---

[1] Fairbairn, *op. cit.* p. 67 *n.*

E

to the question and the answer propounded by Anselm, never appealed to the Western Church until it was restated by Thomas Aquinas.[1]

Origen's doctrine of the Incarnation is remarkable for his clear teaching of the eternal generation of the Son. This relation is supra-temporal ; it is an eternal process within the Divine Being. " In one point he agrees with Tertullian, while in another he advances beyond him. On the one hand he freely interchanges, as Tertullian does, the terms Logos and Son—the abstract term and that which connotes moral relationship ; on the other hand, while Tertullian conceived the Trinity as economic—God as it were in movement, opposed to God *in statu*—Origen, by his doctrine of the eternal generation, replaces the thought of movement by that of an eternal process, ever complete in itself, yet ever continued." [2] But of this movement of Being the Father is the supreme cause and source, and therefore must be regarded as greater than the Son. Thus side by side with his doctrine of the eternal Sonship Origen formulated the notion of the subordination of the Son. This he pushed to extremes which undoubtedly tended to the later Arianism. Thus he refused to allow to the Son essential goodness, or that the highest kind of prayer or adoration may be addressed to Him. Yet, in spite of its limitations, the advance in scientific Christology due to Origen is very great ; how great is unrecognised by an age that can no longer compare him with the Valentinus or Basilides from whose crudities he delivered the Church.

The immediate influence of Origen upon the theology and thought of the Eastern world cannot be exaggerated. In part this was due to the fact that many diverse schools, orthodox and unorthodox, could find in Origen their different arguments, or, failing that, something to arouse their antagonism. Of greater importance was his destruction of the current Gnosticism, and the establishment of

[1] Cf. Ottley, *Incarnation*, ii. p. 30.   [2] Ottley, *op. cit.* i. p. 243.

a philosophy of religion which appealed powerfully to the cultured thought of the age. He was the first of the great theologians of the Church. But, in spite of the influence which at first he exerted, Origen was unable to retain his standing in the Church even in the East. The gradual hardening of theological thought in the fourth century under the growing power of tradition, the change in thought which afterwards set in from Platonic idealism to Aristotelian realism, and the consequent weakened hold of the doctrine of the Logos, after Athanasius, were the causes of this decline. Add the unrest produced by the Arian and other heresies, all of which could appeal to some expression or other of Origen in their favour. At the instigation of Jerome, who in his earlier days had called Origen ' a teacher second only to the great Apostle,' Origenism was condemned in the West. In 496 Origen was branded by Pope Gelasius as a schismatic and the use of his works forbidden, except those sanctioned by Jerome's translation into Latin. This was followed in the East by fresh condemnations by the Emperor Justinian (543), who not only closed the schools of the philosophers at Athens, but the Christian schools at Alexandria and Antioch. Henceforth his name was a byword and reproach in the East. The Orthodox Church no longer allowed even the recollection that once there had been room within it for variety of opinion. But in the West there was respect for his learning, and passages from his works were inserted by Leo III. in the Breviary. At the Reformation Luther's antagonism was followed, though in more seemly language, by Melanchthon. But in the revival of much of his teaching by the Cambridge Platonists of the seventeenth century, as well as by Maurice and Westcott in our own day, we see Origen once more obtaining his own. Under the influence of a truer conception of development Theology recognises in both Clement and Origen two of her great master-builders, though much of their work has not stood the test of time and experience. Yet in many respects (*e.g.* their teaching on the Resurrection) modern thought, in its deliverance from what Bishop Westcott rightly called " the heavy burden of African theology," is now going back to positions first indicated by Origen. " Greek Christian thought has not yet done its work in the West." [1]

VI

The prevailing syncretism with which Christianity had to contend as a religious force manifested its strength in the philosophic world in the system of Neoplatonism, " that splendid vision of incomparable cloudland, in which the sun of Greek philosophy set." [2] This religion or philosophy—both terms are applicable, for Neoplatonism was really a philosophy seeking to transform itself into a religion—embodied in itself the elements of most previous systems, both in the East and West, including not a few ideas and phrases borrowed from Christianity. Two of its leaders, Ammonius Saccas and Plotinus, are stated to have been lapsed Christians, and another, Amelius, made use of the prologue of *St. John.* Numenius seems to have been acquainted with the Gospels, and possibly with the Epistles of St. Paul. Neoplatonism claimed to be " not only the absolute philosophy completing all systems, but at the same time the absolute religion, confirming and explaining all earlier religions." [3] As a philosophy its perfect fruition marked inevitable decay ; as a religion it merits attention by its ethical spirit, as well as the emphasis it placed on the experience of the eternal. In its challenge to Christianity we see the last organised rally of the Hellenic world, with whom the subordination of religion to philosophy was almost an axiom. Neoplatonism, while willing to live and let live, dreaded and detested the absolutist claims of

---

[1] Westcott, *op. cit.* pp. 243, 246. [2] Harnack, *H.D.* i. p. 341.
[3] Hatch, *op. cit.* p. 133.

Christ, and the conquering might of His Church. Its hatred was increased by its consciousness that it had no message save for ' the wise and prudent,' whereas Christianity claimed that none were beyond her reach. Here again we see the mark of an exclusive Hellenism.

The details of the Neoplatonic philosophy as begun in Alexandria in a Jewish setting by Philo, and as set forth in more strictly Hellenic or philosophic form by Numenius, by Ammonius Saccas (†245), in the *Enneads* of Plotinus, in Porphyry (233-305), or by the later teachers at Athens, Plutarch (†433) or Proclus, belong rather to the history of philosophy than of Christian thought. More pertinent is it to note the special challenge made by Neoplatonism, and the effect of the challenge upon Christian thinkers. Neoplatonism supplied for the select few to whom it appealed a religious experience by contemplation of the eternal ideas. Such contemplation involved a withdrawal from the world, the turning of the eye of the soul inward, and presupposed as its condition an ascetic discipline. From this inward contemplation the soul rose by mystic intuition or æsthetic feeling into union with the Absolute. In Neoplatonism, therefore, we have the connecting link between the mystics of the Christian Church and the old Hellenic world of philosophy. And just as the idea of a crucified Saviour is contrary to the whole genius of Neoplatonism, so in Christian mysticism, as we shall see later, the danger ever lies in an inadequate doctrine of the Atonement.

The master-architect of Neoplatonism was Plotinus, one of the profoundest and most religious thinkers the world has known. Though himself outside the Christian Church, no one, except St. Augustine, has had a more lasting influence upon the thought of the Church. Plotinus, a fellow-student of Origen, was born at Lycopolis in Egypt about 205 A.D. In 244 he settled in Rome, where his influence was remarkable. His writings were voluminous,

and were collected by his biographer Porphyry into six
books called *Enneads*. As he died (269) he said to his
companion : ' Now the divine in me is struggling to reunite
with the divine in the All.'

His last words are an exposition of his whole system.
The universe is one, a vast chain in which every being is
a link. The centre of all is the Absolute, who transcends
all thought, even being itself. The Absolute, in fact, is just
nothing except sheer pure oneness. From this Absolute
we have the emanation of Mind (Νοῦς), the second name
in the Trinity of Plotinus—speedily identified by the
Christians with the Logos—which radiates from God as
light from a luminous body, producing thereby the world
of Ideas, the patterns after which our phenomenal world—
i.e. the world as we see it, not as God sees it—is framed.
A second overflow of Mind is Soul—the third name in the
Trinity—the Oversoul which is diffused everywhere, in
animals, vegetables, and the earth itself, which enfolds
within itself all individual souls, being, as it were, the
higher soul within every individual soul. Matter by itself
is No-thing, *i.e.* pure indetermination. This limit or barrier
as it were to which soul comes breaks into endless multi-
plicity that which in its origin was one. Space and Time
are forms only of thought. All progress lies in the attainment of the Absolute, the first step to which is the discovery by the lowest soul, *i.e.* the soul bound up with the
body, of its union with the Oversoul ; the second the grasping that which is ' even more divine, the soul's neighbour
above (*i.e.* Mind), after whom and from whom the soul is.'
The method of such attainment is by ' contemplation '
in the realm of pure thought. The last stage in the quest
of the Absolute is the most difficult, and is reserved
for the initiated. Its method is by vision or ecstasy,
when self-consciousness is transcended. But of this,
therefore, no description can ever be given : ' For how
can a man tell of that as other than himself which

when he discerned it seemed not other but one with
himself ? '

With the intensely scholastic Proclus (†485) Neoplatonism reached its zenith. Forty years after his decease
the schools of Athens were closed by the order of Justinian
(529), and the little band of seven philosophers, all that
were left, were driven into Persia. Orthodoxy, blind to
the facts of its own history, and with eyes from which the
future was sealed, would brook no rival in the teaching of
truth. This defeat and suppression were really for Neoplatonism the beginning of a more lasting triumph. The
schools in which for eight hundred years pagan philosophers
had taught might be closed, but before Justinian was in his
grave the great ideas of the Neoplatonists had begun their
long rule in Christian thought. Through Victorinus, the
converted philosopher, in whose writings Christian terminology only thinly veils his old Neoplatonic ideas;
through Boethius ; above all things through the pseudo-
Dionysius and his interpreter Erigena ; through Eckhart
and the long line of Christian mystics, Neoplatonism, driven
out of Athens by intolerance, found in the Church for a
thousand years a congenial home.

The influence of Neoplatonism upon Christianity was as
many-sided as it was profound. Neoplatonism was always
attracted by certain aspects in the teaching of St. Paul.
Neoplatonism had prepared Victorinus for the doctrine of
justification by faith in opposition to moralism, and from
Victorinus it passed to St. Augustine. On the other hand,
the emphasis by Neoplatonism of ' contemplation ' and
ecstasy as rungs in the ladder whereby we climb to perfection ; that in comparison with ecstasy action is but
' coarsened thought ' ; its identification, especially in
Proclus, of perfection or the Absolute with that which is
emptied of all distinctions, above all of the human ; its
teaching that the phenomenal world is a shadow only of
the timeless Intelligible World of the divine Ideas, tended,

among other causes, to the growth of Monasticism, especially in its eremitical or solitary form as exemplified in the Thebaid. Monasticism, it is true, detested Neoplatonism with a hatred which mistook difference of method for fundamental difference of aim. Nevertheless, it is not an accident that the sway of Neoplatonism in Christian thought, and the domination of the monastery in the Church, perished together. Of equal importance for Christian thought was the Neoplatonist conception of evil as in itself nothing, not merely unreal but unreality itself, the negation or privation of pure being. For this conception, as for much else, St. Augustine is profoundly indebted to Neoplatonic ideas, though no one saw more clearly where Christianity and Neoplatonism must inevitably part company.[1] Through St. Augustine and Dionysius[2] the idea became part of Christian thought, or rather of Christian theology, for Christianity can have little sympathy with an unreal optimism whose note of triumph comes from explaining away instead of overcoming the sin and sorrow which surround us.

[1] *Infra*, p. 116. [2] *Infra*, c. vi. § v.

CHAPTER III

THE PERSON OF CHRIST

Argument

I

No problem of the early Christians was more difficult than
the reconciliation of their doctrine of the Trinity with
Monotheism in such a way that they could justify their
faith, and live by it.   The ascription of deity to Jesus was
not difficult, at any rate for the Gentile who had been
brought up in an atmosphere in which there is no consciousness of the sharp gulf between man and God which Christianity has taught us to realise.   But as the Jewish converts,
among whom Christianity arose, would be the first to point
out, such ascription of deity must not be purchased at the
expense of their monotheistic faith.   Another problem,
the solution of which was equally difficult, and equally
necessary, was the giving an accurate definition of the
Person of Jesus.   This second problem was really historically first, if we view the matter in the order of thought,
and gave rise to the other.   The Early Church started with
the unity of God, at the same time clinging tenaciously
to the deity of the historic Saviour.   Only slowly was the
Church driven to see that the solution of the problem involved must be found in a distinction within the Divine
Unity and in a careful definition of His Person.   From the
earliest days these problems were acutely felt ; in the third
and fourth centuries they became burning questions in the
Church, round which centred its life and thought.   Controversy on both matters was endless.   The battle when quiet
on the main field was renewed in many side conflicts.
Nothing would be more profitless than to go through the
details of the struggle, to fill our pages with the names of
the antagonists, with the details of their arguments.   We

shall content ourselves with pointing out the movement
of thought which may be discerned in the controversies
viewed as a whole.

Discussion on the nature of the Person of Christ was
inevitable, the direct outcome of the genius of Christianity
itself. For the religion of Jesus differs from every other
religion in the relation it bears to its Founder. Christianity
is something far more than the belief in, or the acceptance
of, any principles or doctrines, though these, no doubt,
form no small part of its content. It is essentially adherence to the Person of Jesus Christ. " Who do men say
that I am ? " is still the question that must be answered
by every would-be believer. The avowal of St. Thomas,
" My Lord and my God," is still the one answer to all doubt
that wins the benediction of the Master. The institution
of the Eucharist as the central sacrament of the Church,
with its ever repeated memory of His death, its constant
realisation of His living and real presence, shows that from
the first the Church recognised that this personal relationship was the fundamental fact in its existence. In Christianity, as Dr. Fairbairn well puts it, " the pre-eminence
belongs to His Person, not to His words : His people live
by faith, not in what He said, but in what He is ; they are
governed not by statutes He framed, but by the ideal He
embodied." Thus the supreme end of Christian theology
must be the giving full intellectual expression to the truth
as manifested to men once for all in the person and life
of Jesus Christ. But this is so unspeakably rich that it
needs for its explication the varying study and experiences
of all individuals, races, and civilisations to the end of time.

The study of theology is so often divorced from the
study of history, even the history of the Church, that in-
justice has long been done to the controversies in question.
Abstraction from reality, fatal in any science, is never
so disastrous as when dogma is separated from life and
experience. Nicaea taken by itself is, perhaps, unintelli-

gible ; Nicaea studied in connection with the three centuries of struggle that preceded it becomes no longer the arena of contending syllogisms, but a crown laid at the feet of the triumphant Christ. At Nicaea many of the bishops of the dominant party still bore in their persons the marks of the sufferings they had endured for their Lord. Only a few years severed the council from the three centuries of blood and fire through which the Church had been called to pass. If in the noble army of martyrs we salute the conquerors of the world, we must not forget the cause of their victory. They did not lay down their lives for vague generalities, wider visions, or larger hopes. They knew in whom they believed. Through a confidence in His divine claims, so absolute that they scorned the most awful torments rather than subtract one jot or tittle from His honours, the martyrs had accomplished the most stupendous revolution which the world has ever known, had sapped and dissolved gigantic polytheisms, and had overthrown the Roman Empire itself. *Vicisti, Galilaee* is not merely the self-conscious cry of a dying paganism ; it is the testimony wrung from the reluctant lips of Julian to the personality of the conqueror. That the Church in its hour of triumph should consent to abate in the smallest iota the full measure of the rights of Christ was impossible. Veterans do not so easily forget their chief. For the Church thus to deny the Lord and Master for whom she had suffered all things, by whom she had conquered all, would have been an ingratitude so complete that it would leave the victory she had won more marvellous still, because totally unexplained.

This position will shed light on another matter which has sometimes puzzled the unwary. In the earlier days of the Church the Christological problem was less pressing than in later centuries. Jesus was Himself all the philosophy the Christians needed ; He made them wise unto salvation. They had, it is true, no confident phrases in which to sum up His meaning. They might, in fact, stumble into all sorts of confusions when they expressed themselves about Him, as we see Hermas doing in his *Shepherd*. But, after all, this, at any rate at first, was immaterial. It was enough that they called Him Lord, that, as Pliny found, they sang their hymns to Him as God. From the first His deity was viewed as a simple historic fact, which scarcely called for explanation. With the Ebionite, who claimed that a suffering Christ could not be divine; with the Docetist, who added that if He was divine His sufferings were unreal; with Marcion, who maintained that He had not passed through human birth or development, the early Church refused to argue save by the reaffirmation of the truths denied. " Without knowing how or why, they believed that in Him they had seen the Father, and in His name found power to walk as sons. Their experience carried its own vindication to that distracted later Empire, for joy and strength justify themselves, and men joined their company that they might pass out of weakness and fear." [1] But with the joining of the heathen recruits trouble began; the early fervour gave place to a spirit of criticism. There was a surprising oneness in their experience of Christ, but when attempts were made to give the interpretation or scientific explanation, unity ceased. His very pre-existence, which all allowed, assumed a new meaning when the term passed from the Jewish to the Hellenic world. With the Jew pre-existence is an attribute of all that is real, even of the furniture of the Mosaic tent of meeting, much more of the Messiah (1 Peter i. 20). But with the Greek pre-existence is the mark only of the spirit. Thus we are plunged at once into the whole controversy of the nature of the Person of Christ. For a while the widest freedom of thought was allowed regarding the Lord whom all adored. But the pressure of heathenism without, and of heresy within, forced the Church to

[1] Professor Armitage in *Hibbert Journal*, July 1910, p. 841.

attempt to find some formula of faith which would unite all, satisfy most fully the needful conditions, and interpret Christ to the world.

Nothing would be more interesting than to follow out the development of the consciousness in the Apostles themselves that the Saviour of the world must be far more than the historic Jesus of the Gospels; but this lies outside our scope. By the end of the first century the Church realised that any adequate definition of the Person of Christ could not be simple. In any solution "three things were demanded : a Man who actually lived, worked, and suffered ; a Divine Word whose presence has always been in the world, but has been manifested with a special power since the Incarnation ; and One, Human and yet Divine, who is constantly revealing Himself with increasing clearness to the conscience of man. We want a Christ of the past, of the present, and of the future—of yesterday, to-day, and for ever." [1] But an adequate synthesis of these needs was not reached all at once. The Church needed a long education before she was fitted to expound the complete Catholic doctrine. Nor must we forget that her difficulty was increased by the lack in ancient thought of the modern idea of personality.[2] Only slowly, by bitter experience, was the end attained. As iron sharpeneth iron, so the conflicts of a faith struggling to be articulate wrought out first the terminology of our creeds, and then their precise expression.

At the same time we must aver that the Christological struggle of the second and third centuries was part of the penalty paid by the Early Church for its failure, so marked in more ways than one, to understand St. Paul. The great spiritual conceptions of the Apostle soar clear out of the ken of the early fathers. When they think they understand him they too often degrade him. We have illus-

<hr>

[1] Foakes-Jackson in *Cambridge Theological Essays*, p. 524.
[2] Dorner, *op. cit.* A. ii. p. 510.

trations of this in the hard legal notions which Tertullian
and Augustine imported into St. Paul's great contrast
between Adam and Christ, and in the alteration in the
Roman symbol of St. Paul's explicit denial that the flesh
rises again into the materialistic clause of a belief in the
carnis resurrectionem. So also with regard to the doctrine
of Christ. " In the Apostolic Fathers and in the earlier
Apologists we find indeed for the most part a *practical*
application of the Person of Christ which leaves nothing
to be desired ; but as soon as they venture upon any
directly dogmatic statement we miss at once the firmness
of grasp and clearness of conception which mark the writings of the Apostles. If they desire to emphasise the
majesty of His Person, they not unfrequently fall into
language which savours of Patripassianism. If, on the
other hand, they wish to present Him in His mediatorial
capacity, they use words which seem to imply some divine
being who is God and yet not quite God, neither Creator
nor creature. . . . The true successors of the Apostles in
this respect are not the fathers of the second century, but
the fathers of the third and fourth centuries. In the expositors of the Nicene age we find indeed technical terms
and systematic definitions which we do not find in the
Apostles themselves, . . . but the main idea of Christ's
Person with which St. Paul confronts Gnostic Judaism is
essentially the same as that which the fathers of these later
centuries opposed to the Sabellianism and the Arianism of
their own age." [1]

In this prolonged struggle, whatever fault lay as its root,
we find two tendencies at work " each rooted deep in
human nature, each working inside and outside the Church,
and each traversing the whole field of Christian doctrine.
The first tendency was distinctly rationalistic. Its crude
form of Ebionism had denied the Lord's divinity outright.
And now that this was accepted, it was viewed as a mere

[1] Lightfoot, *Colossians*, pp. 124-125.

influence or power, or, at any rate, as not divine in the highest sense. Thus the reality of the Incarnation was sacrificed, and the result was a clear reaction to the demigods of polytheism. The other tendency, already roughly shadowed out in the docetic evasion of the Lord's humanity, was mystic in its character. Accepting the full deity that was in Christ, they reduced it to a mere appearance or modification of the One. Thus the reality of the Incarnation was undermined on the other side, and the result was a clear step back to pantheism. The first of these tendencies endangered the Lord's divinity, the second His distinction from the Father. The difficulty was to find some means of asserting both. In the fourth century it became clear that the problem required a distinction to be made inside the divine unity ; and as the Lord's baptismal formula associated the Holy Spirit as well as the Son with the Father, it followed that the God of Christianity is not personal but tri-personal. Arianism laid down a merely external, Sabellianism a merely economic Trinity ; but neither the one nor the other satisfied the conditions of the problem. It, therefore, became necessary to reverse the idea of a personality, and acknowledge not three individuals but three eternal aspects (ὑποστάσεις) of the divine, facing inward on each other as well as outward on the world." [1]

We see the same problems when we look at the development of the doctrine of the Trinity, and ask what were the conditions which must be satisfied. First and foremost, the unity or Oneness of the Godhead must be preserved at all costs. The pressure of heathenism, let alone its Jewish ancestry, prevented the Church from forgetting this. But, on the other hand, Christianity was not Judaism, however enlarged or reformed. It was through ignoring this that the Jewish Christian Church wrote its doom. In the meagre Christology of the chief epistle of that Church,

[1] Gwatkin, *Studies of Arianism*, p. 8.

St. James, we see the secret of its decay. For Christianity, as we have already emphasised, centred in Jesus Christ.[1] But experience was to show that no such position was possible which did not grant to Jesus Christ full deity. The relation of such deity to the essential unity must, however, be so stated that heathenism should not claim a ditheistic Christianity as akin to itself. The difficulties were further increased by the need, which the Church soon felt, arising out of its early baptismal formula, of guarding the real personality of the Holy Spirit, and of explaining His relation in the Tri-unity.

The difficulty under which the Church laboured in putting into exact words and definitions its concepts of God, of Christ, and of the Holy Spirit is only natural. Language is never an adequate vehicle for the expression of the deeper facts of the soul ; logic is impotent in the presence of the vivid intuitions of experience. Necessarily, therefore, language and logic, even the subtle language of Greece, proved altogether unequal to the task of wrapping up in cold phrases all that the Christians had experienced as truth in Jesus Christ. The scientific terminology of dogma had yet to be created ; only by slow sifting was the orthodox connotation determined. " The history of the terms used in Greek theology has still to be written, and only when it has been will the continuance within the theology of old philosophical questions be made apparent." [2] Unbelief has never ceased to laugh at the difficulties into which, in consequence, the theologians fell ; the records of their fierce conflicts over differences of an iota, the inadequacy, possibly the unintelligibility, of their resultant definitions. But unbelief has generally failed to see that the questions that puzzled the theologians were the same that were baffling the philosophers, and that philosopher and theologian were seeking a solution upon parallel lines.

[1] Cf. Fairbairn, *Philosophy of Religion*, pp. 532-533.
[2] Fairbairn, *Christ in Modern Theology*, p. 89 *n*.

F

Yet it would be a fatal mistake to suppose that the subtle discussions of the third and fourth centuries were the result of a philosophical spirit alien to Christianity, intruding with its noisy jargon into what would otherwise have been a holy of holies. The mistake is not without some justification. No doubt the controversies of the fourth century, when looked at from a distance, often hide the real life of the Church. But this is due to an exaggerated emphasis upon the details of the controversies themselves, instead of grasping the root from which they sprang. For, in spite of the metaphysical terms in which the struggle abounds, the cause of contention and its issue were not metaphysical at all. The controversies on the Person of Christ were not the outcome of an attempted transformation of the faith into a system of speculative theology, but were due to the richness and breadth of the spiritual experiences which men felt owed their all to Him. This it was that led the Fathers, in the spirit of St. Paul, to become Greek, if only they might win some ; it was their loyalty to Christ, not their love of metaphysics. The test of any definition, whether in physics or theology, is its power of fitting in with the facts of life. Judged by this test, the theologians may be indifferent to criticism. Poor at best as the definitions must be in which they sought to express all that Christ thus meant, yet their definitions have survived the wear and tear of centuries just because in a real way they embodied vital experiences, and made salvation through Christ the central point of theological thought. The twentieth century may not approve of fourth-century metaphysics, may be bewildered by terms some of which have lost their meaning. Nevertheless, the creeds remain because there was in them the dynamic of a living faith. The dogmas of Nicaea and Chalcedon, if they had been but a bold, splendid piece of constructive metaphysics, the completion of the Greek quest after a scientific expression of God would have perished. They have lived because they are

among the affirmatives and imperatives which from time
to time surge up in consciousness, and which carry a larger
authority than belongs to any dialectic. Their value does
not lie in their accordance with objective reality ; for of
that in the nature of things we are unable to judge—'no man
hath seen God at any time '—but in the complete explanation they give of the deepest facts of experience and history.

In this imperfect world there are few issues that are
simple. We may, therefore, own that the Christological
struggles of the fourth century, inevitable as we believe
them to have been, valuable as we hold their issues, exacted
their price. Some writers think that, as a result of the
struggle, Christianity suffered. The resultant theology, it
is said, represents the triumph of " scholastic terms and
moral realities." [1] This view, though often exaggerated,
contains some truth. In many quarters there was an un-
fortunate shifting of the centre of gravity. God was not
sufficiently interpreted in terms of the consciousness of
Christ. For a faith in the living Christ we find the substitution of belief in a complicated theory about His Person.
This is seen in its worst form in certain clauses of the
symbol known to-day as the Athanasian Creed, which the
Eastern Church has always refused to recognise. The
clauses in question appear to be of medieval Frankish
origin. Instead of fellowship and trust in the Redeemer
as the condition of salvation, the acceptance is demanded
of certain verbal subtleties. Apart altogether from the
injury done by thus turning the Gospel into a legal statute
hedged round with sanctions, we have here a fatal inversion
of the true order of life, in which experience must always
come first, theories about experience duly follow. Moreover, the invariable tendency of all such descriptions of
God " in terms neuter and abstract, rather than personal
and moral," is " the de-ethicisation of Deity," [2] and the

---

[1] Fairbairn, *op. cit.* p. 91. Cf. Harnack, *H.D.* iii. p. 8 ; iv. p. 49 *n.*
[2] Fairbairn, *op. cit.* p. 405.

divorce of the concept of God from relation to man. But this was the characteristic of much else that was medieval besides the clauses of this symbol.

II

One of the earliest attempts to grapple with the Christo-logical problem was that of Gnosticism. We have seen its failure. By their insistence that matter was the handi-work of Satan the Gnostics reduced the Incarnation to an illusion. The Divine Man who could be touched with a feeling for human infirmity became a contradiction in ideas. His mission had not been to raise our human nature, but to annihilate it. His Gospel was not the glad tidings of redemption, but the call to warfare with all forms of the seen. Gnosticism thus struck at the root of Christian faith. But when we ask wherein lay the strength and attraction of this Gnostic idea for many Christians in the second cen-tury, it is not difficult to see the answer. The conscious-ness of the value of man as man is one of the results of Christianity itself, the chief factor in which was the realisa-tion of the humanity of Jesus. Priceless as the doctrine of the real humanity of Jesus may seem to the twentieth century, we are guilty of false historical perspective if we imagine that it would appear of such value to the second. The Church was driven to fight for it, if it would be true to its deposit, above all if it was to retain its Gospels and its historical foundations. But the difficulty in fighting, which the Church itself felt, is seen in the fact that for the majority of the theologians, both in the Early and Medieval Church, the real humanity of Christ may have been a dogma of faith, it certainly did not bulk largely either in their experience or their creeds. Harnack, in spite of some exaggeration, is not far wrong when he points out that in the Christology of Athanasius, the one man who more than any other " saved Christianity as the religion of living

fellowship with God," every trait which recalls the historical
Jesus of Nazareth is erased.[1] Only in the school of Antioch
do we find adequate insistence on the fact of Jesus. The
consequences of this will appear later in the growth of
Monophysitism and other heresies.

The answer of the Church to Gnosticism was twofold.
In Rome it would seem to have led to the formation of the
symbol known in its later development as the Apostles'
Creed. On the other hand, in opposition or contrast to
the aeons and emanations of Gnosticism, Justin and Origen
had laid stress on the pre-existence of Christ as the Logos.
With the Alexandrians this was the central point of their
theology. Before the rise of Gnosticism the term ' Logos,'
as Dorner has pointed out, was but " a little used
treasure." [2] We owe it to Gnosticism that its significance
was expanded and realised both in the East and West.
Nevertheless, the doctrine of the Logos, despite its clear
statement and application to Jesus by the author of the
Fourth Gospel, as we see from its later history and from
our creeds and symbols, never became firmly established
in the Catholic Church. Though dear to the Apologist
and theologian, it does not seem to have become part of
the living faith of the common people ; on the contrary, to
them it seemed rather to threaten the simplicity of faith.
Possibly, as at Nicaea, the common people and not the
philosophers were right. The term Logos is too abstract ;
its tendency is " to obscure the personal elements in the
Divine relation." [3] Hence it is difficult to state the doctrine
of the Logos in terms which do not issue in its reduction
to a cosmic or dynamic force, with too exaggerated reference to the universe rather than to salvation, a weakness
common to all the Apologists.

The failure of the doctrine of the Logos to maintain its
hold in the Church gave rise to a set of opinions classed

[1] Harnack, H.D. iv. p. 45.   [2] Dorner, Person of Christ, A. i. p. 257.
[3] Ottley, op. cit. i. pp. 262, 296.

under the general title of Monarchianism. Though in time
Monarchianism degenerated into heresy, it began in a
reaction of orthodoxy. The insistence upon the Lord's
divinity, without adequate explanation of the relation of
that divinity to the Father, was leading back to a refined
ditheism. So in opposition both to Gnosticism and to
exaggerated and involved statements of the doctrine of the
Logos, certain thinkers laid emphasis on the ' monarchy,'
the sole absolute being and rule of God the Father.

'Monarchy,' as applied to God, was a familiar term with
the Greeks, but in a sense fundamentally different from
its use in Christianity. To the Greek thinkers of the second
century polytheism in the sense of a number of Gods of
equal power was a discarded theory. As Plutarch and
Maximus of Tyre are ever insisting, there must be one
god supreme over all others. But this did not prevent
belief in the existence of lesser deities, " mediatised gods "
as Dr. Bigg happily calls them, borrowing a figure from
the relation in the German Empire of the lesser kings
to the Emperor. All this hierarchy, with the underlying
conception of the ' monarchy ' of one God, Christianity
swept away. ' Simple, unskilled people,' writes Tertullian,
' hurl in our teeth that we preach two gods or three gods.
. . . We, say they, maintain the monarchy.' Tertullian
was speaking of Christian laymen ; but the reference
might have been extended to the heathen, some of whom,
as we have seen, maintained the monarchy by means of
a theology of ' daemons,' partly human and partly divine.
Others, for instance Porphyry, reasoned more boldly still
against the Christian conception : " Let us proceed to
inquire about the monarchy of the one God, and the joint
rule of these deities who are worshipped. . . . A monarch
is not one who is alone, but one who rules alone over
subjects of kindred nature with himself ; as the Emperor
Hadrian, for instance, who was a monarch not because he
stood alone, or because he ruled cattle or sheep, but because

he was king over human beings of like nature with his own." [1] In the same strain Caecilius complained that the Christians made the heavens a wilderness and a solitude with their ' one god, lonely and forsaken,' the unutterable isolation and aloofness of whose position in heaven seemed to the Greek mind an " atheistic " impossibility. But Caecilius overlooked that this ' lonely God ' had given place in Christian thought to a doctrine of the Trinity.

While Monarchianism thus failed to appeal to the Greek mind, as in fact the Monotheism of the Jews had failed in previous centuries, it led within the Church to serious difficulties. Those who exaggerated the ' monarchy ' were faced with the problem of the deity of the Redeemer. To those who held the doctrine of the Logos, which Monarchianism tended to displace, this had presented no real difficulty. But any abandonment of this solution drove men to attempt another conception, the recognition, for instance, that the divine nature of Christ was a creation or manifestation of God in time. One class, the " dynamic Monarchians " as they have been called, saved the ' monarchy ' by resolving the deity of Christ into the gift of God bestowed upon the man Jesus, a view practically identical with that which in later times was known as Adoptionism.[2] The beginnings of this doctrine may be traced back to the *Shepherd* of Hermas, always a favourite work in the Roman Church, of which Hermas had been a member, and of which, according to a somewhat doubtful statement, his brother Pius was the bishop.[3] In this school the most important name was Paul of Samosata, bishop of Antioch (c. 260), a high political officer of Queen Zenobia of Palmyra. With Paul the main thought is the ' divine ascent ' ($\mathring{a}\nu\omega\theta\epsilon\nu$) of the man Jesus to Godlike honour by the indwelling of the Logos as His ' inner man,'

---

[1] Macarius Magnes, *Apocritica*, iv. 20.   [2] *Infra*, pp. 76, 86, 145.
[3] A.D. 140-155. The chronology and Christology of Hermas is, however, very doubtful. On Hermas, see Bigg, *Origins of Christianity*, chap. viii.

a view in fatal antagonism to the doctrine of the *Kenosis*. The founder of the school was apparently a 'learned' currier called Theodotus, who about the year 190 preached at Rome that superhuman power—Theodotus refuses to own that this was 'deity'—was conferred upon Jesus at His baptism. It is worth note that the followers of Theodotus, according to Eusebius, were much given to higher criticism and mathematics, and eschewed all allegorical methods of interpretation. They favoured Aristotle rather than Plato. But at that time the standpoint of all educated Christians save the Antiochenes was Platonism.

The danger of dynamic Monarchianism is plain ; it inevitably lowers the claims of Jesus. Between it and the current heathen conceptions of theophanies and apotheosis there was little difference save one of degree. But differences which depend on degree are always unstable. In time the result must have been the degeneration of Christ into a subordinate God, a superior Hercules or Prometheus : redemption would have become a temporary cleansing of the Augean stables, not an eternal fact in the heart of God. Over against all such forms of Adoptionism the Church was bound to assert the eternal Sonship of the pre-existent Christ as the only safeguard of its truths. After the close of the third century no other Christology was possible in the Church, and in the fourth century it found scientific expression in the formula of Athanasius : Λόγος ὁμοούσιος. One practical result of Adoptionism was the omission in all the symbols of the Church of reference to the baptism of Christ. Experience had shown that it was almost impossible to safeguard it from docetic interpretation.

" Dynamic Monarchianism " was so manifestly on a plane with the old heathenism that it can hardly have been a serious difficulty, at any rate until in the fourth century it reappeared in the more subtle form of Arianism. Another class of Monarchians was more dangerous. These saved the ' monarchy ' by resolving the deity of Jesus into one mode or incorporation of the Father, who Himself was born and died. Of these Patripassians or Modalistic Monarchians the most noted leader was Sabellius, the earliest Noetus (fl. 220), and Praxeas (fl. 210)—unless indeed these two are one, masquerading under different names— the latter a stout opponent of Montanism, who, in the caustic phrase of Tertullian, ' did two Jobs for the devil at Rome. He drove out prophecy and introduced heresy. He put to flight the Paraclete and crucified the Father.' In the conception of the Atonement set forth by the Patri- passians there is none of the poverty of the Dynamic Monarchians. But to maintain, as did Noetus, that such a doctrine ' glorified Christ ' by upholding His com- plete deity, shows a curious blindness to its ultimate effect. What this was became manifest when the logic of Sabellius (c. 198-217) resolved the Trinity into three different phases or functions under which the one divine essence manifests itself—three energies in one hypostasis. Such a view is, of course, fatal to the reality of the Incarnation, or to the existence in Christ of a human soul. It is consequently destructive of the conception brought out in the *Hebrews* of the indissoluble union of deity and humanity in the ascended Christ. Sabellianism by thus refusing to recog- nise the Trinity, save as a mere category or form in ex- perience, in reality robs experience of all its sources of consolation. This deeper note the Church rescued when, as the result of the whole controversy, it insisted that Christ must be both true God and true man.

The history of Sabellianism is confused and fragmentary. But it does not appear that it ever obtained a hold in the Church. As an organised heresy it seems rapidly to have perished. Nevertheless, owing to a curious chapter in ecclesiastical history, it has left permanent marks upon Christian thought, as well as upon the text of the New Testament.[1]   For a whole generation, in spite of the oppo-

---

[1] *e.g.* μονογενὴς υἱὸς for θεὸς in John i. 18.

sition of Tertullian and Hippolytus, Modalism in a moderate form was the favourite doctrine at Rome, possibly because of the sympathies between Stoicism, the fashionable creed of Rome, and Modalism, both of which posited a nominalist logic.[1] When Origen (about 215) journeyed to Rome, he seems to have sided with Hippolytus. To the great Alexandrian, with his doctrine of the subordination of the Son, modalistic Monarchianism was intolerable. After the defeat of Hippolytus by Callistus, Rome retorted (231-232) by the condemnation of Origen's writings, and decided that his doctrine of subordination led to Tritheism. Another result of Sabellianism was even more noteworthy. Hitherto, as in the doctrine of the Logos, the tendency had been to emphasise the pre-eminence of the Father. For this cause theologians in the East had looked with suspicion on the use of the *homoousios* formula. According to the common opinion, they had secured its condemnation at the council of Antioch (268), possibly because of its too realistic use by Paul of Samosata. By placing the Three Persons on a parallel line, if we may so speak, instead of on one of economy or subordination, Sabellius prepared the way both for the Athanasian and the Augustinian Christology, including the definite adoption into the creed of the West of the homoousian formula.

Theological opinion rarely develops by moving in straight lines. It progresses rather in a series of actions and reactions, by the strife of which another step forward is taken. Of this we have an example in the reaction of Dionysius of Alexandria (247-251) against Sabellianism. In his anxiety to guard the distinct personality of the Son, among other incautious statements he used a phrase that later became a watchword of Arianism—' the Son did not exist before He was begotten '—and denied the *homoousios*. For this

---

[1] See Harnack, *H.D.* iii. p. 55 *n.* That ' Father' and ' Son' are relative or accidental attributes is really Nominalism. According to Tertullian, the Monarchians contended that the ' word' is ' only voice and sound.'

reason he was condemned by his namesake the bishop of
Rome (259-268), who once more laid stress on the unity of
God.   But the one spoke Greek and the other Latin, and,
in consequence, neither seems to have understood the other's
use of technical terms.   It was necessary to determine more
accurately the connotation of the current terms of theology.
The opportunity for this was given at Nicaea.

Nor must we overlook the importance in this connection
of the " Arius before Arius," Lucian of Antioch (†311), and
the Antiochene school.   In its desire for formal and logical
consistency this school was "impelled to simplify the
Catholic doctrine by dropping one element in Origen's
teaching (the eternal generation of the Son), and pressing
the other (subordinationism) to its logical consequences." [1]
In thus historically linking itself on with the controversies
which closed the third century, the unity of God and the
distinctness of the Son's personality, lay one secret of the
strength of Arianism.

III

The greatest of all the Christological controversies was
that raised by Arius, a presbyter of Alexandria and pupil
of Lucian of Antioch.   The details of this struggle, prolonged for over a century, with its bewildering variations
and cross-currents and its miserable scandals, are accessible
in every text-book.   The imposing council of Nicaea
(325), with the great figures of Constantine, of Ossius[2] of
Cordova (b. 256), of Eusebius of Caesarea (260-340), above
all of the heroic young presbyter of Alexandria, Athanasius,
are set forth at large in all histories, as are also the Arian
reactions, especially in court circles, which followed the first
triumph of the faith.   It must suffice that we note the
inner meaning of the whole controversy, the results of
which we possess summed up in a symbol known as the

[1] Ottley, op. cit. i. p. 307 ; Gwatkin, op. cit. pp. 15, 16 ; Harnack, H.D. iv.
p. 3 ff.   [2] For name, see infra, p. 98 n.

Nicene (Niceno-Constantinopolitan) Creed. This famous
symbol would appear, however, to be more strictly an
edition of the yet older Baptismal Creed of Jerusalem,
enlarged by Cyril of Jerusalem somewhere about the year
362, with Nicene corrections, and ultimately attributed to
the Constantinopolitan council of 381.[1]

When looked at carefully the meaning of the council of
Nicaea is plain. As Carlyle, certainly no prejudiced ob-
server, puts it : " If Arianism had won, Christianity would
have dwindled into a legend." The question at issue was
whether two created and subordinate gods, holding their
existence precariously, *durante beneplacito* of the Father,
very little different from the philosophical triad or duad of
Philo, Plotinus, and the Neoplatonists, should be interposed
between the deity and mankind. For in plain English
that is really the meaning of the Arian formula as regards
Christ—ἦν ὅτε οὐκ ἦν, ' there was when He was not '—with
its necessary consequences as to the Holy Spirit, in spite
of all refinements about leaving out the concept of time
and the rest. The philosophers, with their rationalistic
arguments from the human to the divine, and their conception of a Logos centred in creation, were in favour of the
affirmative ; the great mass of earnest believers in favour
of the negative. The issue was the defeat of the philosophers, much to the surprise of Arius. For Arius was no
deliberate unbeliever. He could rightly claim that many
passages of Scripture were capable of interpretation such
as to prove his argument ; and that, moreover, the Fathers
of Alexandria were on his side. He could adduce, with
some justice, the support of the Alexandrian Dionysius.
He could maintain that Origen's doctrine of subordination must logically issue in the placing of Christ among
the creations of the One God, the ' first-born,' it is
true, of all creation, but none the less a creature. He

---

[1] See Hort, *Two Dissertations*, pp. 54, 138, 139 ; Harnack, *H.D.* iv. p. 98 *n.*
It displaced the original Nicene Creed about the year 530.

could point to the danger that the doctrine of the
Lord's deity, unless further guarded, would lead back to
polytheism.

But, in spite of plausible defence of his doctrine as a
fight for Monotheism, the common consciousness of believers saw clearly that which was hidden from Arius and
the philosophers, because of what Harnack rightly calls
"their childish satisfaction in the working out of empty
syllogisms," that such a doctrine in the long run would be
fatal to Christianity, and was really an accommodation to
heathen conceptions. Arius did not see that his doctrine
issued in hopeless contradictions. Thus Arius maintained
the unity of God, upon which in his cosmology he laid such
stress, by opening the door in his theology to the very
polytheism he detested.[1] He did away with the Rock of
Ages when he affirmed that, like all rational creatures, the
Son is by nature capable of change—a view that strikes at
every basis of ethics. By making a chasm between Christ
and the Divine essence, he denied that Christ was the full
revelation of the Father. Thus he destroyed the conviction of the Christian world that in Christ man had
attained to unity with God Himself. " Those men make
merry in vain who think there was but an iota of difference
between the contending parties at Nicaea, or that it was
a strife about terms. The deepest things of the Christian
life were at stake. For Athanasius belonged to that
small class of men in the Church who have ever sent new
life coursing through its veins. He was of the company of
Paul and Augustine, of Luther and Bunyan. He stood
forth at Nicaea as the exponent of the deeper soul in every
man's soul, for in him was seen a man whose deep spiritual
needs had made him cry aloud for the living God, and who
then declared that in Christ this need had been met. His
whole intense spiritual experience stood to affirm that it
was no delegate of the Most High, no matter how august,

[1] Harnack, *H.D.* iv. p. 40 ff.

that had met him in Jesus Christ, and pardoned his
sins, and filled him with new life, but *very God of very God* ;
and it was with a view to this central experience that he
accepted a term that passed beyond Scripture, and affirmed
of the Son that He was of *one substance with the Father*.
Terms were of little moment, and probably Athanasius
cared little about them ; the fact was everything, and the
terms only had a value if they did justice to the facts of a
profound experience." [1]

The confident appeal which the Nicene symbol thus
makes to the facts of spiritual experience is further verified
if we turn to that larger experience which we call history.
At first Arianism with its easy reduction of Christ to a
demi-god, with its popular methods of appeal, including
much use of songs ($\theta a \lambda \epsilon i a$), found a quick response among
the heathen, as well as among the thousands of nominal
converts to Christianity.   For the barbarians it was a half-
way halting-place in their conversion from paganism.   As
such, Arianism had its mission.   When that was accomplished, it vanished.   For just as the Church was driven,
one might almost say in spite of herself, to eradicate the
Arian taint, so " sooner or later every Arian nation had to
purge itself of heresy or vanish from the earth.   Even the
distant Visigoths were forced to see that Arians could not
hold Spain. . . . Of continental Teutons the Franks alone
escaped the plague of Arianism.   It was in the strength of
orthodoxy that they drove the conquerors of Rome before
them on the field of Vouglé, and brought the green standard of the Prophet to a halt upon the Loire." [2]   As in
secular history, so also in sacred.   Arianism has again and
again in diverse forms laid its spell on the thoughtful.   But
since its capture of the barbarians it has never succeeded in
obtaining the allegiance of the many, while the congrega-

---

[1] Professor Armitage, *op. cit.* p. 848.
[2] Gwatkin, *op. cit.* p. 264.   Cf. Foakes-Jackson in Hastings' *E.R.E.* i.
p. 784.

tions which have embraced it have for the most part
withered away.

Some explanation is necessary of the profound hold of
Arianism upon the East. In the West, Arianism never
made headway in the Church itself. The Western bishops
at the council of Sardica (Sophia in Bulgaria, 343-344)
would have nothing to do with the efforts of the Eastern
bishops to amend the Nicene symbol. In the split which
followed in the council itself we see the beginning of the
final separation. In part this refusal was due to the lesser
interest of the West in subtle refinement. The West with
its tendency, so characteristic of the Roman, to view dogma
from the standpoint of administration rather than intellectualism, worked outward from life and experience to
theory. The East, constructing its *a priori* schemes, destroyed the very experiences which the scheme was called
in to explain. But the victory of orthodoxy in the West
must be traced, in a special degree, to the clear, simple
teaching of Tertullian. For Tertullian had definitely
turned the thought of the West from the splendid but
shadowy doctrine of the Logos, so dear to the more philosophical East, to the clear, definite conception of the Son
of God, with its emphasis of distinct personality. When,
therefore, Athanasius, as the real fruit of his speculation,
dwells on the Christ centred in salvation, instead of, as
Origen and the Apologists, on the Logos working in creation,
the West was prepared. But in the Eastern Church, with
its strong attachment to the philosophy of the Logos,
Nicaea was rather a surprise victory won by the clear
thinking of the minority than the deliberate expression of
general conviction.

IV

In the Nicene Creed we find two remarkable expressions as to our Lord's human nature, all the more remarkable because of their repetition : ' Who was incarnate,' and

' became man.' But the council was so absorbed in
protecting the true deity of Christ that it failed to
guard against the possible errors that might creep in
as regards the Incarnation and manhood. As a matter
of fact, the Arian heresy was just as harmful with
reference to these truths as to the true ' deity.' Its
tendency was to render a human soul in Jesus unnecessary,
to view the Incarnation as merely the ' taking flesh '
by an indefinitely great though not infinite Logos. The
Church soon found that it was as necessary for it to
assert the *homoousios* with reference to humanity, as
it had been necessary to assert it with reference to
deity. The latter was needful, because no true revelation
of love could come from a God who, if Arius was right,
stood aloof for ever from the world. The former was
equally necessary ; if mankind was not to lose its
sense of the dignity of humanity by a theory of the Incarnation which refused to allow that the Son of Man
possessed a human soul.

Controversy on this matter was begun by a zealous
defender of the Nicene symbol. Apollinaris, bishop of
Laodicea (†390), in his defence of Christ's deity, and in his
desire to represent Christ's human nature as impersonal,
sacrificed the integrity of His manhood. His intention was
to safeguard the character of the Redeemer from the possibility of change or fall. The Incarnation, viewed *i.e.* as the
union of God and man, had been eternal in the Logos.
' The Lord from heaven,' who bore within Himself, so to
speak, the potency of the Incarnation, brought with Him
His heavenly humanity, the Incarnation being merely, as
with the Arians, the taking flesh and an animal soul. In
the psychology of Apollinaris, who followed the threefold
classification to which Plato had given currency, Jesus
Christ thus lacked a human soul ($\nu o \hat{u} s$). This further involved the lack of any real human will. Now, whatever
views may be held as to the psychology of both Apollinaris

and his opponents, this much is certain. By the ' soul ' of man both sides alike intended the noblest part, the essential fact in humanity itself. If this were lacking, then, as the Catholic writers, Gregory Nazianzen and others, complained, the Incarnation was incomplete. And lacking, according to Apollinaris, it certainly was, in spite of his subtle argument that all human souls were in a way adumbrations of the Logos, that man's nature pre-existed in God. To this extent therefore—for there is much in his teaching that is still obscure—we may join with the second council of Constantinople (381) in its condemnation of Apollinarian doctrines. One outcome of the controversy would appear to have been the formulation of the symbol known as the Athanasian Creed. This seems, in part, to have had its origin in the opposition of southern Gaul to Apollinarian doctrine.

Half a century after Apollinaris the battle was reopened. The new controversy was an attempt to answer the problem Apollinaris had raised, but which neither he nor his opponents, Gregory of Nyssa and Gregory Nazianzen, had answered, of the unity of Christ's Person. The author of this new heresy was Theodore of Mopsuestia ; its foremost advocate Nestorius (fl. 431), the patriarch of Constantinople. Theodore (350-428) was one of the leaders of the school of Antioch. The logical method of this school was Aristotelian ; its chief interest in anthropology. The tendency, therefore, of its somewhat critical and literal theology was to fix attention on the human element in Christ, as set forth in the simple Gospel narratives. The service which in this matter the Antiochenes rendered to the Church, by insistence on the historical Christ, was unfortunately neutralised by their making the bond between the human and divine merely external, an exaggeration of the moral discipline whereby our High Priest was ' made perfect,' instead of vital and permanent. Vexed with the popular custom, defended by Gregory Nazianzen, of calling

G

the Virgin Mary θεοτόκος,[1] Nestorius, following Theodore,
contended that ' she only gave birth to a man in whom the
union with the Logos had its beginning, but was incomplete
until His baptism.' Christ was thus not ' God ' but ' God-
bearer ' (θεοφόρος), another form of Adoptionism. The condemnation of Nestorius in his absence, by the synod of
Ephesus (431) under the lead of the passionate Cyril,
metropolitan of Alexandria (412-444), was not the end of the
heresy. An energetic Nestorian Church, in its missionary
zeal, carried the condemned tenets first to Edessa, and then,
on the suppression of that school in 489, to the ends of the
earth. Persia, India, China—as the tablets at Si-ngan-fu
(636-781) bear evidence [2]—alike witnessed their activity.
From the eleventh century, until almost blotted out by
Tamerlane, the Nestorian Church was the largest Christian
body in the world, whose patriarch at Bagdad was acknowledged by twenty-five metropolitans. On the conquest of
Persia and the East by the Muslim, Nestorianism was
thrown into an alliance, by no means unfriendly, with the
new faith. To this we trace the rise in Mohammedan
Spain in medieval times of a new form of this Nestorian
doctrine to which the title of Adoptionism is more strictly
applied.[3]

More deadly than Nestorianism was the Monophysite
peril, a heresy as dangerous to Christianity as Arianism
itself. Its author, Eutyches, an old unknown monk, was
its nominal founder because of a few plain sentences in
which, exaggerating the tendencies and formulae of Cyrus,
he maintained that after the Incarnation there was but one
nature in Christ, the fusion of the two natures into one
humanised Logos or ' deified ' man. With Eutyches the
deity completely overshadowed the manhood. The con-

---

[1] The English translation, Mother of God,' puts the emphasis in the wrong
place. It would be better ' who gives birth to God.' Glover, *Conflict of
Religions*, p. 21, points out that " the land which introduced the Mother of
the Gods to the Roman world gave the name of θεοτόκος to the Church."
[2] See Bury's Gibbon, vol. v. App. 7. [3] *Infra*, p. 145

demnation of Eutyches at Constantinople (448), his justification at the violent ' Robber ' Council at Ephesus (449),
was followed by further condemnation at the fourth
Ecumenical Council at Chalcedon (October 451), as also in
the ' Tome ' in which Leo I., the ruling spirit of the age,
condemned Nestorius and Eutyches, and at the same time
advanced the claims of the Roman primacy. In his definition, which was adopted at Chalcedon, Leo pointed out
with great clearness that the true faith is always of the
nature of a *via media* between conflicting errors.[1]

By the adoption of this definition the Christological
controversy reached its logical conclusion. The permanence of Christ's manhood was definitely asserted, though
the council " failed to recognise the ethical aspects of
Christ's humanity as the unique archetype of manhood—
a point which had held such a prominent place in the
thought of earlier writers like Irenaeus." [2] But not without long, dreary years of debate could the Eastern Church
be induced to accept the Western Christology. Monophysitism, though formally banished, was not driven out.
Certain sects in the East to this day still make Monophysitism their main tenet, with, at first, Antioch, then afterwards Baghdad as their patriarchate—the Jacobites [3] of
Syria, the Copts and Abyssinians, the Armenians and
Maronites. Even in orthodox circles, both in East and West,
the real humanity of Jesus was for long ages a conviction
of the study, not a working belief. In Cyril of Alexandria
and Gregory of Nyssa, for instance, " the Redeemer's manhood ceases to have independent existence : it is transformed and ' deified ' to a point which makes it only
nominally 'consubstantial' with ours." [4] The consequences
of this practical Monophysitism were most disastrous.

---

[1] The keywords of the Chalcedonian formula were : as to the two natures,
ἀσυγχύτως without commixture, ἀτρέπτως without conversion ; as to the
One Person, ἀδιαιρέτως undividedly, ἀχωρίστως inseparably.

[2] Ottley, *op. cit.* ii. p. 109.   [3] So called from the monk Jacob Baradai.

[4] *Ibid.* p. 88.

" To its secret prevalence in the Church is due much of the degradation of Christian worship in the Middle Ages. The cultus of the Madonna, of the Bambino, and of wonder-working images, is traceable to the feeling that Christ's divinity had absorbed His humanity altogether." [1]

To the same lack of any sense of the real humanity we must trace the Monothelite controversy formally con-demned at Rome in 649, and at Constantinople in 680. To claim that in Jesus Christ there is but one will is to take from Him the very essence of humanity. Poor and inadequate as the language in which John of Damascus attempted to sum up the Catholic position may be, yet, after all, he attained the right end. His definition of the relation of the human to the divine nature in the unity of the Person as enhypostatic or anhypostatic—in other words, the doctrine of an impersonal human nature in Christ—is not more satisfactory as an explanation than most definitions of ultimate facts. But it has this merit at least, perhaps a negative merit, that it does not lead us away from the fact itself.

With the settlement of the Christological controversy the contribution of the Eastern Church to Christian doctrine became practically exhausted. The Eastern Church had lost its thinkers. In 383, according to Socrates, the Em-peror Theodosius fell back upon tradition for the settle-ment of all disputes. In John of Damascus (†754), the last of the great names, we find all the worst faults of the Western schoolmen. Antioch and Alexandria, for so many centuries the seats of progressive Christian schools, were captured by the Arabs. The life of the Byzantine Church, even when spared by the Muslim, was stifled by political and spiritual despotism, ruined by corruption and super-stition. In place of the soaring thoughts of Origen, Basil, the Gregories, Athanasius, and Chrysostom we have the long and bitter Iconoclastic controversy (726 ff.). The great

[1] Foakes-Jackson in *Cambridge Theological Essays*, p. 490.

Emperor Leo the Syrian,[1] stung by the Muslim taunt that the Christians worshipped idols, and desirous of infusing new life into the Empire by correcting the effete sentimentalism of Oriental Christianity, demanded that images should only be used as architectural ornaments. The common people, goaded by persecution and superstition, rose in defence of these relics of paganism or religious childhood. Such thought as survived in the Eastern Church was confined to the monasteries, and there, under the influence of ' Dionysius the Areopagite,'[2] assumed the form of mystic quietism. With the conversion of Russia (988) the Eastern Church awoke to a wider life. But Russia, alone of the countries of Europe, owed its Christianity to the arbitrary command of its Tsar Vladimir rather than to the usual missionary agencies. Hence the distinctive feature of this new Slav church was not its thought, or even its orthodoxy, but its constant emphasis of an unbending nationalism. In the East religion and nationality are identical; hence unity of religion is the basal principle of the state, and its easiest definition. But though the consequent political importance of the Eastern Church cannot be exaggerated, its contributions to Christian thought after John of Damascus must be dismissed as almost valueless. Like the Rhine, the river, once deep, clear, and life-giving, had ended in the mud-swamps.

[1] Commonly but mistakenly called ' the Isaurian.'
[2] *Infra,* p. 153 f.

CHAPTER IV

THE GENIUS OF ROME

Argument

I

THE influence of the Roman world upon the organisation
of the Christian Church, especially in the development of
the papacy and of a territorial episcopacy, has been so
profound that there is danger lest we overlook its importance for Christian thought. For vast as was the influence
of the Hellenic spirit, Roman thought for more than a
thousand years was the all-important factor in the development of Christian philosophy and theology, at least
in the Western world. To say this is but to state, in different words, the permanent influence upon the Western
Church of the teaching of St. Augustine, in whom Roman
thought finds its highest expression. We propose, therefore, to consider, first, the formative factors in Roman
thought prior to St. Augustine, then to review the work
and influence of St. Augustine himself. From St. Augustine we pass by a natural transition to the further development of thought in the Middle Ages.

We do well at the outset to define the special bent which
the Latin genius gave to Christianity. To state roughly
that it gave it organisation would scarcely be sufficient.
For organisation in itself can hardly be regarded as
" thought." Yet the organisation which the Church received, so largely under the influence of its Roman environment, and as part of its adaptation to the polity, public
and private, of the Empire, is the hall-mark, so to speak,
of definite tendencies in Latin thinking, which as much
claim recognition as the more abstract methods of Hellenism. By a process of thought, gradual but inevitable, the
Church came to be construed in terms of the State.

The Latin genius corresponds, in fact, to a certain clearly marked movement of the intellect. "There will ever exist," writes Neander, "two tendencies of the theological mind, of which while the one will seek to understand the supernatural element of Christianity in its opposition to the natural, the other will endeavour to point out its connection with it. The one will seek to apprehend the supernatural and super-rational element as *such* ; the other will strive to apprehend it in its harmony with reason and nature—to portray to the mind the supernatural and super-rational as being nevertheless conformable to nature and to reason." These two tendencies characterised respectively the Greek and Latin genius.[1] The constructive ideas of the Greek are metaphysical ; of the Latin, political. The Latin sought above all else to fit facts into their ethical or social bearings. Hence his desire to test opinion by a rule of faith, fixed and secured by a definite organisation. For speculation he had an instinctive mistrust. The philosophy of the West, not even excepting Lucretius, is wholly derivative. The Greek, on the contrary, was ever insisting on the continuity of the revelation, judging opinion from within by its harmony with its premises, or its additions to gnosis. Hence the love of subtle doctrinal disputation, at times becoming a malady. ' Every corner of the city,' writes Gregory of Nyssa in a striking picture of Constantinople during the Arian controversy, ' is full of men who discuss incomprehensible subjects ; the streets, the markets, old clothes dealers, money changers, provision merchants all alike.' The Latin has given us the Roman Church ; the Greek the Apologists and Alexandrians. The creed of the West—the so-called Apostles' Creed—is the terse recital of historical facts. The creed of the East—the so-called Nicene—is full of subtle intellectualism. The West is Catholic, the stress is laid upon extension ; the East is Orthodox, with the emphasis

---

[1] Neander, *Church History* (ed. Torrey), ii. p. 197.

upon opinion. With the East faith becomes spiritual
vision; with the West it is primarily assent to external
authority.

In consequence of this, in the Roman genius two matters
stand out prominently, its emphasis of law and its reverence for tradition.   To the Roman conception of law, and
its basal principle that the ordered is the good, we owe
really the Roman power of organisation.   The Greek ideal
of highly developed social atoms seemed lawless to the
Roman.   Law and order demanded that the atoms should
be bound together into a unity.   Thus the Greek πόλις
became the Roman State ; the *ecclesia* of earlier days, the
' Catholic ' Church of the third century.   ' Roman ' and
' Catholic ' had, in fact, a special relation to each other
from the earliest days.   Both alike connote ' universality,'
' organisation,' and ' unity,' and such lines of thought as
are necessary to produce these fundamental marks.

One of the chief results of the Roman genius for law
was the influence exerted upon Western conceptions of
truth.   In the words of an eminent writer : " Theology
became permeated with forensic ideas and couched in
forensic language. . . . The Western Church threw itself
into a new order of disputes, the same which from those
days to this have never lost their interest for any family
of mankind at any time included in the Latin communion.
The nature of sin and its transmission by inheritance,
the debt owed by man and its vicarious satisfaction, the
necessity and sufficiency of the Atonement, above all the
apparent antagonism between Free Will and the Divine
Providence, these were the points which the West began to
debate. . . . Almost everybody who has knowledge enough
of Roman Law to appreciate the Roman penal system ;
the Roman theory of obligations established by contract
and debit ; the Roman view of debts, and of the modes
of incurring, extinguishing, and transmitting them ; the
Roman notion of the continuance of individual existence

by universal succession—may be trusted to say whence
arose the frame of mind to which the problems of Western
theology proved so congenial, whence came the phraseology
in which these problems were stated, and whence the
description of reasoning employed in their solution." [1]

As regards the Atonement, the Eastern Church looked
to the Divine Immanence as the answer to its questions.
Hence its emphasis of the Incarnation. But one result
of the legal attitude in the Latin Church was that the whole
stress of its thought was thrown upon the death of Christ,
and not upon His Incarnation. The Atonement was
looked upon as almost accidental, certainly no necessary
part of the Divine Nature, as distinct from the duty of a
Divine Law-giver. Regarded thus under the category
chiefly of ' satisfaction,' it was almost limited to the Cross,
to which the Incarnation was but ancillary. This narrowed
conception was further assisted by the juridical attitude
whereby the whole race was treated as guilty of one sin
because of one descent—a system of ideas that borrowed
its terms from St. Paul, but its working principles from
the law and polity of Rome.

After the adoption of Christianity by Constantine as the
religion of the State, the Roman genius further demanded
that the unity of the Church be concrete, a visible society
with visible location, headship, and terms of citizenship.
To imagine otherwise was to fall back upon the despised
Greek abstractions, with their futile ' bird-cities ' in cloudland and their unrealisable Platonic republics. Thus the
abstract definition which the Greeks loved, the fruits of
which in the development of theology we have already
studied, became with the Romans concrete determination
of the relations of the society or church—its boundaries,
government, practice, the terms of admission or exclusion,
the nature and power of its officers, and the like. The out-

[1] Maine, *Ancient Law*, p. 356. Cf. Fairbairn, *op. cit.* pp. 108-109, and cf.
infra, c. vii. § 1.

come of all this in the growth of the conception of the Catholic Church, with its territorial episcopate, its fixed ritual, its graded hierarchy, its head centre at Rome, and its ordered Monasticism, is a familiar story.

At the outset of our inquiry it is well to notice one result of the use of the Latin tongue. The abstract ideas so dear to the Greek were abhorred by the practical Roman. As a rule, he had no terms whereby he could express them. When, therefore, attempts were made to translate for the West the subtle terms in which the fathers of the East had expressed their creed, difficulty and serious mistakes arose. The term οὐσία, for instance, should have been rendered by *essentia*, an abstract word that the Romans disliked. So *substantia*, a concrete term that has an undertone of materialism, unfortunately took its place. But as *substantia* was really the translation of the Greek ὑπόστασις (hypostasis), a further difficulty was introduced, which was only met by the use of a legal term, *persona*. Little wonder that the theologians of East and West misunderstood each other ; they too often used words, which they supposed to be equivalent, in contradictory senses. With the severance of East and West the Latin terms alone became recognised in the West, with results that have been disastrous for exact thinking.

II

The struggle with Gnosticism forced the Alexandrian Church to attempt clearer exposition ; it drove the Western Church back upon a more definite statement of apostolic tradition as opposed to speculation. In this matter, so momentous, as after events showed, for the history of the whole Church, many circumstances predisposed the Roman congregation to take the lead. Its accepted double foundation by St. Peter and St. Paul of itself gave it pre-eminence, to say nothing of its importance as the capital of the world. By an early date also the Roman Church had given to the

primitive baptismal formula and to apostolic tradition
the definiteness of a creed and a canon, touchstones to
which it was able to bring all heresies and difficulties.
It is at Rome that the existence of a canon of the New
Testament can first be definitely traced, as we see in the
Muratorian fragment. The Roman symbol also, in the
main substantially the same as that now known as the
Apostles' Creed, was in existence in the second century,
possibly before 150, certainly before Irenaeus.

The Apostles' Creed has been called, not without justification, "the simple but emphatic protest of the Church
against Gnostic heresies." [1] If by the Church we mean the
Western Church—for this creed is unknown in the East—
and if with the Gnostics we include Marcion, the statement
is correct. Its first clause is the negation of Gnostic dualism ; while the simple phrase, 'His only Son our Lord,'
sweeps aside all aeons and emanations. Its affirmation
of 'the resurrection of the flesh' is in opposition to
Marcion's denial. Finally, docetism is absolutely excluded
by the simple recital of the facts of His life, and by the
emphasis of the completeness of His death in the addition ("Descended into Hades") made at Aquileia towards the close of the fourth century.

The advantage for the Roman Church of the possession
of this symbol cannot be over-estimated. Rome was
not only, as Juvenal tells us, the cesspool of the world ;
to its Church all heresies turned, if only in the hope of
capturing the metropolis of the Empire. Of this we have
illustrations in the coming to Rome of Marcion of Sinope
in Pontus, and the Gnostic Valentinus of Egypt. But
against the rock of a definite confession and a fixed canon
they could not prevail. Alexandria, the heart of the
Eastern Church, in the great struggles of the second century
neither possessed a formulated creed, nor was its foundation by St. Mark or St. Barnabas either historically

[1] Allen, *Continuity of Christian Thought*, p. 111.

certain, nor, if proven, such as entitled its traditions to pre-eminence and obedience.

We see the consequences of these Roman advantages in the tendency of the churches of East and West to refer their difficulties or disputes to Rome for settlement or advice. Of this we have the earliest example in the so-called *Epistle of Clement*, in reality a reply from ' the church that sojourns at Rome to the church that sojourns at Corinth' to an invitation to heal a somewhat obscure dispute. This letter, written about the year 96, bears unmistakably the marks of the Roman genius. In place of speculation we have a wide sweep of practical Christian exhortation, while the question uppermost in the writer's mind is that of obedience to the properly constituted officers of the Church. Such claims to counsel as the Roman Church possesses the writer bases on her superior knowledge of ' the ordinances and commandments of God,' and on her adherence to ' the canon of tradition.' We see this tendency further developed in the visits to Rome during the second century of such prominent Eastern Christians as Hegesippus (c. 151), Polycarp (c. 154), and Origen (c. 215), as well as in the efforts of the Montanists to obtain recognition from Pope Eleutherus. In the case of the condemnation of Origen the decision of Rome seems to have been of special importance. All these events bear witness to a widespread anxiety to know the devotional standpoint of what Origen calls ' the very old Church,' of the metropolis. This culminated in the statement of Irenaeus and Tertullian, in his pre-Montanist days, that agreement with the Church at Rome with its detailed succession of bishops was the best safeguard for the transmission of the apostolic faith.[1] By the end of the second century Victor (†197), the first bishop of Rome of Latin

---

[1] Tertullian, *De Praes.* 32, 36 ; *Adv. Marc.* 4, 5 ; Irenaeus, iii. 3, 1-2. On the difficult interpretation of this last (ad hanc enim ecclesiam propter potentiorem principalitatem necesse est omnem convenire ecclesiam) see Harnack, *H.D.* ii. p. 157 *n.*

race, definitely advanced claims to universal headship. In the Quartodeciman controversy he maintained that every congregation which failed to fall in with the Roman paschal arrangement was thereby excommunicated. The action of Victor was imitated by his successors, especially Callistus (†223). By the year 250 the Roman Church possessed an acknowledged primacy, though whether it was not the primacy of the city and church—' a presidency of love ' as Ignatius had called it—rather than of its bishop, may well be questioned. This brief sketch of a movement, the historic consequences of which are as certain as its validity may be disputed, will show the forces at work in the West which produced the type of thought associated with the Catholic Church.

As the type of thought, so the type of man. The typical fathers of the East are to be found in its great theologians, Clement, Origen, the two Gregories, Athanasius, Dionysius, Theodore of Mopsuestia—to name the leaders in a long line of great theologians. The typical fathers of the West will be found among its lawyers and administrators, Tertullian ; Cyprian, the great prince-bishop, as we may well call him, of Carthage ; Ossius[1] of Cordova, the friend and minister of Constantine ; Ambrose of Milan, whose splendid prelacy, especially his humiliation of the Emperor Theodosius, set the ideal of true ecclesiastical *imperium* ; Hilary of Arles ; Leo the Great and Gregory the Great, two popes whose lofty deeds raised the see of Rome to undisputed pre-eminence ; and Bernard of Clairvaux, for so many years the dictator of Europe. The one exception at first sight is Augustine, who had little or nothing to do with practical affairs. Yet, as we shall see later, no one so powerfully contributed to the organisation both of the Church and the world upon a definite ecclesiastical and political basis as St. Augustine.

---

[1] For Ossius, instead of the Greek form Hosius (="Οσιος), see C. H. Turner in *Journal of Theol. Studies*, Jan. 1911, p. 276.

III

The hardening process whereby the liberty of the spirit was slowly changed into a rigid Church was not allowed to proceed without protest. Of such protests the chief was Montanism, a movement first appearing in Phrygia, a country parts of which were only nominally incorporated in the Roman system, about the year 156. After years of struggle and persecution the sect was finally crushed out by Justinian, the last members of it, in their despair, burning themselves in one of their chapels. With the doctrines of Montanus and his followers we are not now concerned, much less with their ascetic practices and puritanic strictness. Some of their tenets were retrograde—a reversion to principles (for instance, chiliastic expectations of Christ's return), the readoption of which would have been a hindrance to Christianity. Others again, *e.g.* the excessive value attached to celibacy and virginity, tended to the development of Christianity upon lines alien to its primitive spirit. But the stress of Montanism was its protest—exaggerated, it is true, as most protests are, but in the main a conservative reaction—against the elimination from the Church of the free life of the Holy Spirit. The Montanists stood for the liberty of prophesying, regardless of tradition —or even, if need be, of primitive regulation, as in their refusal to be bound by St. Paul's views as to the place of women in the Church. They appealed to prophetic rather than apostolic succession, and attached an extreme value to dreams and ecstasies. Montanism, at any rate in its Western form, had no quarrel with the doctrine of the Catholic, or ' great ' Church as it was then called, nor, in the main, with Catholic ritual ; only it wanted to force both back into what it deemed to be apostolic simplicity freed from episcopal innovations. Its work was not to bring forward new doctrine, but to emphasise the primitive gift of the Paraclete, and that, as Tertullian puts it, all

' advancement to better things ' must be ' by that Vicar
of the Lord, the Holy Ghost.' Its ideal was not organisation—this was the note of the ' great ' Church—but
spirituality, or rather what eighteenth-century divines
would have called ' enthusiasm.' To secure this the
Montanist would shut out the world from the Church by
rigorous discipline, and work upon the world not so much
by intercession as by challenge. By one of the familiar
paradoxes of history a movement which began in the claim
of freedom ended in extreme rigidity—the substitution
for the laws of the Catholic Church of the inspired oracles
of the ' prophets.'

The antagonism of Montanism to culture and thought,
especially Hellenism, was inevitable ; nor was this antagonism confined to such distorted forms as Gnosticism. We
see this antagonism in the self-satisfaction which led the
Montanists to call themselves ' spirituals,' as against the
ordinary Christians, who were but ' psychical ' or ' carnal.'
The ' prophets ' through whom, in Montanist judgment,
the Spirit always worked, were the least cultured of all
the orders in the Early Church. Their roving lives, their
ecstasies, their reliance on vague, incoherent oracles, their
tendency to dwell in their sermons on the retribution that
would shortly overwhelm the world—points all noted by
Celsus—did not predispose to thought. In the highest
spiritual state Montanus claimed that the man himself is
passive : ' Behold the man is as a lyre, and I (the Spirit)
sweep over him as a plectrum. The man sleeps, and
I wake.' Such passivity, an early form of Quietism, is
destructive in the long run of both intellectual and moral
effort. But in the Montanist *Passion of St. Perpetua* we
have one of the gems of sacred literature, and in the
Montanist Tertullian, Latin literature, both secular and
ecclesiastical, must always recognise one of its great masters.

The effects of the suppression of Montanism must not be
overlooked. As a result, or rather as a condition of the

Catholic victory, the Church was led to see the necessity of emphasising historical Christianity. In the effort to crush out the 'prophets' and their "enthusiasms" the bishops fell back upon the two conceptions of the canon as the complete oracles of God, and the limitation of the Spirit's special gifts to the twelve Apostles. In this last we note a narrowing down of the significance of the early order of 'Apostles,' which has misled the Church ever since. To the epoch of revelation given to the Twelve all authority belonged. Between the Apostles and the living Church, the channel of communication and, therefore, of authoritative interpretation, was the 'apostolic' office of the bishops. Thus the discredit of Montanism riveted upon the Church the very fetters of traditionalism and authority against which the Montanists had made their protest. Tertullian already defines the position of his adversaries in the saying, 'ecclesia est numerus episcoporum.' To this episcopate it was given to preserve both the unity and holiness of the Church by the use of the keys.

We have referred to the issue of Montanism in the settlement of the canon. To this the Church was driven if it were to oppose an effective barrier to prophetism. But it was not the Montanists only who forced this issue. A section within the Church itself, to which was given the name of the Alogi, in their hatred of Montanism refused to recognise the Johannine writings ; the Apocalypse because of its prophetism, the Gospel because of its stress upon the Paraclete. Curiously enough, the Alogi ascribed both to the heretic Cerinthus. Against Montanists without, and the Alogi within, the Church asserted a completed and defined canon of the sacred writings. That the churches of the East and West have never yet fully agreed on the limits of the canon, and that the twentieth century is inclined to question altogether their arbitrary rulings, should not prevent us from seeing the vast consequences for Christian thought of the step thus taken.

H

IV

The strength of the Empire lay in its power of assimilating diverse races and civilisations. Latin theology was similarly comprehensive and international. Its founders were Irenaeus and Tertullian, the former a native of Asia Minor, the latter of Carthage. That in his latter days Tertullian (†223) became a Montanist does not lessen the force of his earlier works in the development of Western thought. In some respects, as indeed we might expect from his origin, Irenaeus (†202) is in sympathy with Greek theology, especially in his conception of the Incarnation. Irenaeus had no confidence in the reason as an organ of truth, while his view of the episcopate as possessing the *charisma veritatis*, the prominence he gives to the institutional as distinguished from the fiduciary element in Christianity, is Latin rather than Greek. So also is the practical cast of his mind. He will have nothing to do with subtle speculations ; ' such things we ought to leave to God.' In opposition to the Gnostic philosophy, he founds his theology on ' Catholic ' use of Scripture, with the help of allegory. His great contribution to Western thought was his clear formulation of the idea of tradition. Irenaeus will admit nothing, but obedient and acquiescent faith in the words of Scripture. Theology is, therefore, interpreted faith, and the canon of interpretation is authoritative tradition. The tradition of every church must be regulated by its agreement with the tradition of the churches of apostolic foundation, especially the tradition maintained in its purity at Rome. For this he finds his reasons in Rome's ' influential pre-eminence,' whose Church was founded by the two apostles St. Peter and St. Paul, and in the ease with which, owing to the constant intercourse of the capital of the Empire with the provinces, any departure from the Roman tradition could be detected. Tertullian expressed the same view in his *De Praescriptione*

Hereticorum, the title of which (*praescriptio*—a legal technical
term for the limitation of a suit) signifies his argument;
the ruling out of court of all heretics, inasmuch as the true
meaning of Scripture could only be decided by the orthodox.

The reader will recognise the immense importance of the
doctrine of tradition thus clearly laid down by Irenaeus
and Tertullian. To the ambiguous words of Irenaeus
Rome has ever appealed for confirmation of her claims;
while the general argument of Tertullian issued in the
position expressed by St. Augustine that ' he would not
believe the Gospel were it not for the authority of the
Catholic Church.' In the fifth century the relation of
tradition to interpretation was further defined by Vincent
of Lérins († c. 450) in the famous phrase, *Quod semper, quod
ubique, quod ab omnibus creditum est,* which made the antiquity of tradition the decisive criterion of truth. Vincent,
it is true, is careful to guard his doctrine from too rigid
application. Progress he allows is a real fact, but it is
always organic, never by innovation; it is a deeper or
wider growth rather than a change; it is the unfolding
of the implicit; a clearer explanation of views already
held; the growth from infancy into manhood. Throughout the Middle Ages the dogma thus clearly expressed by
Vincent was the unchallenged opinion of the Church.[1]

In his view of the Atonement Irenaeus tried to develop
a dropped line of thought. In opposition to the doctrines
of Origen, with its emphasis on the Logos, he restated the
Pauline ideas, though with an inadequate appreciation of
the meaning of grace.[2] He is mainly concerned with the
historical significance and results of the Incarnation. His
central thought is the substitution of the obedience of
Christ for the disobedience of Adam. He reminds us of
Anselm in his insistence that as man has fallen man must
conquer. Though the Atonement is thus vicarious and
objective, there is little emphasis of the idea of penal

[1] See *infra*, p. 130.　　　[2] Fairbairn, *Christ in Modern Theology*, p. 67 *n*

satisfaction. It is rather the recovery of the lost image of God, the restoration of humanity to his original state, the taking up anew the conflict in which man has been worsted, the reunion of things unnaturally separated— ἀνακεφαλαίωσις (or *recapitulatio*) as Irenaeus calls it, phraseology which he appears to have borrowed from Justin. The mystic Pauline contrast of Adam and Christ, Irenaeus worked out into a definite Christology that, in spite of its tendency so to exaggerate the accidents as to lose the essence, has many affinities with modern thought. Jesus Christ, God and man, becomes the centre of faith and history, who ' joins the end to the beginning,' through whom mankind reaches his consummation and fulfils his true destiny. With Irenaeus " Christianity is real redemption, *i.e.* the highest blessing bestowed in Christianity is the ' deification ' of human nature through the gift of immortality, and this ' deification ' includes the full knowledge and enjoyment of God." [1] This further suggested to Irenaeus the question as to the cause of the Incarnation. With the Apologists the answer had been given by reference to prophecy ; and the humanity was but shadowy. Irenaeus made the Incarnation the pivot. The Deity, he claimed, ' must become what we are in order that we may become what He is.' This answer, worked out by means of a few simple Biblical ideas into a coherent view of redemption, has become part of the permanent thought of the Church. Not the least significant feature in the doctrine is its optimism, so contrary to the Gnostic idea of the divine descent as a fall or degradation. [2]

To Tertullian, the great lawyer and heroic defender of the faith, the Latin Church owes a larger debt than she has always acknowledged. Next to St. Augustine he is the greatest name in Latin Christianity, in spite of what Neander calls the " massive one-sidedness of his nature." His method, rhetorical rather than scientific, leads him into

[1] Harnack, *H.D.* ii. p. 240.   [2] Ottley, *op. cit.* i. p. 219.

many inconsistencies ; his interest, in fact, in systematic
theology is but slight. He disparages reason ; he tells us
frankly : ' credibile est, quia ineptum est ; certum est, quia
impossibile est.' Though saturated with Stoic thought,
he speaks scornfully of philosophy, and yet is one of the
ablest of those who philosophised on a Christian basis. He
sought to be a disciple of the prophets, and yet at the same
time a zealous defender of the established rules of faith.
But owing to what Harnack calls " his masterly power of
framing formulae," Tertullian founded the terminology
of much later Christian thinking. ' Satisfaction,' ' faith,'
' merit,' ' sacrament,' ' original sin,' and many other
technical or legal terms, especially those that bear upon the
doctrine of sin, are all from his mint. Hence in Tertullian
we find the development of the hard legal ideas of God in
His relations to sin. In Tertullian also we first find the
juristic idea of Adam's sin as envolving the race, and the
realistic idea of the physical taint of sin propagated through
procreation of souls (Traducianism), the beginnings of the
later doctrine of original sin formulated by St. Augustine.

As we might expect in a Roman lawyer, Tertullian's conceptions in his treatment of Christology are juridical. The
terms he uses are those of a jurist ; ' substance ' being
' property,' ' person ' an individual with legal rights, and
the like, though the terms, it is true, are always hovering
between their legal and Stoic senses. Hence he approaches
the problem of the ' Monarchy ' of God [1] not from the
standpoint of first cause, but from that of the ' sole
and single lordship.' This unity is not imperilled by the
administration through ' Persons ' of the Divine lordship.
Thus with Tertullian the Trinity, an economic not immanent necessity, " is our name for God in movement or
self-manifestation." [2] As part of this movement or forth-
coming the Word or Reason of God becomes the Son of
God, an event which had thus its origin in time—*fuit tempus*

[1] *Supra*, p. 74 f.   [2] Ottley, *op. cit.* i. p. 255 ff.

cum Filius non fuit ; language which reminds us, though with different connotation, of the later watchword of Arius.[1]

In reality Tertullian was travelling along the same line of thought as " those who at a later period tried to show that the Trinity is the eternal process of the Divine self-consciousness confronting itself with itself "[2]; though the concrete, not to say materialistic, images in which he expresses his thought lead him into difficulties. As part of his tendency to change " an absolute process into a concrete relationship,"[3] the title Logos with Tertullian gives place to that of Son. The expansion of this term is his special contribution to Christian thought. This term, with its greater sharpness of definition, its harmony with human analogies and experience, and its greater simplicity, henceforth became predominant, at any rate in the Western world, driving out the more abstract Logos with its mystic lights and shadows, beauties and obscurities. The subordination of the Son, a doctrine characteristic of all the Alexandrians and Apologists, is treated in his usual juristic method, as the free exercise of a delegated power ; while the ' monarchy ' is saved by his emphasis that this delegated power must hereafter be delivered up to the Father again.[4] With docetism in any form he will have nothing to do. Hence he insists, as no writer had done so fully before him, on the reality of our Lord's human soul, and on the dignity of the flesh [5] He assumed. To the Christology of Tertullian Novatian (fl. 250) added little save increased emphasis on the subordination of the Son, in which, in fact, he finds a proof of the unity of God.

Owing to his lapse into Montanism the influence of Tertullian on the Church was indirect and unacknowledged. His leading conceptions were appropriated by Cyprian (†258), whose importance lies in his establishment of the

---

[1] *Supra*, p. 80.　　　　[2] Dorner, A., vol. ii. p. 63.
[3] Fairbairn, *op. cit.* p. 394.　　　[4] Ottley, *op. cit.* i. p. 259 ff.
[5] With this should be compared the clause σαρκὸς ἀνάστασιν in the old Roman symbol, contemporary with Tertullian.

rule of the hierarchy and, in consequence, the identification
of the Church with its priesthood, the episcopate of which
constituted its essential unity. From this unity it is impossible that good men should separate. That which is
blown away from the wheat is self-convicted as chaff. With
Cyprian the separatist is worse than the apostate ; the
latter sins once, the former daily. Though the opposite of
his intention—the emphasis of the ecclesiastical parity of
all bishops—no one so effectively assisted as this metropolitan of Carthage in the building up of the Roman
primacy, with all its vast consequences for history and
society. The supremacy of the bishop in the local church
passed insensibly into the doctrine of the supremacy of
the *episcopus episcoporum*, who could be none other than
the bishop of the capital city. The foundation of the
Church on this institutional basis, begun by Ignatius,
strengthened by the quarrel between Callistus and Hippolytus, formulated in a definite theory by Cyprian, was
completed, as we shall see later, by St. Augustine and the
Donatist controversy. Unlike the Reformation, the theory
of Cyprian reigned almost unchallenged.

No step more momentous for good or ill has ever been
taken by the Christian Church than its adoption of the
sacerdotal and hierarchical idea. Unfortunately the matter
is one round which there still rages the fiercest controversy.
The time has not yet come for the dispassionate historian
to lay down, with general approval, the genesis of the idea,
its relation to the original concepts of the Apostles and the
Master, and the stages of its growth. Into this thorny
subject it is no part of our purpose to enter. But even
those who claim for the theories of Cyprian the primitive
authority of Christ would not deny the factors and forces
which made its acceptance the easier. The earliest Christians were Jews. They naturally interpreted the New
Testament through the law and priesthood of the old covenant. For Gentile converts also a priestless religion was

an anomaly ; the old habits of a lifetime would predispose
them to a church of sacerdotal form. Of equal importance
was the whole drift of Roman political life. In the old
Greek πόλις the centre of life was the ἐκκλησία of its free
citizens ; but in the *civitas* of the Romans the *imperium*
was exercised by an *imperator*. Cyprian's theory thus
accorded perfectly with the whole atmosphere of imperialist
rule, and, on the adoption by the Empire of the Christian
religion, would naturally form the basis in the new State
Church. How completely it was helped by its environment is shown by the researches of ecclesiastical archae-
ologists. M. Desjardins, for instance, has given cogent
reasons for believing that in Gaul every city which had a
flamen to superintend the old State religion, the worship of
' Rome and Augustus,' became the seat of a Christian bishop
in the new State Church ; while metropolitan archbishops
are to be found wherever there was a provincial priest of
the imperial cult.[1] Thus " the conquering Roman Church
took its hierarchic weapons from the arsenal of the enemy." [2]

In the play of these three forces—whatever may have
been the original intentions of the Master and His Apostles
—we see the causes which led to the triumph of the ideas of
Cyprian. Believing as we do that the development of the
sacerdotal idea was invaluable for the taming of the barbarians, and that in no other way could the chaos of the
dark ages have been reduced to order,[3] we may allow that
in its triumph we have the work of the Spirit. At the
Reformation new forces and ideas came into play. But
the consideration of their sanction and place in the up-
building of the kingdom of God falls outside our scope.

One effect of the triumph of the theory of Cyprian and
Augustine outlived the Reformation, and, alas ! still
survives. We allude to the spirit of intolerance and perse-

[1] M. Desjardins, *Géog. hist. et administrative de la Gaule Romaine*, iii.
pp. 417, 418 ; cf. Hatch, *D.C.A.*, s.v. Primate, Orders, Ordinations, etc.
[2] Mommsen, *Provinces of Roman Empire* (1st ed.), i. p. 349.
[3] See my chapter on this in Dr. Garvie's *Christ and Civilisation* (1909).

cution, so alien to the teaching of the Master, so characteristic, alas! of Christian thought in all ages. We must remember, in partial mitigation of sentence, that toleration, even as a speculative idea, is essentially modern, and that intolerance, especially in the Early Church, was oftentimes the only effective opposition to indifference. Nevertheless, there is nothing more sad in history than to trace the steps whereby Christianity, in the growing bitterness of theological strife, especially over Arius, forgot the incongruity between persecution and the Gospel. The first result of Christianity becoming the religion of the Empire was the attempt by Constantine to enforce uniformity. In an Imperial Church there can be no right of the sects to separate existence, just as there can be no right of the nations to be independent kingdoms. The world-power secular (Imperial) or spiritual (Catholic) must crush all revolt. Individualism of thought or religion was regarded as a thing impossible; for thought and religion had become questions of society. In their unity men found the basis and bond of continued existence. Whatever, therefore, tended to destroy this unity was held to be as much a hurt to the State as the work of thief or coiner. So in the fourth and fifth centuries the State, aided by the Church, tried to destroy all Christianity that lay outside the Imperial or Catholic Church. The State, openly encouraged by so great a man as Ambrose, in its persecution of Montanists, Donatists, Priscillianists, and others, confiscated their churches, prohibited their meetings, banished their clergy, and sometimes even butchered their members. The worst outcome of this Latin spirit was the story, written in fire and blood, of the medieval inquisition. But the growth of intolerance, and the disasters it has inflicted upon civilisation, would require a volume to itself. Nevertheless, in a history of Christian thought it was impossible not to mention the rise of a spirit so destructive of thought, and to mark out the underlying causes,

CHAPTER V

ST. AUGUSTINE

Argument

I

AURELIUS AUGUSTINE [1] requires a chapter to himself. Since St. Paul no equal name has arisen in the Christian Church. From his conversion until the present day his teaching has swayed the opinions of men and moulded their most potent beliefs. His direct influence upon the East was not great, with the exception of the Antiochenes. Nevertheless, indirectly, through Leo, he gave to the Eastern Church at Chalcedon the final form of its Christological definitions. But no one did more by his life work to give to the Western Church the specific character of its theological thought, one outcome of which was the widening of the gulf already existing between East and West.

The most remarkable thing about St. Augustine is that men of every variety of school look back to him for their inspiration, and trace their most sacred convictions to his writings. Romanist and Anglican, Mystic or Covenanter, Lutheran and Methodist, to say nothing of other schools, all alike revere his memory, and are eager to quote his authority. As early as 431 Pope Celestine sharply rebuked certain bishops of Gaul who had allowed his writings to be questioned. For centuries he has been the one Father of the Church recognised by all, to whom many have assigned 'irrefragable authority.' To St. Augustine we owe the formation of scholastic terminology. From the doctrines he taught have sprung the greatest movements and their most violent reactions. Though the result of her

[1] Born 13th November 354 at Tagaste; baptised by Ambrose at Milan, Easter 387; died at Hippo, 28th August 430.

teaching was the slow but effectual elimination of Augustinianism, Rome still looks back to him as her chief doctor.
Gottschalk, Wyclif, Luther, Jansen are only a few names
in a long line of leaders of revolt who owed their inspiration
to his writings. An order of canons, and an order of friars
—Luther himself was at one time an Austin friar—alike
claimed him as their founder, with disregard of historical
accuracy, but with true insight into his importance in the
development of monachism. Upon the ideas which under-
lie his *De Civitate Dei* of the kingdom of God as an actual
organised visible polity, as old as the world, identified
with the Church yet closely connected with earthly rule, was
founded the theory of the Holy Roman Empire, which for
a thousand years dominated the political development of
the Middle Ages. The opposition which Augustine constantly posits between the *civitas Dei* and the *civitas
terrena* or civil society was reproduced in the edicts of
Hildebrand, Innocent, and Boniface. Augustine was the
first of the leaders of the Church to give full expression to
the truths called evangelical, that religion is a personal
relationship between the soul and God. At the same time,
he gave powerful support to the conception of grace as
objective, as something imparted by sacraments or Church.
" The Biblicism of later times is to be traced back to
St. Augustine ; and the resolute deletion of Scriptural
thoughts by an appeal to the authority of the Church's
doctrine may equally refer to him." [1] Though the statement is exaggerated, there is yet truth in Harnack's claim
" that the whole of the Middle Ages presents itself in the
sphere of dogmatic history as the period when the Church
was fixing its relationship to Augustine and the numerous
impulses originated by him." [2] In certain of its aspects
the Reformation was but the triumph of Augustine's doctrine of grace over his doctrine of the Church. That with
the twentieth century his influence seems on the wane is

---

[1] Harnack, *H.D.* v. p. 99.   [2] *Ibid.* p. 8.

only to state in other words the transitional character of
the age in which we are living.

The greatness of St. Augustine lies in his synthesis
of opposing tendencies. His rich, many-sided nature
appropriated from all sorts of sources, but gave a new
significance to all. No one before or after has so success-
fully fused into one doctrines that are really contradictory.
Attempts to harmonise them are worthless, and lead only
to what Harnack rightly calls "theological chatter." [1]
They are united, however, in the rich inner life of their
originator. This it is, rather than the possession of any
clear, logical system, which has led Eucken to call him
"the single great philosopher, on the basis of Christianity
proper, the world has had." [2] For the success of his synthesis is due to his deep sense of the continuous evolution
of the divine purpose in all things, and of the unity and
reality of the spiritual life. With Augustine everything
is dominated by the deepest wants of mind and heart, of
love and hope. His own desire is ' to know God and the
soul : nothing more.' Hence his ability to grasp all his
problems with his whole being, and not with his heart alone,
or with his mind alone.

This astonishing synthesis can only be explained when
we remember the age in which St. Augustine lived, and
above all his own spiritual experiences. "He stood on
the watershed of two worlds. The old world was passing
away ; the new world was entering upon its heritage, and
it fell to him to mediate the transfer of the culture of the
one to the other." [3] The result, as might be expected, was
too often an impossible fusion. So also in the more
spiritual sphere. Throughout his life he was intent on
reducing to a consistent unity the various elements of
history, nature, and revelation as they presented themselves

---

[1] Harnack, *H.D.* v. p. 167.
[2] Quoted by Warfield in Hastings' *E.R.E.* ii. p. 222.
[3] Warfield in *E.R.E.* ii. p. 220.

in the consciousness of the believer. As during a long life his views expanded and changed, it is often possible to appeal—as we shall do more than once in this chapter—from the later to the earlier Augustine. The synthesis he attempted is imperfect even within the limits of his own experience. But this should not surprise us. His theological treatises are not *a priori* architectonic systems. They grew up without definite sequence, out of the needs of his life and ministry. His theories are but his interpreted experiences. In his *Confessions* we have the key to his doctrine of grace, the love of God seeking him and prevailing within him in spite of himself. In the troubles of his age, above all in the fall of Rome before Alaric, we have the explanation of his *City of God*. He was driven by the crash of the old order to find an apology for Christianity in the philosophy of history, of which science he was really the creator. To understand the dogmas of St. Augustine apart from the age and the man is an impossible task. But in these pages, through limitations of space, such knowledge must be assumed in the reader.

As we might expect from this emphasis of experience, Augustine lays unusual stress upon psychology. With St. Augustine self-knowledge becomes one of the roads to knowledge of God. The acuteness of his psychological observations is remarkable, and is one of the many features in which we may claim that he is essentially modern. Nowhere is this more clearly brought out than in his answer to the philosophical scepticism of the Academies. There is, he pleads, one matter over which there can be no mistake : ' Even though I err, still I am ' (' *Si enim fallor, sum* ')—a curious anticipation of the ' *cogito, ergo sum* ' of Descartes a thousand years later : My very doubt is a proof of the existence of myself. Again and again he returns to this argument in new forms and with new illustrations. Throughout his system he makes the inner life the starting-point of reflection upon the outer world. As a rule, his

philosophical position is that of Plato, but in his explanation
of the origin of knowledge he rejects the Platonic theory
of reminiscence for that of the divine truth borne in
directly upon the human soul. "The ideals we cherish,
the intelligible relations we all recognise, are the thought
of the Eternal Creator—His Eternal Being manifested in
space and time among things of men, through which we
may see Him as in a glass darkly." [1] Both these thoughts
were afterwards worked out into Christian Mysticism, as
was also St. Augustine's statement that there was a
stage in spiritual experience in which men passed beyond
Scripture.

St. Augustine did not draw merely from Catholic or philosophic sources. He began his spiritual history as a Manichaean. For nine years he was one of their 'auditors'
or catechumens. But his acute intellect and unsatisfied
spiritual nature finally escaped, through the help of Ambrose, from this pessimistic fatalism, with its doctrine, so
uncompromising in its dualism, that nature, man's body, and
half man's soul are the work of an evil being. 'There is no
health,' he discovered, 'in those who find fault with any
part of Thy creation, as there was no health in me when
I found fault with many of Thy works.' Nevertheless,
Manichaeism or Gnosticism left its scars. His view of life,
on the whole, is pessimistic; life here is but a preparation
for the hereafter. Moreover, "His confidence in the
rationality of Christian faith had been shaken to the very
depths, and it was never restored." [2] Hence the contradictions in his teaching, which certainly did not distress
him, inasmuch as, unlike the Apologists, he did not expect
that everything in his creed would be clear, consistent, and
demonstrable. Hence, also, the tendency in St. Augustine
to fall back upon the Church for the guarantee of faith—
a doctrine that was to develop in later ages into that of
infallibility. Moreover, Augustine was never able to shake

[1] Cunningham, *St. Austin*, p. 34. [2] Harnack, *H.D.* v. p. 79.

himself free from the Manichaean doctrine of a twofold morality, one for the small body of the elect or perfect, the other for the general mass. In the monks of his new faith and in their higher service Augustine found the old distinction, though in a more reasonable form.

Another stage in his spiritual history was his relation to Neoplatonism. Through Neoplatonism he was first snatched from Manichaean darkness. Before his conversion, or rather as one stage in it, Augustine seems to have studied the *Enneads* of Plotinus as translated into Latin by Victorinus.[1] From Neoplatonism he learned that God is a spirit, immaterial, eternal, incorruptible, unchangeable, the supreme Unity that is the Soul of souls, ' the Life which never dies,' ' Who governs the whole world down to the leaves that flutter on the trees.' At one time even he seems to have attained the adept's goal of the mystic vision, the ecstasy in which ' with the flash of one trembling glance he arrived at That which Is.' But the Neoplatonic idea that moral evil can be got rid of by moral discipline did not satisfy his craving for deliverance or meet the demands of his conscience.[2] He accepted, it is true, as did his teacher Ambrose, the contention that all evil is ' a privation,' that apart from good there is no real existence. Evil, therefore, was not, as the Manichaeans taught, an eternal power in opposition to God. But this ' privation,' he held, was a taint, the mark of God's just judgment, ' a perversity of will which turns aside from Thee, O God, flinging away its inner treasure.' The one remedy for this he found to lie, subjectively in deep humility, objectively in the Cross of Christ. ' The books of the Platonists tell nothing of this. Those pages give me not the lineaments of this religion, the tears of confession, the troubled spirit, the broken and contrite heart. . . . No

[1] For Victorinus, see *infra*, p. 198.
[2] St. Augustine's account of his release from Neoplatonism is found in the seventh book of his *Confessions*.

one there hearkens to Him that calleth : Come unto Me all
ye that labour. They think it scorn to learn from Him
because He is meek and lowly of heart.'

II

The details of the Donatist controversy—a continuation,
as it were, under a new form of the issues at strife in Montanism—belong to ecclesiastical history. But the real
question in dispute was far wider and deeper than the re-
baptism of those who had received the rite at the hands of
heretics or of the lapsed. The result of the controversy was
to fasten upon the West the conception which dominated
the Middle Ages, that the Church in its sacraments and
ministry possessed virtues that were objective and inalien-
able, whatever the character of its members. Logically, of
course, St. Augustine was right. It is impossible to put
the reality of the means of grace and the existence of the
Church at the hazard of the worthiness of its ministers.
This would be to found it not on the rock but on the quick-
sands. But the victory of his logic had its perils. The
revolts of Wyclif and Hus in the fourteenth century against
this dogma were followed by the later revolts of Luther
and Wesley. It is no small testimony to the greatness of
St. Augustine that the inspiration in their revolt against
this Augustinian doctrine was their grasp of another, the
Augustinian doctrine of grace.

Though to St. Augustine the Church is the *congregatio
sanctorum,* he yet unconsciously transfers to the institutional Church the predicates which rightly belong only to
the ideal. To St. Augustine, be it remembered, the ideal
is the only real, and that which is not good and eternal has
no real existence. Hence he identifies the ideal Church
with the visible Church. When pressed with the difficulty
of the presence of the wicked in the Church he falls back
upon the number of the elect, without seeing that he had

thus reduced the visible Church to an empirical Church, the bounds of which lie outside human cognisance. The result was complete confusion. In one direction the influence of St. Augustine was thrown upon the side of the belief in the Church as the sphere of salvation and authority, the sole agent in grace. Through St. Augustine, working in alliance with other forces, and building on the foundations of Cyprian, this Roman conception—to which really his fundamental doctrine of grace was opposed— became the dominant thought of the world. At the same time, his conception of the Church as the elect who never obtained their election through the Church but directly by grace, who might even lie outside the visible society, undoubtedly tended to overthrow the idea he had otherwise built up. Another fruitful idea, in practical, though not necessarily logical, opposition to the arguments whereby he had overthrown Donatism, was Augustine's insistence upon love as the note of the Church, without which the sacraments themselves were deprived of their efficiency.

III

The central fact with St. Augustine, the starting-point of his thoughts, is his realisation of Sin and Grace. Through these, more than any other, he has won his supreme place. By their revival he first gave to St. Paul, their real author, his right place in Christian thought. Hitherto these great Pauline truths had been so little recognised that their emphasis by St. Augustine came upon the Church with all the surprise of a new discovery. To this discovery he was guided by his own spiritual experience. Between the *Confessions* and the spiritual history of St. Paul before his conversion, as given in *Romans* vii., there was probably much similarity. The consciousness of the radical, sinful condition had been driven in upon him by Ambrose. In his revolt from Manichaeism Augustine had discovered

that evil was no physical power. His own failures refuted
the ruling Stoic conception that virtue was the supreme
good, that in the concentration of the will upon its attainment lay the essence of redemption. It is characteristic
of the man and of the whole drift of his experience that
in his closing days at Hippo the penitential psalms, written
in large letters, were hung where he could see them.

   In our estimation of every movement associated with
some great thinker there is a danger lest we overlook the
influence of the age. Not by accident was it that the
question of the relation of sin and grace was raised in the
West and not in the East. The doctrine of sin can never
be properly treated except by a society in which the individual is strongly conscious of himself. To a corporation,
whether state or trading company, the sense of sin is always
difficult to bring home. In the Eastern world, where the
new Empire laid its paralysing grip upon all, individualism
could only find expression in the eremite life. Moreover,
Greek philosophy, which was in the ascendant in the
Eastern Church, owing to its imperfect sense of personality,
had never troubled itself much over the question of Free
Will. In the West the fall of the Empire had thrown back
the individual upon himself. One result was the adoption
by the West, under the lead of Martin of Tours and others,
of Eastern Monasticism in a form more suitable to itself ;
another, the development, through the teaching of St.
Augustine, of the doctrine of sin and grace. For the
constant burden of the thought of Augustine is the relation
of God and the soul, of the soul and its God, and such an
inquiry necessarily leads to the doctrine of sin and grace.
Moreover, in the East there was always a reluctance to
assume the corruption or depravity of the race; in the West,
since the teaching of Tertullian, there was full recognition
of a bias towards evil. As in the West there was a readiness
to accept the freedom of the will, the doctrine of the prevalence and potency of evil brought in as a corollary the

doctrine of the potency and prevalence of the grace which could thus redeem and restore.

With St. Augustine the origin of evil is through the defect of will, the negligence of a changeful will. ' For as a snake does not creep on with open steps but by the very minutest efforts of its several scales, so the slippery motion of falling away from good takes possession of the negligent only gradually, and beginning from a perverted straining after the likeness of God, arrives in the end at the likeness of beasts.' Unfortunately St. Augustine did not stop there, but added other elements of more than doubtful character. In an acute criticism of the first chapter of *Genesis* Augustine had pointed out that the narrative of creation was not a history of actual facts, but was allegorical, for the coming into being of Time could not take place in periods of time. But when he came to the third chapter he dropped his criticism, and treated it as actual history instead of as the unfolding of truth under allegorical language. This, possibly, was because of his desire to be able to give to the Manichaeans, with their insistence on the eternal character of evil, an account of how, as a matter of fact, evil had arisen in time.[1]

As to the punishment of sin, St. Augustine would not agree with the ' Platonists who hold that all punishments tend only to the purgation of sin.' Punishment is the assertion of the moral order which crime has disturbed. If punishment were in itself fully remedial the Incarnation and Redemption of Christ would be superfluous. The punishment of sin is not necessarily physical, it consists rather ' in the ignorance and incapacity that befall every soul that sins ' ; these in their turn lead to deeper alienation from God. Unfortunately Augustine is again led by a literalism that is out of harmony with his usual principles of Scriptural interpretation into insistence that the punishment after death is material as well as spiritual ; nor does

[1] Cf. Cunningham, *op. cit.* p. 56 ff.

he notice the intellectual difficulties involved in his giving
an everlasting significance to certain physical conditions,
i.e. to phenomena in space and time. Rightly or wrongly,
Augustine's doctrine henceforth dominated the Church,
to the exclusion of Origen's larger hope of the final salvation of all.

In his treatment of reward Augustine accepted the idea
of ' merit ' with which the Church had been familiarised
by Tertullian and Cyprian. In the final decision of character merit alone would be considered. St. Augustine
reconciled this with his doctrine of grace by teaching that
all our merits are, after all, only the gifts of God. 'When
God crowns our merits He is only crowning His own gifts.' [1]
Faith, Love, and Merit are the successive stages in the
road of salvation, faith being the preliminary, and love the
active agent in the new life.

We must note, moreover, a further deduction of immense
consequence. With St. Augustine evil was not, as the
Manichaeans held, " a real substantial existence opposing
God. It was a defect in things otherwise good, and which,
despite their defects, still made a harmonious whole. In
so far as a being persists it is because it has elements of
goodness." [2] In this idea of the " harmonious whole " we
see the source of Austin's dogma, destined to grip so terribly
a later age, of hell itself witnessing to the glory of God, as
part of the ordered fitness of creation.

IV

We pass next to the consideration of Augustine's conflict
with Pelagius, a pious British or Irish monk whose secluded
cloister life had never wrestled with the deeper sins of the
soul. Pelagius had been roused to anger by the flabby
Christianity of the day, that excused its degeneracy by

---

[1] See Harnack, *H.D.* v. p. 87.
[2] Cunningham, *op. cit.* p. 71, and Harnack, *H.D.* v. p. 114.

pleading inability to fulfil the commands of God. In Augustine's conflict with the Manichaeans the question at issue was metaphysical; in his conflict with Pelagius, and his abler allies, Caelestius and Julian of Eclanum, the question was more psychological. There are few errors or opinions which have not some root in the past. So with Pelagianism. The historical connections of this heresy with the current Nestorianism seem fairly certain; its theological links are more evident, and were first traced out by Cassian of Marseilles. The doctrine that Jesus was a sinless man promoted to the dignity of being assumed by God is not far removed from the Pelagian idea that all men can become by their own efforts what Christ became, or, at least, may avoid sin and earn eternal blessedness. In neither doctrine is there the essential exaltation of the Saviour. Both doctrines are extreme forms of individualism. In neither is there any sense of solidarity religious or social, and this, after all, is a note of no small importance in the doctrine of original sin. The ultimate effect of both Nestorianism and Pelagianism, as well as of its modern counterpart Deism, is to deny the need and power of the Atonement, or, at least, to reduce it to a mere question of God and the individual. This is only to state in other words that Pelagianism fails to grasp the reality of evil, which it regards as a momentary self-determination of the will instead of as the result of a deeper cause. For the doctrine of original sin teaches the great truth of experience, that behind all separate sins there lies sin itself, expressing itself in a want of rest, joy, harmony, and love. Moreover, in their exaltation of the nature of man Nestorianism and Pelagianism alike overlook the cardinal factor in religion as distinct from morals, the ' grace ' or condescension of God, and, consequently, both undervalue the means of grace.

Nor is it only with Nestorianism that Pelagianism has contact. The Stoic doctrine, as prevalent in the time of

Augustine as in new forms it is prevalent in the twentieth century,[1] of a life according to nature, of virtue, and of the spiritual as only natural forces—nature itself being regarded as independent of the notion of God—is practically only another, if more philosophical, expression of the same error. For the crucial question in the whole controversy was whether ' grace ' should be reduced to ' nature,' man's ' glorious constitution,' and the like, upon whose primitive innocence Julian, the acutest of all the Pelagians, insisted. Pelagianism, in fact, is only another aspect of the age-long conflict of " morals as against religion, free will as against grace, reason as against revelation," [2] and, we may add, of culture against conversion. Not without cause does Julian appeal to Aristotle, without whose categories he regards theology as valueless.[3] For Aristotle was ever the prophet of the natural man.[4]

In the broad outlines St. Augustine was undoubtedly right. His victory over Pelagius was a victory for which all subsequent generations may be thankful. But the same high praise cannot be given to all the details of the controversy. His great adversary Julian riddled much of his doctrine, and showed how untenable it becomes. His whole doctrine of grace in the Adamic state, apart altogether from what modern science would say about it, is itself an illogical Pelagianism, in complete conflict also with his doctrine of irresistible grace. In his doctrine of original sin he argues, as his adversary Julian pointed out, as if all would be well, could children be born by being shaken from trees.

The student should be careful not to confuse with the teaching of Augustine opinions which later writers, especially Calvin, read into him. Thus in our judgment—the question, it is true, might fairly be debated—St. Augustine

[1] In the eighteenth century we find it best in the teaching of Rousseau.
[2] Rainy, *Ancient Catholic Church*, p. 468.
[3] See Harnack's elaborate note, *H.D.* v. p. 191 f.
[4] See *infra*, p. 228.

did not always hold the doctrine of total depravity in the
form commonly imputed to him, that through the Fall man
both wills and does nothing but evil,[1] with the added rider
of inherited sin in itself sufficient for damnation. For
Augustine at times clearly teaches that, in spite of its depravity, the power of the will is still a noble power, in the
possession of which lies the kernel of our nature.[2] But
Augustine did not see that in admitting that sin springs
from the will he reduced his theory of original sin to a contradiction. Moreover, Augustine had written in defence
of Free Will against the Manichaeans, and distinguished,
though in an uncertain fashion, divine prescience from
divine foreordination. God predestines because God fore-
sees what man will do. Augustine held, it is true, that unre-
generate man is so bound by sin that he is not ' free ' to
do right. But this denial of ' freedom ' is really a denial
of capricious choice ; the assertion of self-determination
on the lines of one's real character.[3] In the same way
God Himself is not ' free ' to do wrong ; for St. Augustine
in his earlier days refused to separate the Will of God from
the character of God, and so saved himself from the divine
arbitrariness which is the great blot in Calvinism. But
Calvin was only following the repulsive teaching of St.
Augustine's later days, as set out in his letter to Sixtus
(417 or 418).

Another doctrine of Augustine destined to bear much
fruit in later centuries was that the election of grace is
irresistible—as indeed with his premises it is bound to be—
though no one can be certain that he possesses this grace.

[1] In his final survey of his teaching in the *Retract.*, St. Augustine, however,
adopts the extreme form. The modern revolt against his doctrine can, however, appeal from the later to the earlier Augustine. Unfortunately the later
Augustine, and the crude interpretations of Augustine, usually held the day
in the Church.

[2] On this see Harnack, *H.D.* v. p. 123 *n.*

[3] It would be interesting to compare this with the teaching of T. H.
Green, *Prolegomena to Ethics.* The gap between the two does not seem to
be very great, except in the greater precision and consistency of the Oxford
scholar.

As Harnack rightly remarks : ' With all his horror of sin Augustine had not experienced the horror of uncertainty of salvation.' [1] Augustine never saw that his doctrine of predestination must issue in the destruction of the conception of the Church and its sacraments, upon which he had enlarged in the Donatist controversy. Where grace is irresistible all else becomes needless, and man himself can scarcely be said to be a moral creature at all. The doctrine of predestination is also, as Dr. Bigg points out, only a form of Gnosticism, for " it makes no real difference whether our doom is stamped upon the nature given by our Creator (Gnosticism) or fixed by an arbitrary decree." [2]

It is impossible to pass away from Pelagianism without glancing at another allied controversy. The question of original sin is strictly bound up with the question of the origin of the sinning soul. To this question three different answers were given in the Early Church. Origen, following out his Platonic philosophy, taught the pre-existence of the soul. Human life is only a disciplinary process for the spirits that sinned. Such a theory, while it secures responsibility and accounts for original sin, becomes really an extreme form of individualism. Solidarity may have existed in previous worlds ; there is none among mankind. By this theory the body becomes, as in the great poem of Wordsworth, merely a prison-house. A second theory, current in the East, as also with Jerome and Hilary, was Creationism, or the new creation by God at the time of birth of every individual soul ; the body in which it tabernacled being, however, derived by natural processes of generation. Such a theory is bound logically to issue in the belief that the body is the source of sin, a view akin to the old Gnosticism. A third theory was Traducianism. This was the theory of the West, forcibly expounded by Tertullian, and

---

[1] Harnack, *H.D.* v. p. 210 *n.*
[2] Bigg, *Christian Platonists*, pp. 284-86.

made a part of the Catholic faith by Leo. In this conception body and soul are alike formed by natural generation.
The indirect adoption by St. Augustine of this theory, above
all the logical issues of his conflict with Pelagianism, led
to Traducianism becoming the recognised creed of the
Church. Whatever its truth—and modern biology, as well
as the facts of experience and psychology, have much to
say for it [1]—it gives to the doctrine of original sin, even
in its crudest forms, a certain logical unity. But this
unity was purchased at too great a cost, since it tended
to lay the whole stress of sin upon the sexual desire. We
see the outcome of this doctrine in the stress which for a
thousand years was laid upon celibacy as the supreme grace
of the would-be saint.

We have spoken of St. Augustine as the greatest of
Christian philosophers. His greatness consists as much
in his method as in his teaching. His teaching we may
reject ; at any rate we cannot on his *ipse dixit* accept it
as a ready-made solution of the difficulties of modern
thought. His doctrine of predestination was a novelty
in the Church, and as such was regarded with strong suspicion. Even in his own days John Cassian of Marseilles,
and Faustus, bishop of Riez in Provence, set aside the extreme teaching of St. Augustine in favour of a more rational
account of the relation of Grace and Free Will to Original
Sin. Their semi-Pelagianism, though formally rejected by
the council of Orange (529), was, however, the doctrine
which prevailed long before Trent, and which, through the
discredit of Calvinism, is now dominant. But neither this
nor other departures from his dogmas touch his real greatness. "It is easy to show that in every single objectionable
theory formulated by Augustine there lives a true phase
of Christian self-criticism." [2] "Old controversies return,

---

[1] To the present writer Traducianism seems logically to lead to the
Deistic notion of God starting a series to which He was once related, but
which now runs on by its own laws or caprice.

[2] Harnack, *H.D.* v. p. 221.

but in new forms; yet the way which he pursued in his search for truth is open to us too; it is still the path of faith that leads to knowledge." [1] With Augustine, as with every true thinker, 'the fear of the Lord was the beginning of wisdom.'

[1] Cunningham, *op. cit.* p. 9; *Nisi credideritis, non intelligetis* was Austin's motto. Cf. *infra,* p. 186.

CHAPTER VI

THE DARK AGES

Argument

I

MEDIEVAL thought begins with pope St. Gregory the Great (590-604). He is the connecting link between the ancient and the medieval period, the last of the Fathers and the first of the Schoolmen. Various events tended to bestow upon Gregory this mediating position. He marks in more ways than one the beginning of a new era. In the year before he ascended the papal throne Spain renounced her Arianism at the council of Toledo, and proclaimed her return to the Roman unity. In the West the old Roman Empire had passed away, while the onset of the barbarians had for the moment ceased. The first monk to become a pope, Gregory was also the first of the popes to turn to the new races in the West to restore to Rome her lost empire. By his writings, his zeal, his fame for sanctity, his quickness to grasp opportunity, and his administrative wisdom, Gregory succeeded in making effective in the West the primacy of his see. Through the bloodless weapons of his missionaries lawless countries bowed before the supremacy of the new Caesars. Illyricum, Gaul, Spain, and Africa acknowledged his metropolitan claims; while Italy, swept by the Lombards, recognised in Rome her head in temporal as well as spiritual matters. On the firm foundations thus laid by Gregory the life of Western Europe was established anew. The Innocents and Hildebrands of later centuries but carried out with greater detail the principles which we find in germ in Gregory.

In Gregory's administrative reconstructions the ruling idea is not new. It was the reversion in a new form to the old conception of the Roman Empire. The formal

inauguration of the Holy Roman Empire, by the coronation
of Charles the Great on Christmas Day 800, was but the
consummation of Gregory's efforts to secure continuity
with the past. Equally lacking in all claims to originality
was his theology. What Gregory did was not to develop
new ideas so much as to introduce the old creeds and faiths
to the barbarian races conquered by the Church, in a form
adapted to their crude intelligence. In all his writings, however naïve, we discern the practical administrator, more
anxious for the accommodation of thought to immediate
need than for its purity and truth. As his *Dialogues*
show, no superstition is too gross if only its acceptance
served in the taming of barbarian tempers. His theology and thought are a debased Augustinianism, but as
such it was so perfectly adapted to its environment that
for centuries Gregory was looked up to by the Western
world as the wisest of the fathers, more read even than
St. Augustine himself. If to-day we are tempted to wonder
at this success, it is because we forget his practical work.
Gregory's doctrine fitted his practice of Church government
as perfectly as hand and glove ; the two became one.

This administrative character of medieval theology was
in reality the effect of a change in thought itself, or rather
was due to the complete development of the ideas of the
Latin world. The restless intellectual activity, both
within and without the Church, which led the great fathers
to formulate the doctrines of the Church, had been succeeded by a period of stagnation. The investigation
of doctrine, the attempt to reconcile dogma with mental
needs, was no longer the predominant question. Doctrine
was a sacred deposit, handed down from the fathers, to
be transmitted unimpaired to the new nations. Of this
inheritance the guardians were the Roman hierarchy, the
Church alone its recognised interpreter. As, moreover,
the content of dogma was fixed and complete, the field of
inquiry was limited to the giving precision and harmony

to the accepted doctrines. The attempt, as we shall see, was not always successful. Interpretation of the old often passed, by unconscious gradations, into the promulgation of the new. Nevertheless, for nearly a thousand years the attempt at restriction was made. There were, no doubt, certain intrusive elements, the influence of the Saracens, and the like. But these chiefly manifested themselves in the formation of diverse heresies of limited extent and influence.

Thus, speaking broadly, the first characteristic of medieval thought is its essential unity. Differences rarely touched the deeper centres ; for at bottom the diverse schools, however apparently opposed, were fundamentally one. Viewed from the standpoint of a more divided age, the matters which separated Gerson from Hus, to take a noted illustration of antagonism, were as nothing compared with the doctrines in which they were agreed. Here and there the unity of the Middle Ages was broken, but such breach was generally political rather than theological or philosophical.

This unity of medieval thought must not be misunderstood or exaggerated. There never was a time in the Middle Ages when men were so cramped by dogmatic system that there was no room left for individual opinion. On the contrary, the student of medieval thought is often surprised at its freedom. But, as a rule—for the exceptions rarely exerted any wide or lasting influence—this liberty of individual judgment always adjusted itself in the last resort to certain fundamental positions of the Church ; though the method of adjustment is often violent, involving contradiction between the actual and the assumed premises. But for our present purpose it is of importance to notice that the attempt at reconciliation is always there ; the contradictions so familiar to-day did not exist ; or rather, where they existed, they speedily disappeared, logically or otherwise, in the all-pervading consciousness of ultimate unity. Friction between theology and science could not be permanent, for theology, as in the story of the conflict between the rods of Moses and those of the Egyptian magicians, swallowed up the rest.

But though medieval thought was thus a unity in itself, to a degree utterly unknown either in the Roman world or in the world since the Reformation, it nevertheless possessed well-defined periods. These were determined, as is natural where the chief question is one of authoritative interpretation, by the discovery or promulgation of certain recognised text-books. The importance of text-books for the medieval mind cannot be exaggerated. The influence of Gratian's *Decretum*, or of Peter Lombard's *Sentences*, may be instanced. For centuries law and divinity centred itself round their study. But the authoritative text-books, *par excellence*, were to be found in the works of Aristotle. It is by its relation to these that the periods of medieval thought may best be defined. In the first period, which closes with St. Bernard, the works of Aristotle were known only in misleading and partial Latin versions. In the second period fuller and more accurate translations were introduced from the East to the Western world, and were made the basis of a vast superstructure of Christian theology. In the third period, which begins in the fourteenth century, the growing knowledge of letters made it impossible that men should remain satisfied with the confined outlook of the past, or with the narrow philosophical foundations upon which the current thought rested.

As is usually the case, the transition from the one period to the other was by no means abrupt, though each was marked by certain well-defined characteristics. In the first period, in spite of its general barrenness, we find in unexpected quarters considerable originality of thought, and the emphasis of the value of individual opinion. In the second period the appeal to an authoritative text-book was often attended with intellectual disaster, and the restriction of liberty. The third period, at any rate in its fruition, scarcely falls within our scope, though the reader should always remember that the revival of Greek letters and the rise of the new intellectual spirit considerably ante-dated the Reformation, and only in the early years of the sixteenth century became part of a great religious move-ment.

II

The first period, often known as the Dark Ages, covers the centuries from the fall of the Western Empire to the discovery of Aristotle. Outwardly it was a period of stress and strain, the upheaval of a world already broken in pieces. Successive flights of barbarians—Saxons, Huns, Northmen, and the like, each one no sooner settled and comparatively civilised than overwhelmed in its turn by some new invasion—led to the destruction of such little culture as had survived the fall of the Empire. Viewed from within, the period was marked by superstition and terror. Amid the chaos of society men found in these the groundwork of authority, and the main element of order. Without and within alike the Church was fighting a des-perate battle. At times she nearly succumbed, and it is undeniable that she degenerated in the contest and absorbed some of the surrounding barbarism.

The student would do well to realise the intellectual equipment with which Western theologians in the Dark Ages advanced to their task. Of the great inheritance of classical culture little had survived ; of the thoughts of Hellas almost none. Such secular knowledge as remained was represented by the well-known division of the seven arts into the elementary *Trivium* (Grammar, Rhetoric, Dialectics), and the more advanced *Quadrivium* (Music, Arithmetic, Geometry, Astronomy). The text-books in use were two in number, Boethius and Cassiodorus—for the *Satyricon* of Martianus Capella, often mentioned as the third, was really a grotesque allegory. Of the two the most valuable was that of Boethius, a writer in the early years of the sixth century, probably the author of a much-suspected treatise, *De sancta Trinitate*. But his importance for later generations did not spring from his theological beliefs, but from his being the chief means whereby such scanty knowledge of Aristotle as modified his Platonism had been preserved to the Western world. In his famous *De Consolatione Philosophiae* we have the source to which, for the most part, the scholars of the Dark Ages turned for their knowledge of classical culture.

Little, however, of real value had been saved. The gold of past culture as distinct from strictly dogmatic or exegetical science had sunk ; it was only the lighter rubbish that had floated down the stream of time. Even in Boethius there is of the *Quadrivium* but the scantiest outline ; the real secular education of the period was confined to the *Trivium*. Under grammar were included not only the technical rules of Priscian and Donatus, but also the few survivals from the wreck of pagan culture, though the study of these was hindered by a lurking uneasiness of conscience in the teacher. Vergil and Cicero were pagans ; Vergil, in fact, a great magician who had fled from Rome to Naples, and enriched that city with his black art. The study of such writers was often regarded as like unto the sin of Achan. Even so enlightened a statesman as Gregory the Great had written to Desiderius of Vienne to condemn his teaching of grammar and the reading of the poets : ' A report has reached us which we cannot mention without a blush, that thou expoundest grammar to certain friends ; whereat we are so offended and filled with scorn that our former opinion of thee is turned to mourning and sorrow. The same mouth singeth not the praises of Jove and Christ. . . . If, hereafter, it be clearly established that the rumour which we have heard of thee is false, and that thou art not applying thyself to the idle vanities of secular learning, we shall render thanks to God, who hath not delivered over thy heart to be defiled by the blasphemous praises of secular men.'

The loss of classical culture was most disastrous for medieval theology. There was nothing to save it from itself, or to keep it in touch with the human. The result was of necessity a pretentious dogmatism. The hardening of all thought into formulae was also assisted by another influence. The knowledge of Roman law did not die with classical culture. In the towns, especially of northern Italy, as the history of the great law university of Bologna shows us, a knowledge of Roman law survived the conquests of the barbarians; like Roman roads, aqueducts, and bridges, it had been built too solidly to be easily swept away. The effect of this survival cannot be over-estimated. We see it in the Church in two directions. The one was the rise of Canon law, confessedly moulded upon the Roman model. The other, more germane to our present inquiry, was the permeation of medieval theology with forensic ideas and their expression in forensic language. To the effect of this survival of the Latin spirit we have already alluded.

As regards its content, so far as theology was concerned, the inheritance transmitted to the Middle Ages by Gregory the Great was little better than a confused Augustinianism. Of the great thinkers of the Greek Church, and of their broad, comprehensive outlook upon life, the Western Church became almost completely ignorant, save for a few elements assimilated from Hilary, Ambrose, Jerome, and Augustine, or from 'Dionysius the Areopagite.' Here and there writers like Alcuin or Paschasius Radbert show their indebtedness to Greek Christology; but they were voices crying in the wilderness. The scientific study of the Bible, begun by Origen, was a lost art. Of Augustine the most valuable element, his doctrine of grace, was practically suppressed until the Reformation. The consequences of this suppression manifested themselves in different forms, the most disastrous being the system of the penitentials. This great instrument for Christianising barbarian tempers, the doctrinal basis of which may be found in the acts and teaching of Ambrose, was probably in its origin the creation of the Irish Church in its most flourishing days, and in especial of Columban. Thence, through the English Archbishop Theodore of Tarsus (668-690), the penitentials passed into the general Church of the West. An attempt at codification of the different systems in vogue formed part of the reforms of Charles the Great ; this was one of the forces upon which he relied for reducing his empire to order. In time the older penitentials gave place to the scholastic sacrament of penance, though many of the earlier prescriptions were embodied in the text-books of Gratian and Gregory IX.

In condemnation of the principles and methods of the whole system of the penitentials, historians and theologians are now substantially agreed. Nevertheless, the student should remember the law, illustrated on every page of ecclesiastical history, " that those beliefs or institutions which seem irrational, or absurd, or unworthy of the Christian spirit, have come into vogue in order to kill some deeper evil, not otherwise to have been destroyed." [1] The penitentials were, perhaps, necessary if the Church was to bring the masses that had nominally passed into the kingdom of Christ, yet remained in many respects heathen at heart, into a working acquaintance with the elementary laws of decency and hygiene, let alone any real experience of religion. In the early medieval Church baptism came first—ofttimes the baptism of whole races received as they were into the Church of the Empire which they had conquered ; training and discipline must needs follow. Penance, to adopt for this system of discipline the familiar title nowadays somewhat restricted in its appli-

[1] Allen, *Christian Institutions*, p. 408.

cation, was thus no mere creation of sacerdotalism, but to some extent a response to popular needs, the outcome of the barbarian invasions. In the decaying Roman world no state, save the Church, was strong enough, or civilised enough, to enforce obedience to moral law, or hold down the usages and reminiscences of heathenism.

The punishments of the Church were at first limited to those sanctioned by the pains and fears of the wounded conscience, and the humiliation which public confession involved. Unfortunately the Latin Church, in which the feeling of the legal relationship of the individual to the Church was always prominent, soon yielded to the Teutonic custom of commuting misdeeds by a money payment, or by means of substitutes, combining with the custom Roman systematic legal codification. Hence the opening of the door to the abuses of indulgences, not the least of which was its mercantile scale. Thus the deepening of the conception of sin, which the system at first effected, degenerated later into the stupefying readiness with which men acknowledged themselves to be sinners.

The other evils of the system have often been expounded, and are sufficiently familiar. The student of ethics will point out the tendency—always natural to the Roman spirit —to stiffen all morality into legal restrictions, and to confound the inner law with the regulations of the Church. The theologian will dwell on the result in making sin something arbitrary and external to the soul, and the Atonement, in consequence, arbitrary also, a matter to be effected by constant haggling and bargaining over the degree of sin, or its classification, and the value of merit. This last idea, the origins of which we find in Tertullian and Ambrose, developed into the doctrine of the common treasury of merit, out of whose inexhaustible store the Pope, as the vicar of God, could dispense to the spiritually destitute.

This doctrine, first suggested by the English doctor, Alexander of Hales (†1245), and perfected by Thomas

Aquinas, was really the logical development of the idea, incorporated by Gallic influence into the Roman symbol in the fifth century, of the ' communion of saints ' ! The Church triumphant was one ' family ' or ' clan ' with the Church on earth, and therefore, in accordance with the common Teutonic idea, could equally discharge the debt of any member of the clan. The result was inevitable. The priest who could release from the punishment of sin on earth (for to this, officially speaking, the system alone had reference), or whose prayers had power with God in the mysterious other world of retribution, took the place of the Christ who could purify the heart. The Pope and not the Holy Spirit became the administrator of mercy and pardon. The human race became afraid of dealing directly with God, and sacerdotalism won its long triumph. When Abailard laid down the principle that the essence of sin lay in the motive, he was condemned ; such teaching was a blow at the dominion of the Church. When Dante proclaimed in his *Divine Comedy* that hell, purgatory, and heaven correspond to an inward condition of the soul, men heeded not, the mystics apart, the voice crying in the wilderness. Religious consciousness had handed over to the successors of St. Peter not only supremacy on earth, but an actual dominion over vast circles of the unseen world.

The doctrine of penance underlying the penitential system was supplied by Gregory. In penance four points were included : perception of sin, and ' contrition '—these two may be considered as one—' conversion,' ' confession,' and ' satisfaction ' ; and the greatest of these was ' satisfaction.' The consequences of this exaggeration of ' satisfaction' were writ large in more ways than in a theory of the Atonement. The historical Jesus became almost wholly identified with the suffering Saviour ; the Gospel of the Incarnation was lost in the suggestion of the physical agonies of Calvary ; the Fatherhood of God became an almost unknown idea, hidden especially by the universal belief in the need for the intercession of Virgin and saints.

To Gregory's theory of the Atonement as a deception of the devil we have already referred.   In all his expositions of the work of the Redeemer, " Christ's death and penance appear side by side as two factors of equal value." [1]   Sins of a lower grade may be atoned for, and the soul purified in the fires of purgatory.   The rites and sacraments of the Church are the channel of salvation.   The Atonement, in fact, becomes so completely external in character that Gregory frankly owns that the death of Christ was not absolutely necessary.   An arbitrary fiat would have done as well, more especially as Gregory limits down the elect to the number needed to supply the place of the fallen angels.   One other matter demands attention because of later conflicts.   As regards images of saints, Gregory favoured the popular custom : ' The picture is used in churches that those who are ignorant of letters may, at least, read by seeing upon the walls what they cannot read in books.'

III

The two centuries from Gregory to Charles the Great, though of great importance for the historian, were almost sterile in their contributions to thought.   Such authorship as existed took the form rather of abridgments from the Fathers, *e.g.* the *Sentences* of Isidore of Seville (†636).   Only among the Irish—or rather, to give them their proper name, the Scots—whether in Ireland or in their numerous mission centres in every part of the Continent, was there any true intellectual activity.   Before the inroad of the Danes, Ireland was the university both of northern England and of the kingdom of the Franks.   The monasteries founded by its missionaries from the Atlantic to the Apennines— Iona, Melrose, Luxeuil, Fulda, St. Gallen, Reichenau and

[1] Harnack, *H.D.* v. p. 265.

Bobbio, may be cited as illustrations—were the libraries and schools of whole kingdoms.

From Ireland the literary life passed to England. Aldhelm at Malmesbury, Benedict Biscop at Wearmouth, Bede at Jarrow, Alcuin at York, carried on the work of the Scots, combining the current which flowed eastward from Ireland with that which came westward through Theodore of Tarsus, Benedict Biscop, and others from Rome and even Greece. For a few years the surviving culture of East and West converged to the court of Charles the Great, so that, in the words of his biographer, ' the dark expanse of the kingdom entrusted to him by God was filled with the new radiance of all science.' The old temper which regarded religion and culture as irreconcilable enemies, an instance of which we have seen in Gregory, passed into an anxiety, to which in 826 the Church gave official sanction, ' to search out masters and doctors who should teach the study of letters and learned arts.' The Carlovingian reforms, especially of the monastic institutions, for instance the canons established by Chrodegang of Metz (760), all bear witness to the anxiety of Charles to promote education and to establish schools. In collegiate churches the first duty of the chancellor or dean was either to be himself a schoolmaster or else provide a substitute.

The educational work of Charles did not last ; it was submerged in the general deluge which followed his death, and finally swept away by the new invasion of the Northmen. But the impulse given by the intellectual activity of Charles's reign manifested itself in the ninth century in a remarkable outburst of criticism, both philosophical and theological. To this freedom of thought, no doubt, the welter of the age contributed. The intellectual ferment was no longer checked by the watchfulness of Charles the Great, the vigilant organiser of social and political order whether in Church or State.

But Charles had himself contributed to the ferment of the

day by his own independence. In the *Caroline Books,*
written at his instigation and sanctioned by him, we find
the author—whether Alcuin or not is uncertain—quoting
certain wrongs as ' allowed rather by the ambition of Rome
than sanctioned by apostolic tradition.' At the council
of Frankfurt (794), in spite of the opposition of Pope
Hadrian I., Charles succeeded in procuring the rejection of
the decrees passed by the Eastern Church at the council of
Nicaea (787), that images of the Saviour, of the Virgin, and
of angels and saints should be set up in the churches and
given their due worship ($\pi\rho o\sigma\kappa\acute{\nu}\nu\eta\sigma\iota\varsigma$, not $\lambda\alpha\tau\rho\epsilon\acute{\iota}\alpha$). A synod
at Paris under Lewis the Pius (825) was even more em-
phatic in its condemnation of superstition.

The controversy thus begun by Charles was carried on
after his death by a Spaniard, Claudius, bishop of Turin
(†839). In his warfare with the gross materialised Christianity of the age, Claudius condemned in unsparing terms
the belief in the mediation of saints, the efficacy of pil-
grimages, the authority of Rome. He forbade throughout
his diocese the observance of saints' days, and called,
though in vain, for the destruction of all images and
pictures. The worship of the images of saints seemed to
him but a new form of the old worship of demons. ' Why
dost thou humble thyself and bow down to false images ?
Why bend thy body, a slave before vain likenesses ? God
made thee erect, thy face is raised towards Him. Thither
look, therefore ; seek God above.' He quotes with approval the argument of the Apostle : ' Though we have
known Christ after the flesh, yet now henceforth know we
Him no more ' ; and carried it on to revolutionary conclusions of his own. ' You worship,' he writes, ' all wood
formed after the manner of a cross because for six hours
Christ hung on a Cross. Worship then all virgins, because
a virgin bore Him ; old rags, for He was swaddled in
them ; asses, for He rode thereon.' As for the papacy,
the authority of St. Peter ceased with his death, and is

possessed by his successors only in so far as they imitate his life.

Claudius, protected by the Emperor Lewis, died in peace, in spite of his condemnation by an assembly of clerics—' a council of asses,' as he called them. Too much importance must not be attached to his outspoken utterances. In his extremer opinions, especially as regards the invocation of saints, he stood almost alone. But in his fight against current superstition he was supported by another Spaniard, Agobard, archbishop of Lyons (†840). Agobard was an abler man, of more statesmanlike spirit, and of more commanding influence, who not only attacked images and the like, but popular customs, such as the ordeal by fire or water, and the wager of battle, to which even theologians like Hincmar had assigned a sacramental value. How modern is his spirit is seen in his rebuke of Fredigis, abbot of Tours, for the ' absurdity ' of holding that the words of Scripture are inspired ; its sense is no doubt divine, but its form is human.

Another of the Caroline controversies—the addition of the *Filioque* to the Nicene Creed, in spite of the opposition of the East—has produced more lasting results. The clause came to the Frankish theologians from Spain, whose Church had been involved in a struggle with the Gnosticism of Priscillian, and with the militant Arianism of its Visigothic invaders. The struggle resulted, as is so often the case, in the hardening of dogma by the conquerors. The opposition to Arianism expressed itself in the claim—an implicit but logical consequence, as Augustine pointed out, of the unity of the Godhead—that the Holy Spirit held to the Son a relation in no whit diverse from that which He held to the Father. In 447 Bishop Turibius of Astorga received from Pope Leo the Great the sanction of this doctrine, which is also mentioned in a confession of faith given that same year by a synod at Toledo. When in 589 King Reccared and his subjects abjured Arianism, the

Spanish bishops presented to him a creed with the words
'*et Filio*' added, in spite of the prohibition of the council
of Chalcedon against any innovation. From Spain the
addition made its way to southern Gaul, and was there
incorporated into the symbol now known as the Athanasian
Creed. This symbol, probably composite in character
and Frankish in origin, took its present shape certainly not
earlier than the sixth century, possibly a little later.[1] In
680 the clause was accepted in England by Theodore of
Tarsus at the synod of Hatfield. In 781 the seventh
Ecumenical Council (the second of Nicaea), under the lead
of the patriarch Tarasius, approved of the Greek formula,
the procession from the Father through the Son (ἐκ τοῦ
Πατρὸς διὰ τοῦ Υἱοῦ), and Pope Hadrian I. had not challenged
the decision. But in 809 the theologians of the court of
Charles formally requested that the Western formula
Filioque should be incorporated in the Creed. With his
usual independence, Charles had already introduced the
clause into the symbol as chanted in the imperial chapel
at Aachen. But in spite of the pressure of the Franks,
Hadrian's successor, Leo III., though assenting to the doctrine, was too cautious to estrange the Eastern Church by
any official pronouncement. Even as late as 880 the papal
legate at Constantinople still subscribed to the older form
of the Nicene symbol, nor is it known how or when the
clause was formally admitted by Rome.

The date and manner are of little consequence; the effects
were the same, though the final catastrophe arose from the
personal ambition and violence of one man. In 857 the
supple Photius supplanted the austere Ignatius as patriarch of Constantinople, and appealed to Pope Nicholas I.
for recognition. On hearing of the enormities by which
Photius had procured his elevation, Nicholas excommunicated him (865). Photius met the anathema with arraign-
ing the Roman Church for heresy and schism, especially by

[1] Harnack, *H.D.* iv. p. 134 ff. See also *supra*, p. 71.

the insertion of the *Filioque* in the Nicene symbol. In
879 a synod of Constantinople, under the presidency of
Photius, launched anathemas against all who should countenance this addition. The revolt of the Eastern Church
culminated in the definite schism in 1054 under the patriarch Michael Caerularius. As one result of the Crusades,
attempts were made to bring East and West together once
more, and at a council at Bari (1098) the Greek bishops
tried to reopen the question. On behalf of the Western
Church, the dispute was taken up by Anselm in his *De
Processione Spiritus Sancti*. The unity of the Godhead,
Anselm maintained, demands that whatever is predicable
of God, as such, must also be predicable of the Three
Persons, save so far as their individual characteristics may
prevent. Either then the Son, if begotten of the Father, is
also begotten of the Holy Spirit, or else in proceeding from
the Father the Spirit proceeds also from the Son. As the
first assumption must be dismissed, we are driven back
upon the second, and thus secure the procession from
the unity of the Godhead. The procession is not from
the Father and Son as distinct persons, as in the
Greek doctrine, but from one God who is both Father
and Son.

The logic of Anselm, though formally correct, was of no
avail. Deeper forces than theology kept East and West
apart. Twice did the Eastern Church acknowledge, or
appear to acknowledge, the validity of the Western addition ; once on its definition by Clement IV. at the second
council of Lyons (1274) ; again in 1439 at Florence.
Nevertheless, the two churches are still apart, and, so far as
can be foreseen, there is no likelihood of their being brought
together except indeed by the operations of that same
Holy Spirit over the technical definition of whose ' procession ' they have split asunder.

IV

From this survey of the great controversy begun or
accentuated by the action of Charles the Great we must
return to another, to which the title of Adoptionism has
been given from its chief position, ' the Son adoptive in His
humanity but not in His divinity.'   This heresy was by no
means new.   We have already pointed out its existence
in the *Shepherd* of Hermas, in Ebionite writings, in Theodore
of Mopsuestia, and in Nestorius.[1]   Latin translations of
the works of Theodore in all probability were carried to
Spain.   In the eighth century these gave rise to Adoptionism, strictly so-called, assisted, possibly, by the tendency
of the Mohammedan rulers of Spain and of the East to
patronise Nestorian rather than orthodox Christians, in
this following the example of Mohammed himself.

The heresy in its Spanish form arose with Elipandus,
archbishop of Toledo (c. 780), but was more clearly taught
by his younger ally, Felix, bishop of Urgel, the charm of
whose character was acknowledged by his opponent,
Alcuin of York.   In his teaching we find the emphasis of
the reality of the human nature of Jesus, with all its limitations, including the defilement of the Fall.   The raising
of this human nature (*assumptio hominis*) to the divine,
Elipandus and Felix called ' adoption,' from a word in
common use in the Mozarabic liturgy.   The Son of Man,
urged Felix, has two births : a natural birth of the Virgin ;
a spiritual birth by ' adoption,' begun in His Baptism,
completed by the Resurrection.   Thus the Son of Man
became the Son of God not by nature but by grace.   The
unity of the Son of God and the Son of Man was preserved
by the *ego* of the Son of God being the true *ego* of the Son
of Man.   Nevertheless, Adoptionism " ultimately implies
the independence and juxtaposition of two personal beings
moving in parallel lines, but never really united." [2]   When

---

[1] See *supra*, pp. 75, 76.   [2] Ottley, *op. cit.* ii. p. 160.

Felix was summoned before the council of Regensburg
(792), Charles the Great deemed his defence unsuccessful,
and sent him to Rome. There he signed a recantation ;
but this, on his return to Urgel, he recanted, and fled to
Toledo to the Saracens. On the appeal of Elipandus that
Felix should be reinstated, Charles summoned a council
at Frankfurt (794). After much discussion, in which
Alcuin took part, Felix made a fresh recantation. He
was received back into the Church at Aachen (799), but
detained at Lyons for the rest of his days. After his death
Agobard published certain of his papers, which showed that
his recantation had been far from complete. Adoptionism
itself speedily perished. This was inevitable, for its main
idea of the natural body of Jesus was in vital conflict with
the prevailing Eucharistic conceptions, in which the body of
Christ was regarded as the mystic omnipresent Host, the
principle of eternal life. Even if the conception had been
more logical and orthodox, even if it had won greater
approval from theologians, popular sentiment would have
decreed its doom. In passing we may note that, since the
suppression of Adoptionism, Spain has contributed nothing
to Christian thought, unless we count the transformation
by the Jesuits of religion into military obedience.

The Caroline age is specially notable for the hardening
of the doctrine of the Eucharist. The belief in the real
presence of the King of Kings in the consecrated wafer, and
in the power mysteriously given by the imposition of hands
to the lowest priest to work this stupendous miracle, had
overawed and tamed the rudest barbarians. Whatever
be its theological truth, it must be confessed that the
medieval doctrine of the Sacrament had accomplished
wonders for civilisation where a more spiritual conception
might have failed. Now the Middle Ages were powerless
to realise an idea without turning it into the concrete. Of
Christ and the saints they must have visible images. By
a sort of logical inversion they went one step further.

Where the image was, there was the spirit; thus the image became the vehicle of grace, possessing not only sanctity but life, while the spiritual, on the contrary, was constantly assuming form and colour. To the most subtle spiritual influences the medieval mind would have applied literally the words of St. John : ' That which we have seen with our eyes and our hands have handled.' Equally real, on the other hand, was the conviction that the material was but the veil or covering of the spiritual. That the spiritual could be apprehended by the senses was an axiom of faith, as also the belief that the senses alone could never exhaust or even understand the spiritual meanings of the material.

As yet men had not attempted to compress into definitions and syllogisms the supreme mystery of their faith. But in 844 Paschasius Radbert, a monk of New Corvey, brought out a monograph on the *Sacrament of the Body and Blood of Christ,* which marks an era in the development of doctrine. Radbert, a learned and constructive theologian, familiar with Greek theology and Augustinianism, attempted to put the current faith upon a more philosophical basis. He starts with claiming that faith is always related to the invisible; the believer must ever withdraw into the invisible world. For the unbeliever the *virtus sacramenti* does not exist; Christ's flesh cannot be eaten except through faith. But for the believer Christ's flesh is the nourishment of both soul and body for immortality, our flesh being renewed by it into corruption. Up to this point there is nothing in the views of Radbert to distinguish his teaching from that of St. Augustine or John of Damascus. His importance lies in his introduction of the idea, though not the name, of transubstantianism.[1] Though the sensuous appearances remain unchanged, the bread becomes the veritable Body of Christ. The sensuous

---

[1] The word transubstantiation seems to have been first casually used by Hildebert of Tours at the beginning of the twelfth century. See Migne, *P. L.* clxxi. p. 776.

In many ways this is my own view.

appearances thus become the symbols of a spiritual essence or reality, to the apprehension of which faith alone can rise. Thus Radbert unites the Augustinian emphasis of faith with the Greek conception of the reality prior to all faith. Radbert owns that his theory involves the constant repetition by God of a stupendous miracle. But to the men of his age the miraculous was the commonest occurrence of daily life, a necessary result from their conception of God's will as absolutely arbitrary and without law—the miraculous and the arbitrary are always connected.

Radbert was opposed by Ratram and Rabanus Maurus. To the question of Charles the Bald whether the Body and Blood of Christ were actually received in the mouth of communicants, Ratram replied in a work that was at an early date ascribed to John the Scot. He maintained that the wafer was the memorial of the spiritual body existing under the veil of the material ; that which lies on the altar was not the historical body of Christ, but only the *mystery* of the body, an interpretation that is even more strikingly expressed by John the Scot in his exposition of ' Dionysius.' But on inquiry as to what then the believer actually receives, we find that the question is left unanswered, or rather is wrapped up in undefined, even contradictory, statements that at times remind us of Zwingli, at other times come close to Radbert. One thing alone is clear, the emphasis that Ratram, and even more strikingly John the Scot, would lay upon faith. If in this Ratram coincides with Radbert, he differed from him in his refusal to look upon the Eucharist as a constant miracle against nature, instead of being in harmony with the spiritual world behind the phenomenal.

The fact that Radbert left most questions unsolved, or even untouched, in nowise lessened his influence. He had opened up, or rather expressed dogmatically, views which coincided with popular belief and desire, while his unsolved difficulties allured the thought of generations of students.

By the doctrine of transubstantiation the medieval doctrine of the Mass became firmly established, both as a popular institution and as a fundamental theory of the schools. To the developments that the doctrine assumed later we shall return.

The ferment of the times is also seen in Gottschalk's revival of an unconditional doctrine of predestination. Gottschalk, a monk of Orbais in the province of Rheims, condemned, against his desire, to the monasticism into which he had been forced as a child, taught the doctrine, which he claimed to have found in St. Augustine, of the predestination of both the wicked and the good. But the growth of the sacerdotal system in the medieval Church made this extreme form of the doctrine of predestination an impossibility. For if saint and sinner were already predestinated, of what use were the intercessions of saints, or even the Eucharistic sacrifice ? For if all is immutable decree, there is neither need nor logic in prayer, penance, or worship. These things are but the idle beatings of the wings against the prison bars. The Eucharist itself becomes powerless, as Gottschalk owned, ' for those who perish.'

Such a doctrine, as its later developments in Geneva show, inevitably struck at the power of the priest. The extremer Augustinian doctrine thus revived by Gottschalk was therefore rejected by the Latin Church, not because of the inhumanity which such a doctrine appears to the present age to possess—squeamishness on that head was still far distant—nor even because its ultimate issue was to make the life and atonement of Jesus, at best, a work of supererogation, but in the interests of its priestly orders. Consciously or unconsciously medieval theologians were driven to the limitation of election to the good ; in the case of the wicked election became foreknowledge only. But when his opponents, chief of whom were Rabanus Maurus and Hincmar of Rheims, founded their doctrine of the election of the saved on the divine prescience of their ' right use of grace,' they overlooked the fact that in his extreme anti-Pelagianism Augustine had really cut away any logical basis for 'right use of grace.' Logically or not, semi-Pelagianism was necessary for a sacerdotal sacramental church, as, in fact, Gregory the Great had already seen. So, first at the council of Mainz (848), then at the synod of Quierzy (849), Gottschalk was condemned, cruelly scourged, and imprisoned until his death (869) in the monastery of Hautvilliers. But the controversy which he had revived touched issues too vital for the life and thought of the Church, to be thus easily quashed.

V

Among the opponents of Gottschalk was one of the most remarkable thinkers of the Middle Ages, or for that matter of any age, John Scotus Erigena,[1] the last representative of the Greek spirit in the West, and one of the earliest torch-bearers in the long line of Christian mystics. In the final words of his chief work John the Scot tells us all that we really know of his life : ' Nothing else is to be desired except the joy that comes from truth ; nothing is to be shunned except its absence.' Somewhere about the year 847 John the Scot drifted from Ireland, and settled at the court of that patron of scholars, Charles the Bald. His opposition to Gottschalk's predestination sprang from a bold development of his Neoplatonic ontology. In his tract, *De Predestinatione* (851), written at the instance of Hincmar, John claimed that true religion and true philosophy are identical. True philosophy rests on the basis of the unity of God, ' who is the totality of all things which are and which are not, which can and which cannot be.' To conceive of predestination to evil is thus to conceive a duality

---

[1] I have kept the common, but less accurate, name of Erigena instead of Eriugena, 'the Erinborn.' As Dr. Poole has pointed out, Erinn, less accurately Erin, is the dative case of Eriu, the old name for Ireland. The dative has supplanted the nominative.

in the divine nature, or of some power above God determining His will. But the will of God is absolutely free;
and man, as created in His image, must possess the same
freedom. Sin is simply the negation of good, *i.e.* of ' being,'
for Erigena claims that there can be no ' being ' without
' goodness.' Its punishment is not imposed from without,
but is the inner necessity or nemesis of sin itself, the consciousness of lacking good. 'The loss of Christ is the
torment of the whole creation, nor do I think that there is
any other.' But as all things proceed from good, so in
good must they all be reabsorbed. Sin exists merely in
time, and can have no material punishment in the eternal.

The views of John the Scot, when they depart from the
teaching of Augustine, were naturally too daring for an age
that cared little or nothing for philosophy. At the synod
of Valence (855) they were condemned as ' Scot's porridge,'
and the abjuration of his ' barbarous barking ' was repeated
at the synod of Langres (859). Both synods also showed their
sympathy with Gottschalk by reaffirming the double predestination, though careful to avoid the question whether or
not God willed to save all men. That they were conscious of
the contradiction thus involved between the creed and life
of the Church is seen in their further contention that in the
Sacraments of the Church ' nothing is futile or delusive.'

Erigena's activity was by no means limited to this
controversy. In his important work, originally written
in Greek, but translated into Latin under the title *De
Divisione Naturae,* John the Scot unfolds a system of Neoplatonic mysticism, in which we mark his indebtedness
to his study of 'Dionysius.' The supreme nature, he holds,
is absolute, and cannot be described by any categories.
In this sense God is 'nihilum,' and can only be expressed by
alternate affirmation and negation—this method is, in fact,
the keynote of all John's philosophy, and the solution of
many of his difficulties—and manifests itself in a series
of ' theophanies,' of which the number is as many as the

number of saintly souls. From this it follows that the universe is an eternal divine procession, the reality of which is found in the Divine Ideas. Creation is the necessary self-realisation of God, the passage from the eternal ideas to their appearances under the mental conditions of time and space. As such it finds its meeting-place in the twofold nature of Christ, whose incarnation is the expression of the eternal connection of the ideal and the real, of the immanent relation of God and the world, ' the visible and the invisible.' [1] By this supreme ' theophany ' the whole animated creation ' is restored and recalled to unspeakable unity, now in hope, hereafter in fact.' ' Everything shall return into God as air into light.' Such ' restoration ' is not difficult, for matter, as such, has no existence, save in our thoughts, as the ' concourse of the accidents of being.' Scot holds further that the notion of being existing in the human mind is the substance of being itself—a remarkable anticipation, following St. Augustine, of the famous argument of Descartes. Evil is but the accident of material existence ; it marks the transition from the world of thought to that of matter ; it is the ' shadow of some virtue,' and will cease when man returns to the primal unity.

In his statement of the relation of reason and authority John is not less daring. Authority is secondary to Reason, to which it is related as species to genus. Reason is not only the dwelling-place of the ' word ' of God ; it is itself a ' theophany,' the revelation of God to man, and a sure guide to the interpretation of the Bible. Not less emphatic is his protest against the current conception of total depravity ; even in the wicked the ' natural goods,' in which they were created, cannot be taken away. The universa tendency is upward, ' for the divine goodness, which ever worketh not only in the good but also in the wicked, is eternal and infinite. . . . Our nature is not fixed in evil. It is ever moving, and serves naught else but the highest

[1] Cf. John i. 3, ὃ γέγονεν, ἐν αὐτῷ ζωὴ ἦν, to adopt the older punctuation.

good, which is both its source and end.' The pantheistic
bias of much of Erigena's writings is perhaps exaggerated
by not paying due regard to his method of reasoning by
successive antinomies. His doctrine of the immortality of
the individual, the permanence of the spiritual self 'without
any confusion or destruction of essence,' is fatal to any
pantheistic disappearance in a ' general soul.' But in the
thirteenth century, in connection with the controversy
raised by Amalric of Bena, stress was laid on this danger
of parts of Scot's work, and the book, after being condemned by the council of Paris in 1209, was suppressed by
Honorius III. (1225) because of its ' abominable heresy.'

To his own generation, and to the three centuries that
followed, John the Scot was unintelligible, when not unknown. He was too much of a Greek to have any hold
upon a barbarian age. His influence, such as it was, was
due almost wholly to his translation of the writings currently attributed to Dionysius the Areopagite.

Few writers have exercised greater influence upon the
life and thought of the centuries than ' Dionysius the Areopagite ' ; few stories of literary pseudonym have obtained
larger acceptance. In the general desire of the various
countries to date back the foundation of their Christianity
to apostolic times, France created the myth of Dionysius,
or rather procured the acceptance of a myth already
created. Though with more plausibility Gaul might have
claimed Mary Magdalene or Trophimus as the first to introduce Christianity into the Arelate, it preferred, possibly
by the confusion of some actual but obscure hero of the
faith, to find its apostle in the Areopagite, who was buried,
according to popular tradition, in the abbey (St. Denis) to
which he had given his name. The actual date is unknown
of the writing of the bold forgery—if by this harsh modern
name and idea such common literary form of seeking
greater authority should be called—but cannot have been
earlier than the fifth century. The earliest mention of

the writings of Dionysius occurs, it would appear, in the records of a conference held at Constantinople in 533, when their genuineness was challenged by the Severians, a sect of the Monophysites. ' These so-called works of the Areopagite,' they said, ' were unknown to Cyril and Athanasius, and if no one of the ancients quoted them, how can you establish their truth ? ' Early in the sixth century they were turned into Syriac by the Aristotelian physician Sergius. In the next century they found a zealous editor and defender in the ' confessor ' Maximus (580-662). By the close of the ninth century, in spite of attacks, the works of Dionysius were generally accepted as genuine by the Greek Church.

In the Western Church, though casually referred to by Gregory the Great, and quoted in the acts of the Lateran Synod of 660, the writings of Dionysius were long unknown. Occasional copies were found ; for instance, in 757 Pope Paul I. sent the works of Dionysius to Pippin. Their influence, however, was slight until in 827 the Greek Emperor, Michael the Stammerer, sent a copy as a present to Lewis, the son of Charles the Great. The arrival of these books at the royal abbey of St. Denis, on the feast-day of its sainted founder, was marked by nineteen miracles. The translation of the Greek into Latin by John the Scot, at the command of Charles the Bald (†860), introduced to the Western world the teaching of Dionysius, and the sublimity of the ' heavenly mysteries ' with which he dealt. Erigena's translation, it is true, did not escape suspicion, owing, probably, to the estranged relations between the Churches of East and West, and the daring verses affixed to the work extolling the glories of Greece at the expense of Rome. Scot's translation was followed by two other versions, one in the twelfth and the other in the fifteenth century, as also by numerous commentaries, some of these by the leading scholars of the times. Such was his influence over Aquinas that four folio pages are needed to tabulate the references to Dionysius in his *Summa*. Alone of the Schoolmen, Abailard, who identified Dionysius with the historical bishop of Corinth, hesitated as to the genuineness of this manifest pseudonym, the exposure of which by Laurentius Valla was amongst the earliest results of the Renaissance, though the printing of Grosseteste's commentary (1235) at Strassburg in 1503 showed the tenacity of the old belief. But with the overthrow of the myth, that they were the writings of an inspired apostle, the work was forgotten. Its rediscovery is one of the results of recent historical theology.

The student who to-day turns over the pages of Dionysius is in danger of being misled by their wordy froth. But beneath their wild symbolism, concealed by their metaphysical jargon, there is a basis of truth and the throb of a living experience. The Dionysian writings were probably composed by the Edessene school. They bear marks of the Monophysitism that characterised so much Syrian speculation. They also acknowledge indebtedness to 'Hierotheus,' the assumed name of a mystic monk of Edessa, Stephen bar Sudaili, who wrote towards the close of the fifth century, giving himself out as a convert of St. Paul and instructor of the real Dionysius. Dionysius gives us a philosophy of Being, the nature of which is indicated by his title, *The Heavenly Hierarchy*. Step by step we pass by measured stages and successive manifestations from the Absolute to the Absolute. What we see is but a part of a vast scheme, the visible and invisible parts of which are strictly connected, a ' Jacob's ladder '—the idea is taken from Hierotheus—linking earth with heaven. In this ascent to the One, participation in whom is a universal condition of Being, sense-perceptions have a sacramental value, inasmuch as even ' things inanimate ' partake of ' fellowship with the super-essential and all-efficient Godhead.' But, above all, this communion is shared by, this illumination bestowed on the angels—under this Christian title, and their different orders and degrees, the details of which are borrowed from Hierotheus, we recognise the old system of emanations—whose nine ranks, or stages in the ' progression ' of divine revelation, exercise upon men a beneficent influence, which, however, may be fatally resisted. 'To be made divine, as far as may be, and to be made one with God, is the common end of any hierarchy,' one means for the attaining thereof being the Holy Eucharist, or ' the feast of the Beatific Vision.'

In the most important of his treatises, *On the Divine Names*, Dionysius deals with the mystery of the One and the Many ; with the relation of partial being to the Absolute, of God to time and eternity, and with the problem of the nature of evil. The details of his reasoning would exceed our limits. Here and there we meet with an answer with a strangely modern ring, as in his distinction between time and eternity : ' Things that *are* are expressed by eternity ; things which *become* by time.' For the most part, however, though the Bible is the professed starting-point, they are adaptations of Neoplatonism " slightly sprinkled with baptismal water from a Christian font." [1] Evil, for instance, Dionysius tells us, does not exist ; ' all things so far as they are deprived of the good are neither good nor existent,' a necessary outcome of his Neoplatonist position that the ' ideal ' is the only real. As Browning puts it in his *Abt Vogler* :

"There shall never be one lost good ! What was shall live as
    before.
The evil is null, is naught, is silence implying sound ;
What was good, shall be good, with, for evil, so much good
    more ;
On the earth the broken arcs ; in the heaven the perfect
    round."

Even the devils 'are called bad because of weakness in

[1] R. Jones, *Mystical Religion*, p. 110

respect of their natural energy.' Every creature is good
up to the limits of its capacity. Whatever is, is only by
the inherence of His presence ; whatever becomes, becomes
by the communication of His presence. In every form of
life there is this participation in the one life. The end of
all knowledge is to rise above the conditioned, in other
words the definite, into the unconditioned and absolute.
As the ' hidden and nameless ' Absolute cannot be known,
it is only by ' love ' that this can be accomplished. As
Colet paraphrases it : ' Whoso loveth God is known of
Him. Ignorant love has a thousand times more power
than cold wisdom ' ; but the ' love ' of which Dionysius
wrote has no idea of projection out of itself—it would never
have founded a school for boys. The Atonement, as is
so customary with Neoplatonic speculations, is reduced
to the deliverance of being from the negative influences of
disorder and failure. The conception of reconciliation is
thus altogether absent, our Lord becomes our example
rather than a ' sacrifice for sin.' In consequence, we search
the pages of Dionysius in vain for any doctrine of grace.

The writings of Dionysius are essentially Eastern and
Greek. There is little in them—if we leave out the one
conception of a celestial hierarchy with its antitype on
earth—that is in sympathy with the ruling Latin ideas.
With Dionysius, as with the Eastern Church of all ages,
the highest conception of life is the solitary eremite ; its
monasticism looks to the Thebaid and not to Monte Cassino
for inspiration. Hence doctrine and the organised life of
the Church are regarded as on a lower level than mystical
experience. They only give relative knowledge. But by
experience we are brought into contact with things that
transcend mind, when by ' a resistless and absolute ecstasy
from ourselves we are carried up to the super-essential
ray of the ' Divine Dark ' by casting away all, and becoming
free from all.' Even Dionysius' treatment of the Sacraments, though detailed, is mystical ; there is little that

leant itself to the materialistic conceptions of the later
Latin Church. Their significance is considered to be entirely subjective, personal experience the primary fact in
religious life. In his doctrine of the Atonement, moreover,
there was no place for the priest. The power of binding
and loosing is dependent upon the spiritual communion of
the ministry on earth with the Spirit of God, so that what
is already bound or loosed in heaven is only disclosed on
earth. In this last we may discern the influence of the
Eastern idea of pre-existence.[1]

To this Greek origin and colour we must attribute no
small importance. At a time when the treasures of Greek
thought were lost to the Western world, Dionysius brought
the Latin Church into touch with a set of ideas, so foreign
to its spirit that they would, probably, have received no
lodgment, had it not been that they were protected by an
apostolic name. Their place in medieval thought may,
therefore, be likened to the faults and flaws in some geo-
logical contour ; they are evidences of forces long since
extinct, the visible memorials of which are now intruded
into alien strata. In Dionysius we have the link that con-
nects the medieval world with Proclus, Plotinus, and other
Greek thinkers, whom the medieval Church, if only it had
known them, would have excommunicated or burnt. To
this Greek atmosphere we must attribute the attraction of
Dionysius for John Colet, the English scholar of the New
Learning, as well as for Ficino and the Neoplatonists of
the Italian Renaissance.[2] In art we find that the *Celestial
Hierarchy* is " on all points relative to the representation
of angels, the inexhaustible mine which was worked,
directly or indirectly, throughout the whole of the Middle
Ages, and from which the ideas are derived which are even

---

[1] *Supra*, p. 65.

[2] Colet's abstract or translation of Dionysius (*Two Treatises on the
Hierarchies of Dionysius*, edited by J. H. Lupton, 1869) was published in
1497 (?)—Ficino's in 1492 and 1496. Three other of Colet's writings show
the profound influence of Dionysius (see Seebohm, *Oxford Reformers*,
p. 60 ff.).

to this day current." [1] But the profoundest influence of Dionysius was over the medieval mystics, all of whom came under the spell of his thought. His celestial ladder was one of their commonplaces ; his One Reality above all knowledge the object of their search. Above all, they adopted his method of 'contemplation' passing into 'ecstasy.' But to this we shall return.[2]

[1] J. Fowler, *Works of Dionysius in Relation to Christian Art* (Sacristy, February 1872). Probably the words in the Communion Office, "Therefore with angels, etc.," should be traced to the *Celestial Hierarchy*, vii. 2 (*l.c.* p. 10).

[2] *Infra*, p. 192.

CHAPTER VII

THE RENAISSANCE OF THE ELEVENTH AND TWELFTH CENTURIES

Argument

I

THE two centuries that followed the fall of the empire of Charles the Great are among the darkest in history. The Holy See sank to the lowest depths of impotence ; popes, wretched when not wicked or the tools of infamous women, rapidly pass across the stage—in eight years eight popes were elected and overthrown ; shadowy emperors struggle for the rent mantle of Charles ; over all a deluge of barbarism, Saracens, Huns, Normans, and a darkness that could be felt. Dean Church has well pointed out that by the end of the tenth century " Christian teaching can hardly be said to have leavened society at all. Its influence on individuals, so vast and astonishing, was no measure of its influence on society at large. It acted upon it doubtless with enormous force, but it was an extraneous and foreign force, which destroys and stifles, but does not mingle or renew." The traditions of society at large were still undiluted heathenism. In its conflict with the barbarians who had overwhelmed the degraded Latin civilisation Christianity had conquered, yet at times it might seem as if the chief result had been to make barbarism more superstitious, and cruelty more ingenious.

But in the latter part of the tenth century a great change passed over Europe, culminating in the intellectual and religious awakening of the next generation. Everywhere men aroused themselves from despair to hope and enthusiasm. In this new birth of the human spirit the religion of superstition, which had hitherto formed the groundwork of authority and the main element of order in the

chaos of society, began to shed from it some of its grosser
elements. It was fitting that the new era should open
with a pope who would have been remarkable in any age,
but shines out like a solitary torch in the darkness of
that night. Gerbert of Aurillac, Pope Sylvester II. (999-
1003), was the stout opponent and the stout asserter of
the rights of Rome. But his political actions, though
sufficiently original, were the least part of his claim upon
posterity. This austere monk was the most learned man
of the day, and its foremost teacher. Mathematician,
scientist, mechanician, he spent his nights in watching the
stars from a tower of the Vatican. Naturally, he suffered
the fate of all men who are before their times. But, except
in the dominion of science, Gerbert added little or nothing,
save a larger outlook, to Christian thought. The one theological work commonly ascribed to his pen, *De Corpore et
Sanguine Domini*, is, probably, the production of Heriger
of Lobbes.

Nevertheless, Gerbert witnesses to the new life already
stirring the dry bones of piety and thought. The centre of
that new life was found in the great monastery of Clugny.
The idea which underlay the work of a series of able
Clugniac reformers, among whom we must reckon the
greatest of the popes, the illustrious Hildebrand (Gregory VII., 1073-1086), was the government of the world by a
Church purified by being brought under monastic discipline
and infused with the monastic spirit. The effect of Hildebrand's policy upon the fortunes of the Church belongs
more strictly to history. It must suffice that we note that
in the intellectual world, as well as in the world of action,
for over a century after the rise of Hildebrand, the
monastic ideal prevailed. But towards the close of
the twelfth century the intellectual vitality of monasticism became exhausted, while the revival of the ideals
overthrown by Hildebrand led to the transfer of
thought and education from the cloister to the secular

universities. The leader in this momentous revolution
was Abailard.

There was another direction in which the triumph of
Hildebrand's policy influenced Christian thought. We
allude to the development of the law systems of the Church.
From the first the Church had stood outside the Teutonic
law system. "In the early days of the Frank dominions
the churches lived under Roman law. For one thing, the
Christian emperors had legislated pretty freely on ecclesiastical matters long before the Teutons were converted to
Christianity ; and the Merovingians could hardly venture
to meddle with the organisation of that mighty power
which had destroyed their ancient gods, and done so much
to give them the victory over their enemies. For another,
the churches were corporations ; and it took the Teutonic
mind a long time to grasp the highly complex notion of a
corporation." [1] So from the fall of the Empire onward
we have the Church with a law of her own, and necessarily,
therefore, courts and punishments of her own, living in the
midst of Celtic or Teutonic tribes in which law was a
matter of the clan or fief. In all Western Europe the only
law that was not local or territorial was the ' common law,'
as it was called everywhere except in England, *i.e.* the
universal law of the Roman Church.

The law of the Church was at first the Roman code
modified by such enactments of councils as had received
imperial sanction. But when the popes stepped into the
place of emperors, the Church of the West quietly repudiated the system which had been her foster-mother,
and substituted in its place the canons of councils and the
case-law of the popes. Charles the Great, it is true, in his
general revival of older traditions reduced the Church once
more under the control of the State, but in this, as in much
else, he was both before and behind his age. The wide
recognition within a few years of his death of the authority

[1] E. Jenks, *Law and Politics in the Middle Ages*, p. 27.

of the pseudo-Decretals—the boldest and most successful forgery that the world has ever seen [1]—shows the real drift of the times. From Pope Nicholas I. (858-867) onwards the law of the Church is neither the old Roman jurisprudence nor the *Capitularies* of Charles the Great—codes, in fact, which in the general anarchy sank almost into oblivion—but the papal system of decretals and canons.

With the triumph of Hildebrand's ideals it became necessary to codify the law of the Church, for if the Church was to govern the world the law of the Church must be clear and distinct. Hitherto this law had been gathered from a chaos of papal rescripts, conciliar canons, and civil enactments. But the renaissance of culture in Italy early in the twelfth century took expression in a renewed study of Roman law. Bologna, long noted as a school of liberal arts, became under the teaching of Irnerius (1100-1130) the great university for the study of the *Code* and *Pandects* of Justinian. The advantages which the Empire of the Hohenstaufen derived from this possession of a definite, venerable system, in which the Emperor was recognised as the fountain of all authority, impressed upon the papal jurists their want of a similar code. In the *Concordia Discordantium Canonum* (1142) of Gratian, a monk of Bologna, the Church found the exact instrument she needed. In this work Gratian applied to the materials collected by a succession of canonists the scientific method of Abailard. Influenced by the success of Abailard's *Sic et Non*, Gratian presents his reader with the authorities on both sides of every question. The *Decretum* of Gratian, to give the book its more familiar title, at once supplanted all rivals, and became the recognised text-book of the schools. The importance of the work cannot be exaggerated. The *Decretum* is one of those books, not necessarily great in themselves, which sweep aside all rivals because

[1] This forgery has recently been shown to have been the work of priests in Touraine.

they first clearly embody certain latent tendencies of the age. The success of Gratian led Raymond de Peñaforte in 1234 to publish for Gregory IX. five books of recent *Decretals*. These were followed by further editions, known as *Extravagants* and *Clementines* (1318). With these the golden age of papal legislation came to an end.

The effects of the development and partial triumph of Canon Law upon the history, both ecclesiastical and secular, of Europe cannot be exaggerated. But the disaster for Christian thought has sometimes been overlooked. All questions, ecclesiastical and theological, became subordinated to legal conceptions, at all times the bane of the Latin Church. Faith and grace became secondary to ordinance. The spirit of the jurist governed all theology. Dogma was recast under the categories of judge, accused, satisfaction, and penalties. With his usual insight, Luther saw that the overthrow of the ecclesiastical jurisprudence of the Middle Ages was a prime necessity if the Augustinian doctrine of grace was ever to receive its old place in the life of the Church, and the claims of the papacy to be overthrown. When he cast the *Decretals* into the flames before the doctors and populace of Wittenberg (10th December 1520), Luther claimed more than his civil freedom; he asserted the need for a spiritual theology emancipated from the categories of the law. In his failure to see this great blot upon medieval theology we find the chief weakness of Calvin, as also the evidence of the continuity of his position in general with that of the Middle Ages.

The quickened thought of the age of Hildebrand manifested itself also in the reopening of the Eucharist controversy by Berengar of Tours (†1088). Led on by pride of intellect, or by keener spirituality, Berengar, the head of the cathedral school in Tours, protested against the current materialistic conceptions of the Real Presence. These left out all the refinements in the doctrine of Paschasius Radbert, and declared that the consecrated wafer was a physical

M

portion of the body of Christ ' as born of the Virgin Mary '
' broken by the hands of priests and chewed by the teeth of
the faithful.' The watchword of orthodoxy was ' *vere et
sensualiter*.' Berengar, adopting the standpoint of Ratram,[1]
though with much greater precision, declared that the
Real Presence was but spiritually conceived and received.
The popular doctrine he held to be contrary to reason or
' the image of God wherein we were created.'

Berengar's chief opponent was Lanfranc.[2] Lanfranc
repeated in a hardened form the arguments of Paschasius
Radbert. But Paschasius would not have approved of his
elimination of all faith by his affirmation that even sinners
eat the true body of Christ in spite of themselves, a
development which did more than anything else to materi-
alise the Eucharist. In spite of the attacks of Lanfranc,
Berengar succeeded in maintaining his position until the
second Lateran Council (1059) gave him the choice of death
or recantation. " Logic," says Milman sententiously,
" makes no martyrs "; and for a time Berengar yielded.
Twenty years later Berengar once more retracted, but
through the clemency or personal sympathy of Hildebrand, after abjuration, was dismissed without further
penalty. In spite of his vacillations Berengar is entitled
to this praise : he had set the whole world thinking,
questioning, and disputing. One result of this dialectic
tournament must not be overlooked. When Guitmund of
Aversa maintained that the whole Christ was in every
particle, the foundation was laid for the practice, developed
later by Aquinas into a dogma, that the blood was
contained in the consecrated wafer, and that therefore
the cup could be withheld from the laity. The issue of
the controversy was seen in the passing by the fourth
Lateran Council (1215) of the dogma of transubstantiation :

---

[1] *Supra*, p. 148. As was usual at the time, Berengar thought Ratram's
work was by Erigena.
[2] Born about 1005 at Pavia ; 1070 archbishop of Canterbury ; died 1089.

' The body and blood (of Christ) are truly contained in the
sacrifice of the altar under the appearance of bread and
wine, the bread being transubstantiated into the body,
and the wine into the blood by divine power.'

II

Whether in monastery or university, whether dealing
with law or theology, medieval thought is known to-day
as Scholasticism. The reader misled by current tradition
or frightened by the unattractive tomes in which scholars
buried their thoughts, will enter upon the study of Scholasticism with hesitation, if not aversion. He has probably
thought of the Schoolmen as idle babblers, making
bricks without straw, erecting stupendous syllogisms
upon foundations of sand. We must beware of despising
the ladder whereby we have climbed. No age, however emancipated, can afford to disdain the thoughts
and struggles of the ages that preceded it. Ignorance
may scorn, but a more humble wisdom will ever realise
that the Schoolmen were no ordinary men. " In the chilly
squalor of uncarpeted and unwarmed chambers, by the
light of narrow and unglazed casements or the gleam of
flickering oil-lamps, poring over dusky manuscripts hardly
to be deciphered by modern eyesight, undisturbed by the
boisterous din of revelry and riot without, men of humble
birth and dependent on charity for bare subsistence, but
with a noble self-confidence transcending that of Bacon
or Newton, thought out and copied out those subtle master-
pieces of medieval lore, purporting to unveil the hidden
laws of Nature, as well as the dark counsels of Providence
and the secrets of human destiny, which, frivolous and
baseless as they may appear under the scrutiny of a later
criticism, must still be ranked among the greatest achievements of speculative reason." [1]

[1] Brodrick, *Memorials of Merton*, p. 35.

A definition of Scholasticism is almost impossible. But certain features may be pointed out which mark off Scholasticism from modern thought. In the first place, we must beware of supposing that Scholasticism was neither scientific nor critical ; for it was both, at any rate in its intention. Scholasticism, by its insistence on reason, marks the distance that the Latin Church has travelled since Tertullian's ' Credibile est, quia ineptum est,'—' I believe because it is absurd.' [1] Scholasticism was, in fact, the effort of the thought of the age to arrange itself under such scientific conditions and forms as it possessed. Its weakness did not lie in its contempt for the scientific spirit, but rather in its daring assumption of the all-sufficiency of its method, its refusal to step outside the charmed circle of its system. By means of his logic, with its intricate formalism, the schoolman constructed a complete scientific system, which, however, knew neither the limitations of observation nor the fetters of induction. The analytical power of language was mistaken for the interpretation or discovery of facts. The consequent want of correction of deductive dialectics led to a dogmatism in the end disastrous both for faith and knowledge. The schoolman was, if possible, even more certain of the truth than the materialistic disbeliever of a more scientific generation. To the one to doubt was as certain to be lost, as to the other to believe is to be intellectually damned.

Another result of the absence of any adequate observation of the external world was the absorption of all forms of thought and knowledge within Theology. To the schoolman Theology was even more than the queen of sciences ; it was really the science of science, inasmuch as it dealt with the relation of all things to God. Unfortunately, as this view was not sufficiently guarded, the results were disastrous. All science became ecclesiastical in outlook and origin. Even Geography resolved itself into an

[1] See *supra*, p. 105.

a priori study, the basis of which was not the mariner's compass, but the Bible. Men found the maps of the times in the tabernacle of Moses, for this formed the only possible model of the globe. To imagine, said one writer, that the world is round would be ' to abolish the kingdom of heaven, the future state, and to make of none effect the resurrection of Christ.' [1] In the same spirit St. Augustine had started the controversy as to the effect of the Fall upon stars and vegetables, and on the atmospheric changes due to angels. Modern science cannot sufficiently express its contempt for the vast superstructure which the schoolmen raised on their narrow and flimsy foundations. Modern hermeneutics cannot sufficiently condemn a method of interpretation of the Scriptures which took no account of time, circumstance, development, or history. Nevertheless, that strange system which repels us to-day was in a true sense preparing the way for better things.

A third feature of Scholasticism is summed up in the phrase *pectus facit theologum* ; theology is the affair of the soul. Hence it follows that if theology is the basis of all knowledge, personal piety must be one of the presuppositions of science. In theology proper this expressed itself in the position of St. Augustine, reasserted by Anselm's *credo ut intelligam*, that faith must ever be the foundation of dogma. The extensions of this idea are of considerable importance. For there was no way in which medieval piety could better express itself than in ascetic contemplation. Hence the development, under the help, no doubt, of other factors, of Scholasticism, or the attempt to view things as a whole in their relation to God, into Mysticism, or the knowledge through ' contemplation ' of such relation.

Scholasticism thus possessed certain features which gave it unity. Nevertheless, the divisions and developments of Scholasticism proper must not be overlooked. In the first

[1] See details in Beazley's interesting *Dawn of Modern Geography*, vol. i.

period, as in the Dark Ages before Scholasticism, though portions of Aristotle were known, we note the prevalence of the so-called Platonic Realism, chiefly derived from St. Augustine. "The relation of philosophy to theology in the initial period of Scholasticism was essentially different from what it was at its maturity. In the earlier periods a proper philosophic system, a view of the world developed on different sides, had as yet no existence. Only logic was known with some completeness. As a distinct discipline metaphysics did not exist for the philosophers of that period. What they had of it consisted in single propositions, partly Platonic, partly Aristotelian." [1] In the second period Scholasticism obtained full possession of the writings of Aristotle, both of his logical and physical treatises. In consequence theologians attempted the construction of systems of thought passing beyond formal logic into metaphysics, and a complete view or *summa* of the world. But the treatment of this second period must be reserved for another chapter.

The changing outlook of Scholasticism as it passed from the predominance of Realistic Platonism to Aristotelianism corresponded inevitably with the varying fortunes of the great battle over Universals, which in popular thought it identifies with Scholasticism itself. In the earlier period Realism was predominant ; in the later, Nominalism waged a more equal warfare. In the days of its triumph Realism condemned Nominalism as a heresy, and was in its turn condemned by it. The never-ending controversy formed for centuries the central question of education and theology ; its ceaseless tournaments drew crowds of eager students to the lecture halls of the masters. The precise problem involved cannot be better put than in the famous words from the *Isagoge* of Porphyry, which have played a greater part in the history of thought than any outside the Bible : ' Next concerning genera and species, the question indeed

[1] Deutsch, *Abälard*, p. 96.

whether they have a substantial existence, or whether they exist in bare intellectual concepts only, or whether if they have a substantial existence they are corporeal or incorporeal, and whether they are separated from the insensible properties of the things, or are only in those properties and subsisting about them, I shall forbear to determine. For a question of this kind is very deep, and needs fuller investigation.'

For the various stages and opinions in this long controversy the student should refer to the histories of medieval logic. But there are certain matters of general moment connected with it that should not be overlooked. The reader should above all beware lest he undervalue this dispute. There are few matters of philosophical discussion which do not in their ultimate analysis involve some aspect of the controversy. The medieval doctrine of transubstantiation, as we shall see later,[1] is inseparably wrapped up in it: "Indeed the solution of the most momentous questions to which the human intellect can address itself is inextricably bound up with the solution of a question which ' common-sense ' will undertake to clear up in five minutes, or which it will indignantly pronounce too trifling to be asked or answered. Yet he who has given his answer to it has implicitly constructed his theory of the universe." [2] Those who imagine that there is here nothing but the dust of the past should remember that of Nominalism "the sensationalist scepticism of Hume, or the crude materialism of Haeckel, is but an illogical attenuation." [3] The danger of Realism, on the contrary, was an undeveloped Pantheism. God is regarded as the ultimate substance, the entity common to all species, and identical in each. Such a view must ultimately resolve all existing things, and all individual differences, into accidents of the *summum genus*.

---

[1] *Infra*, p. 236.　　[2] Rashdall, *Univs. in Middle Ages*, i. p. 39.
[3] *Ibid.* i. p. 45.

Nor must we forget that in spite of all the objections that may rightly be urged against the logical positions of the thirteen different schools of Realism which Prantl, in his great history of medieval logic, has discriminated, this much may be said, at any rate about the more moderate Realists, that their Realism was a protest against any doctrine of illusion. They held that mental ideas are, in some sense of the word—in the explanation of this lay their difficulty—strict realities. Realism was their protest against the question, so dear to a diseased subjectivism :—

> Is all that we think or seem,
> But a dream within a dream ?

Thus their Realism was, as Carlyle would have phrased it, the affirmation of the Everlasting Yea ; the emphasis of a doctrine of assurance. The medieval thinkers characteristically sought this assurance in reason and the objective world ; religious minds to-day sometimes seek it in their subjective experiences. Both have grasped the half only of the complete truth.

III

Though Lanfranc and Berengar must be regarded as the first-fruits of the new Scholasticism, Anselm [1] more than any other is entitled to be called its father. As the great Archbishop of Canterbury, to whom England owes the subjection of its Church to the ideas of Hildebrand, the life of Anselm belongs to general history. His place in the history of Christian philosophy is of equal importance. To the general tendencies of his thought it will be more convenient to return after dealing with Bernard and Abailard. Meanwhile it is important to note certain special details of his writings.

In his *Monologion de Divinitatis Essentia*, Anselm gives

---

[1] Born at Aosta 1033, died 1109. For Anselm, Abailard, and Bernard I may refer for further detail to my articles in Hastings' *Encyc. of Religion and Ethics*, vols. i. and ii.

us the famous so-called *a priori* proof of the existence of
God, which has thence found its way into most theological
treatises, ancient or modern. This argument is really a
Realist application of the Platonic doctrine of Ideas to the
demonstration of Christian doctrine by a logical ascent
from the particular to the universal. In the world of experience we are confronted by transitory, imperfect phenomena which invariably lead the mind upwards toward an
eternal, necessary, perfect Being. Our recognition of
goodness, for instance, in phenomena drives us to believe
in a supreme nature that is good *per se*, and which must be
the final *causa causans*, the supreme objective reality in
whom our ' ideas ' inhere. Thus the existence of God is
implicit in ordinary experience.

This argument was further developed by Anselm in his
Proslogion, so called because it is in the form of an address
to God. In this work Anselm attempts to prove the existence of God by a single deductive argument, instead of as
in the *Monologion* by a long inductive chain. The fool's
very denial of God, so Anselm argues, involves the idea of
God, and of this idea existence is a necessary part. In
other words, thought leads by an inherent necessity to the
postulate of the Absolute. When Count Gaunilio († *c.* 1083),
a monk of Marmoutier, pointed out in his *Apology for a
Fool* that the idea of the fabled Isles of the Blessed does
not prove their existence, Anselm replied that there is all
the difference between the *Summum cogitabile* or eternal
necessary idea and any particular empirical idea of things
which had a beginning and will have an end. Contingent
existence as such contradicts the idea of the *Summum
cogitabile*, which cannot be conceived save as existing.

The after history of these ontological arguments, in part
built up by Anselm upon Augustine's *De Trinitate,* belongs
to the history of philosophy.[1] But we may point out that

[1] For a judicious criticism, see John Caird, *Phil. of Religion* (1880),
p. 153 ff.

they were too Platonic to be accepted by the Aristotelian Schoolmen, with the exception of Duns Scotus. They have found their way in various forms into the systems of Descartes, Spinoza, Leibniz, and Hegel, but have been rejected by Kant. We see the same Platonic outlook in Anselm's *De Veritate*, in which he maintained that truth is the accurate perception of the archetypal ideas in the mind of God.

In his *De libero Arbitrio*, Anselm deals with the problem of free will. Freedom, he claims, is not the power of choosing between alternatives, but of persevering in righteousness for its own sake—a doctrine afterwards more fully developed in Kant's *Metaphysic of Ethics*. Anselm pointed out that original sin need not involve total depravity. Man is still left in possession of a real, if impaired, natural freedom, the power of the will to govern motives.

But the most important of Anselm's works is the *Cur Deus Homo*, finished at Schiavi in the Alban Mountains in 1098. This little book marks an epoch in the history of the doctrines of the Atonement. Anselm destroyed once for all the old conception that the Atonement was a ransom paid to the devil. In place of this disastrous dualistic doctrine which had dominated the Church since the days of Origen—with the possible exception of Faustus of Riez (fl. 500)—Anselm put forth a theory of the Atonement as the satisfaction rendered to the honour and justice of God. Anselm shows by deductive reasoning that man could not have been saved without Christ. All the actions of man are due to God for the promotion of His honour. But sin has defrauded God of that honour, and thereby has created a debt due to God. As the lost honour must be restored, the sinner cannot be exonerated of his debt by the mercy or fiat of God; for this were to let sin go without being brought into relation with the righteousness of God. But God's honour cannot be restored by further obedience; for this is due in any case, and cannot, therefore, be a discharge for the past debt. The honour, it is true, may be vindicated by punishment which exhibits God's supremacy, or by ' satisfaction,' *i.e.* the giving back to God more than has been taken away by the sinner. Such satisfaction must be made by man according to the measure of his sin ; yet for man this is impossible. <u>Hence God became man in Christ Jesus, and the infinite superabundant merits—</u> a doctrine very congruent, as we have seen, to medieval developments of thought and practice—<u>of His voluntary death outweigh the number and greatness of all sins.</u>

This treatise may be described in brief as the interpretation of the relationship between God and man in the terms of the Roman law familiar to Anselm. Of Teutonic law it is probable in our judgment that this Italian would know little or nothing. Anselm's argument has produced a lasting effect upon subsequent theology. In the substitutionary form stamped upon it at the Reformation, it has remained the doctrine of much evangelical orthodoxy to this day. " The *Cur Deus Homo*," writes Dr. Denney, " is the greatest and truest book on the Atonement that has ever been written." [1] To many students this verdict, we think, will seem conventional and exaggerated. The chief service Anselm rendered was in sweeping away the old patristic idea of the debt due to Satan, and in this Anselm seems scarcely aware how great was the work he accomplished. In spite of his emphasis of the moral necessity of the Atonement as distinct from the arbitrary fiat of the Divine Will, the fulfilment of prophecy, or the inversion of the Fall ; in spite of the stress Anselm places upon ' satisfaction ' rather than punishment, upon the person and work of Christ rather than upon an ecclesiastical and penitential system, to many the work will seem mechanical and unreal,[2] and its theory to be limited, dangerous, and full of Scholastic abstractions. Anselm's

---

[1] J. Denney, *The Atonement and the Modern Mind*, p. 116.
[2] Cf. Moberly, *Atonement and Personality*, pp. 367-371.

worst fault is his tendency to destroy the essential ethical unity of the Godhead by his revival of the old Gnostic [1] Dualism within the Divine Nature itself between justice and law, and his emphasis of the antagonism between the Son and the Father as representatives of different attributes, the One who pays and the One who exacts. The theory also posits an opposition between God and the external world which ends in the idea of arbitrariness on the part of God, and on the part of man in the Absence of the consciousness of his own personality as an essential factor in the Atonement ; this last, we may remark, a common defect of Scholastic Realism. With Anselm salvation is almost wholly external and institutional, corporate rather than experimental. Thus sin becomes " high treason, not moral corruption. . . . It remains outside the human conscience ; it is indeed a great fault, but it is hardly a moral fault." [2]

The complete absence in the book of any assurance of salvation is, of course, thoroughly medieval. All that Anselm does is to show that salvation is possible—the rest was always left to the Church. Moreover, the theory absolutely disregards the whole life and teaching of Jesus, and abstracts the Atonement as a matter of Calvary alone. " This God-man need not have preached and founded a kingdom, no disciples need have been gathered : He only required to die." [3] That Anselm so completely ignores the immanence of God and St. Paul's mystical conception of union with the Risen Christ is remarkable, for the Pauline ideas would have appealed strongly to Anselm's cast of thought if he could have freed himself from his feudal, forensic fetters. But instead of the mysticism of St. Paul we have the superabundant payment by Christ of a debt due from man to the justice of God, which debt, by reason

---

[1] Bigg, *Christian Platonists of Alexandria*, p. 290.
[2] Stevens, *The Christian Doctrine of Salvation*, p. 242.
[3] Harnack, *H.D.* vi. p. 76.

of his original sin, man cannot discharge. The keynote of the treatise is thus the paradox, 'man must, man cannot.' Moreover, Anselm's theory of the Incarnation is far from satisfactory. In his desire to avoid conceptions now known as kenotic he limits the sufferings of Christ to His human nature: 'The Divine Nature, we assert, is impassible.' Such opposition can only end in Nestorianism; it is fatal to any true conception of the Person of Christ as the unity of the God-man.

The influence of Anselm upon the Scholastic doctrine of the Atonement is of great importance for the student of theology. As regards the old patristic doctrine of ransom paid to the devil, Anselm's refutation was decisive, though shadowy survivals lingered on, sometimes in unexpected places. His idea of 'satisfaction' was widely embraced, though with both additions and subtractions, as for instance by Alexander of Hales, who made much of the added idea of 'equivalence,' developing thence the idea of a 'treasury of merit,' the basis of all medieval doctrines of indulgence. At the Reformation Anselm's idea of 'satisfaction' became predominant, almost banishing the Scriptural idea of 'sacrifice.' Even Luther, who detested the idea as belonging ' to the schools of the jurists,' was forced to retain it; while in the Anglican liturgy 'sacrifice' and 'satisfaction' were indissolubly linked together in the familiar phrase, 'A full, perfect, and sufficient sacrifice, oblation, and satisfaction for the sins of the whole world.'

In Thomas Aquinas we have the fullest acceptance by any schoolman of Anselm's doctrine. Nevertheless, there are differences. Aquinas dwells at some length on the superabundant 'satisfaction' of Christ's death. But in so doing he is not prepared wholly to accept Anselm's attempt to justify the crude dogma of Augustine that sin against an infinite God is necessarily infinite in character. 'The acts of the creature as such,' he allows, even when sins, 'cannot be infinite,' though he owns that they have a

' sort of infinitude.' His conception of the obedience of Christ which gave ' satisfaction ' is also wider, for it extends not merely to the death but to the whole life and suffering of Jesus. Aquinas owns, what Anselm always denied, that God could have pardoned sin without any satisfaction. To Aquinas the position of Anselm seems a limitation of the absolute freedom of divine omnipotence as to choice of means. But the greatest difference is in the approach by Aquinas to a substitutionary theory of the Atonement, the transference of the merit of the atoning work to the sinner, not as in Reformation theology by imputation, but by his mystical union with the Redeemer.

The chief opponent of Anselm among the Schoolmen was Duns Scotus. His contribution to soteriology is his repudiation of Anselm's position that the Atonement was the motive of the Incarnation. Christ, he claims, would have come even if man had not sinned, for only by His Incarnation could He be the head of the Mystical Body. As with much else in Duns' theology, the ' merit ' of Christ's death depends almost wholly upon the arbitrary fiat of God ; for the merit of the sufferings of Christ could only be finite, inasmuch as Christ suffered in His human not in His divine nature. Nevertheless, this nominal satisfaction is accounted by God as infinite. Thus a good angel, or even a sinless man, could equally well have secured the plan of redemption. Duns Scotus calls this theory of thus accepting something as the imaginary equivalent of a contract *acceptilatio*, a familiar term in Scots civil law to this day. The acceptilatian theory of Duns has had considerable influence on later theology, especially on Grotius.[1]

IV

The importance of St. Bernard (1090-1153) in the history of the Church cannot be exaggerated. For a few years the

[1] D. W. Simon, *The Redemption of Man*, pp. 20-23, 413-415.

centre of Christendom was virtually transferred from Rome to Clairvaux. As a theologian, the influence of Bernard was always thrown against all change or progress. In his antagonism to all that Abailard represented, in his belief that the application of dialectic to theology was both dangerous and impious, Bernard was the refuge of a reactionary school destined to be swept away by the rise of Scholasticism. In later years his hatred of heresy became almost a monomania. As his contemporary, Otto of Freising, tells us, ' Bernard was, from the fervour of his Christian religion, as jealous as from his habitual meekness he was in some measure credulous; so that he held in abhorrence those who trusted in the wisdom of this world, and were too much attached to human reasonings ; and if anything alien to the Christian faith were said to him in reference to them he readily gave ear to it.' Hence a want of fairness in dealing not only with Abailard but with Gilbert de la Porrée. Gilbert (†1154) who, according to his learned contemporary, John of Salisbury, ' was a monk of the clearest intellect and of the widest reading, in culture surpassed by none,' had published a commentary on the *De Trinitate*, a collection of treatises currently assigned to Boethius. In this work Gilbert, by distinguishing " God " from " Deity " (in which last he found the universal that his Realism demanded), had laid such stress on the absolute unity of the Trinity as almost to exclude the existence of the Three Persons. At the council of Rheims (March 1148) Gilbert was put on his defence before Bernard's pupil, Pope Eugenius III. Bernard's attack ended in complete failure, or rather in a measure of victory for freedom of thought. When Eugenius proposed that Gilbert's commentary should be handed over to him that he might erase whatever was needful, Gilbert claimed that it was his own duty to erase what was amiss, a declaration received with loud applause by the cardinals. The council ended with the Pope's mysterious ruling, ' that the essence of God should not be predicated in the sense of the ablative case only, but also of the nominative ' ! and Gilbert returned ' with his honour unabated to his own diocese.'

The most lasting contribution of Bernard to the thought of the age lies in his mysticism. The most important of Bernard's mystical writings is his *Homilies on the Song of Solomon*. They were actually preached to the monks of Clairvaux, and still bear signs of interruptions and other local circumstances. The mysticism of Bernard is really not systematic, but the outcome of his persuasion that faith receives all truth ' wrapped up ' (*involutum*). All that reason can do is to add clearness by a certain limited measure of unwrapping ; for the highest knowledge is that which comes not by intellect but by intuition or spiritual vision. Of this there are three stages, the highest of which is ' contemplation.' " The great importance of Bernard in the history of Mysticism does not lie in the speculative side of his teaching, in which he depends almost entirely upon Augustine. His great achievement was to recall devout and loving contemplation to the image of the crucified Christ, and to found that worship of our Saviour as the ' Bridegroom of our Soul,' which in the next centuries inspired so much fervid devotion and lyrical sacred poetry." [1] In this connection we must not overlook the influence of the Crusades, in whose development Bernard's preaching had proved so potent a factor. In the nobler crusaders, *e.g.* in Godfrey of Bouillon, we see the moral power that sprang from the realisation of the suffering Saviour. "Salve caput cruentatum" ("O Sacred Head once wounded ! ") was for the crusader more than a hymn. In medieval piety the image of the historical though dying Jesus was thus formed side by side with that of the sacramental eternal Christ. But with Bernard the historical was secondary to the mystical and experimental. By his

[1] W. R. Inge, *Christian Mysticism*, p. 140, also Appendix D. p. 369 ; Harnack, *H.D.* vi. p. 9 ff.

treatment of the fact of Christ he gave to the romantic, erotic side of mysticism a great stimulus. It is true that he always speaks of the Church and not the individual as the bride of Christ, but the enforced celibacy of monasticism soon led to the transference to the individual of the luscious language of the *Canticles*. Of this sensuous presentation, so akin to the method of allegory, the beginnings appear to be found in Origen's commentary on the *Canticles*. From Origen it passed to the Greek fathers, in few of whom the figure does not occur. Its most extreme form was found in the tendency current in the thirteenth century to give veneration to the specific limbs of the Virgin—'uterum quo Christum portavit, ubera quibus eum lactavit,' etc.

We see the same mystical principles in Bernard's *De Diligendo Deo*. God is the ground and cause of a love in which there are four stages. The first stage is carnal love, in which the man loves himself. The second is a love of God which is selfish, inasmuch as it is due to suffering and experience. In the third stage he loves God for God's own sake. In the fourth stage the spirit, ' intoxicated by the Divine love, wholly forgets itself, becoming nothing in itself, and becoming one spirit with Him.' To be thus affected is to be ' deified,' the annihilation of self " in the immense sea of a luminous eternity." Whether this fourth stage is possible in this life seems to Bernard more than doubtful : ' Let them assert it who have experienced it : to me, I confess, it seems impossible.'

V

With Abailard's lifelong conflicts with authority, whether at Paris in his early attacks upon the crude Realism of his master, William of Champeaux, or at Laon in his struggle with Anselm of Laon, or at St. Denys in his dispute with the monks over " Dionysius," or in the more prolonged duel with St. Bernard, we are not here concerned, save to point out that they were the outcome of his system.

N

For the real cause of Abailard's offending was his constant appeal from authority to reason, and in this he was necessarily misjudged by an age which cared little for reason and everything for authority. In reality Abailard was no heretic. He always maintained that he was the obedient son of the Church. In the verdict of Peter the Venerable, in whose monastery at Clugny he passed away (1142), he was ' ever to be named with honour as the servant of Christ, and verily Christ's philosopher.' In his last letter to the famous Héloise, Abailard had pleaded : ' I would not be an Aristotle if this should keep me away from Christ,' he owes his importance to his demand for reverent though thorough inquiry in matters of religion. Modern Roman scholars have no hesitation in saying that both the synods at which he was condemned, Soissons and Sens, were conspicuous for zeal rather than knowledge. It is well known also that the work of his disciple, the famous *Sentences* of Peter Lombard, is largely the *Sic et Non* of Abailard in a more reverent form. Yet the *Sentences* became the accredited text-book in theology, the very canon of orthodoxy of the later Middle Ages, though many of its views were those for which Abailard had been condemned. But we need not marvel at the misfortunes of Abailard. In part they were the results of an ill-balanced judgment, always in extremes ; in part the retribution of a pride intolerant of all obscurantism ; in part the necessary outcome of his real greatness.

For Abailard was so great intellectually, so completely in advance of his age, both in the extent of his knowledge and the width of his outlook, that his positions were bound to seem heterodox to a generation that leaned wholly on the past. Abailard, in fact, belonged to the future. We salute the herald of the Renaissance " in his joyful recognition of a world of divine teaching of old outside the borders of Judaism." [1] The very spirit of Protestantism is contained in his declaration that the ' doctors of the

[1] Poole, *Medieval Thought*, p. 175.

Church should be read not with the necessity to believe, but with liberty to judge.' We seem transported to the twentieth century when Abailard claims that the interpretation of Scripture may err or the text be faulty. In the preface to his *Sic et Non* he lays down a defence of all criticism : ' By doubting we are led to inquire, by inquiry we perceive the truth.' In the very form of his *Sic et Non* —a collection of contradictory opinions from the fathers on all the leading disputes of theology—Abailard shows his belief that error or contradiction may be but stages in the discovery of truth. Of those who argue that we must not reason on matters of faith, Abailard asks : ' How, then, is the faith of any people, however false, to be refuted, though it may have arrived at such a pitch of blindness as to confess some idol to be the creator both of heaven and earth ? As according to your own admission you cannot reason upon matters of faith, you have no right to attack others upon a matter with regard to which you argue that you ought yourself to be unassailed.' The dilemma of unreasoning pietism has never been better expressed.

Of particular doctrines which illustrate Abailard's drift, we select the following as of especial theological interest. In his doctrine of inspiration Abailard is very bold. This he limits down to matters concerning ' faith, hope, charity, and the sacraments.' The rest is largely ' for the adornment or enlargement of the Church.' Even ' prophets and apostles may err,' while a place must be found for the revelation given to the heathen philosophers, especially Plato. As regards the humanity of Christ, Abailard is in striking contrast to his age. The common theory of the times was a sort of transubstantiation theory of Christ's person ; that in the assumption of flesh the human person though not the nature had perished. In opposition to this Abailard claimed that the humanity was essentially real. He goes so far even as to urge that it includes ' humanae infirmitatis veros defectus.'

Abailard's doctrine of sin may be best gathered from his work *Scito te ipsum*. Its very title shows the emphasis he places on self-knowledge or intention. In this Abailard is in complete opposition to the formal practice of his age. Virtue, he maintains, cannot be attained except by conflict. Ignorance in the case of the unenlightened does not constitute sin, and the Jews who ignorantly crucified Jesus must be judged accordingly. Original sin is thus the penal consequence of sin and not sin itself. ' It is inconceivable that God should damn a man for the sin of his parents.' He thus emphasises the ethical determination of the divine action. From this doctrine of sin it is an easy transition to Abailard's moral theory of the Atonement, the creating within us by His passion or service of love of a love which itself is the deliverance from sin. He rejects totally any theory that makes the Atonement a redemption from the right of the devil, but, except for this agreement, he may be said to have ignored the work of Anselm, as did also his disciple, Peter Lombard. The merit of Abailard's theory is that he emphasises reconciliation through personal fellowship with Christ [1]; its defect that he lays so little stress upon the work of Christ in its relation to guilt. The emphasis is " not so much really upon the love of God manifested to us, as upon the love of God, generated within us. He dwells upon the Cross very finely, as an incentive to love ; but hardly conceives of it more profoundly than as an incentive. He has lost the emphasis upon the thought of humanity as a corporate unity, summed up and represented in Christ, which was so strong and clear in the earliest Christian theologians." [2] We owe also to Abailard the renewed emphasis of the doctrine of the *Epistle to the Hebrews* of Christ's unceasing intercession as part of His atoning work.

Abailard's teaching of Logic amounted almost to a re-

[1] Deutsch, *Abälard*, p. 382.
[2] Moberly, *Atonement and Personality*, p. 381.

volution. Though not the first to discern, he was the first to popularise a theory that to-day we should call conceptualism, midway between the extreme nominalism of his former master, Roscelin, and the crude realism of William of Champeaux, whose lectures Abailard had also attended. William seems to have asserted the full immanence of the universal idea in every individual, " a view which must necessarily have led to the doctrine of the *one* latent substance, and of the negating of all that is individual as mere semblance or mere contingency." [1] Abailard set himself to combat the logical position of both ; by conceding to each the truth of their affirmative positions, while denying the correctness of their negations. He held that we arrive at the general from the particular by an effort of thought. Thus he allowed to the Nominalist the reality of the individual, and to the Realist the reality also of the universals, in so far, that is, as they were the necessary creations of the intellect. Abailard thus returned to the position of Aristotle, probably without any direct knowledge of Aristotle's arguments. Hence the reputation of Abailard in dialectics when Aristotle became dominant.

We have alluded to the theological struggle between St. Bernard and Abailard. The differences of the two men were fundamental, of the kind that no argument or personal intercourse can remove. That Bernard was a realist goes without saying. Realism in the early part of the twelfth century was almost identical with orthodoxy. But this was not the chief difference. The two were representatives of opposing forces. Abailard summed up in himself the spirit of a premature revolt against unreasoning authority. Bernard was the embodiment of all that was best in the old faith ; a reformer in morals and life, a rigid conservative in creed and ritual. Abailard, profoundly religious in his way, was the representative of a creed full of dry light and clear of cant, but which had shown, both

[1] Harnack, *H.D.* vi. p. 35 *n.*

at St. Denys and St. Gildas—two monasteries in which
he had passed some years of stormy life—little power in
turning men from their sins to the higher vision. With
all his narrowness of intellectual outlook compared with
Abailard, put St. Bernard down at St. Gildas, and that
abode of loose livers who flouted Abailard would have felt
at once the purifying power of Bernard's zeal. Bernard's
was that baptism with fire which not only cleanses but
warms ; but of this the cold, intellectual religion of Abailard
knew little or nothing. To Bernard ' Faith is not an
opinion, but a certitude. " The substance of things hoped
for," says the Apostle, not the phantasies of empty con-
jecture. You hear ; " the substance " : you may not dispute
on the faith as you please ; you may not wander here
and there through the wastes of opinion, the byways of
error. By the name " substance " something certain and
fixed is placed before you ; you are enclosed within boundaries, you are restrained within unchanging limits.'
Abailard, on the contrary, proclaimed that reason was of
God, and had, as philosophy showed, found God. He
argued, quoting from the *Wisdom of Sirach*, that " he that
is hasty to trust is light-minded." Conflict between the
two men was inevitable.

The circumstances of the times flung Abailard into
controversy with Bernard. Intellectually the only foeman
worthy of his steel would have been Anselm of Canterbury.
At first sight there seems to be between these two philosophers an impassable abyss, unconsciously summed up
by Anselm in the preface to his *Cur Deus Homo*. ' Some
men seek for reasons because they do not believe ; we seek
for them because we do believe. This is my belief, that if
I believe not, neither shall I understand ' (*credo ut intelligam*). It is the same teaching as we find in St. Augustine
and in all mystics. ' He who would know,' writes the
author of *Theologia Germanica*, ' before he believeth cometh
never to true knowledge.' The rule of Abailard is the

exact opposite. He argues that men believe not because
of authority but because of conviction. Doubt is his
starting-point, reason his guide to certitude. But a
deeper study reveals that the conflict between the two
may be exaggerated. Abailard owns that the highest
truths of theology stand above the proof of our understanding ; they can only be hinted at by analogies. But
through knowledge faith is made perfect. Anselm was no
less anxious to satisfy reason than Abailard, only he
wanted to make sure of its limits before he began. Thus
the difference between the two great thinkers was one
rather of order of thought than real divergence. If the
chronological order be regarded, Anselm is right ; if the
logical, Abailard. In the order of experience, faith precedes
reason ; in the maturer life, reason leads up to faith.[1] It
is in the clear perception of this last that the true greatness
of Abailard lies. But, as Bacon, he had to leave his name
and memory to the next age, that age which he had done
more than any man to usher in. His spirit lived, though
unrecognised, in the victories and movements of later
thought. In more ways than one he prepared the way for
the conservative constructions of the great Schoolmen.
The school of Paris in which he taught developed within
a generation into the greatest university of Europe largely
through his influence. With Abailard also closes the first
period of Scholasticism. The thoughts which he had
worked out for himself the next age assimilated directly
from authority ; the ideas which the Church had condemned were henceforth accepted. For in 1128 James of
Venice translated into Latin the works of Aristotle hitherto
for the most part unknown. Within a century the ' New
Logic,' as it was called, dominated Europe. In the place
of St. Bernard we have Aristotle as the canonised leader
of the Church.

[1] Cf. Fairbairn, *Christ in Modern Theology*, p. 120 ff.; Deutsch, *Abälard*,
p. 172.

CHAPTER VIII

THE MEDIEVAL MYSTICS

Argument

I

As the importance of Mysticism in Christian thought cannot be exaggerated, it were well to understand clearly to what that importance is due. In his remarkable examination of Mysticism the late Professor James [1] tells us that there are two necessary marks or qualities of the mystical. The first he calls Ineffability, by which he means " that no adequate report thereof can be given in words." He goes on to add : " It follows from this that its quality must be directly experienced ; it cannot be imparted or transferred to others. No one can make clear to another who has never had a certain feeling in what the quality or worth of it consists." The second quality of Mysticism, Professor James tells us, is the Noetic quality : " Although similar to states of feeling, mystical states seem to those who experience them to be also states of know- ledge. They are states of insight into depths of truth implanted by the discursive intellect. . . . As a rule they carry with them a curious sense of authority for after-time."

Professor James adds " two other qualities, less strongly marked." The first he calls Transiency, the second Pas- sivity. "Transiency" seems to us to be rather a matter for the psychologist ; it is the mark of certain psychic or pathological states which are by no means an essential of Mysticism. But of the truth of the other three qualities of Mysticism indicated in this analysis by Dr. James there can be little doubt.

To these qualities Mysticism owes its importance in Christian thought. Take, for instance, the Noetic quality.

[1] William James, *Varieties of Religious Experience*, lectures 16 and 17.

Medieval mysticism arose at a time when all theological knowledge was being reduced by logical rules to various '*summas*,' when Aristotle was becoming the dominant factor in the thought of the Church. Mysticism proclaims that the soul has faculties, that there are states of its own for the discernment of spiritual truth, knowledge none the less true because they are reached by direct intuition, and escape clean beyond all syllogism or systems. The more, in fact, that theology became the sport of the schools, the greater the need that there should be voices, if only in the wilderness, proclaiming that the kingdom of heaven was within.

As regards Ineffability, or the appeal of Mysticism to an experience of which "no adequate report can be given in words," we note in Mysticism the revolt of the spiritual against a religion which gave little place to experience in comparison with formal or sacramental religion. In the medieval Church the individual, *qua* individual, had little or no place. His salvation was conditioned from first to last by his belonging to a corporation, in whose privileges and functions he shared ; through whose sacraments his life was nourished ; by whose graduated hierarchy, though but the meanest servant of the Church, he was linked to the supreme Head ; whose saints shielded him by their 'merits,' or helped him by their intercessions. Through this corporation alone was he brought into touch with his Saviour ; outside the corporation his soul was lost. The grandeur of this idea few will dispute ; its extraordinary hold for centuries upon the conscience of men testifies to its appeal. Its dangers, however, in the suppression of the individual, are equally clear. Against this danger medieval mysticism raised its constant protest. Mysticism never wearied in its insistence that spiritual results can only be attained by inward, spiritual processes :

"God is not dumb, that He should speak no more.
If thou hast wanderings in the wilderness,
And find'st not Sinai, 'tis thy soul is poor."

But such experience in its ultimate analysis is always "ineffable," and this in several ways. It is ineffable as contrasted with the disputations and syllogisms of the schools. The mystic maintains that such knowledge or experience is not obtained by reason, but by a faculty that works in a sphere above reason. As such it cannot be otherwise than ineffable. As Eckhart puts it : ' All the truth which any master ever taught with his own reason and understanding, or even can teach to the last day, will not in the least explain this knowledge.' In the words of Tauler : ' The dwelling in the Inner Kingdom of God where pure truth and the sweetness of God are found ' is not something that can be learned from ' the masters of Paris.' ' What it is, and how it comes to pass, is easier to experience than to describe. All that I have said of it is as poor and unlike it as a point of a needle is to the heavens above us.' The soul-stuff that rises to the surface of consciousness only when the depths of the heart are stirred is nearly always inarticulate. Or, to change the metaphor, the human soul is like some great iceberg ; its foundations are submerged in hidden depths.

There is a corollary to this emphasis of experience, the understanding of which is of great importance. We cannot do better than expound it in the oft-quoted words of the Neoplatonist Plotinus : ' Even as the eye could not behold the sun unless it were itself sun-like, so neither could the soul behold God if it were not God-like.' For the vision of God there must be likeness to God. Hence the emphasis laid by the mystics on the ' Spark ' or ' Ground,' or ' inward man ' or ' eye ' in the soul—the names vary, the thought is one—that is of the same nature as the ' Ground ' in God. Whether this ' Spark ' or ' Ground ' was uncreated, immanent, and basal, or a remnant of the sinless state before the Fall—with the corollary that salvation consists in realising our true nature—or was something infused, imparted, or added, was a matter over which mystics were never united. Some, with the *Theologia Germanica*, declined to decide at all : ' The true light is that eternal light which is God ; or else it is a created light, but yet Divine, which is called grace.' If this ' ground ' was uncreated, the further question arises of its relation to the Divine Essence or Ground. If it was ' imparted,' we open the door to the doctrine, upon which so many of the later mystics loved to dwell, of ' the birth of Christ ' within the soul, an idea materialised by certain highly wrought nuns into the actual travailing in birth with Christ.

' Passivity,' the belief that the soul simply is and receives, is no accidental note of medieval mysticism. To say that ' passivity ' is, strictly, a Neoplatonist term is not sufficient explanation : " Passivity goes on figuring in Christian Mystics (in spite of its demonstrably dangerous suggestions and frequently scandalous history), because the Christian consciousness requires a term for the expression of one element of all its deepest experiences, that character of ' giveness ' and of grace which marks all such states in exact proportion to their depth." [1] Moreover, in the Church for a thousand years the chief note of the ' religious ' was the ascetic or monastic. In early monasticism or eremitism, the solitary recluse of the Nitria, or the monk plunging into the dense forests to escape his fellows, asceticism was necessarily ' passive.' This is seen most clearly in the records of the early hermits, especially in the *Historia Lausiaca* of Palladius. But as monasticism ceased to be the refuge of the individual soul, and became instead an organised-community life, ' passive ' asceticism was bound to find its refuge elsewhere. This is found in mystic ' contemplation,' the note of which was the same passivity as is so striking a feature in the oldest records of the monastic life. The result of such ' contemplation ' was the ' darkness ' or ' nothingness ' of soul—the human correspondence to the ' quiet Desert of the Godhead,' ' the Divine Darkness,'

[1] F. von Hügel, *The Mystical Element of Religion*, ii. p. 132.

negative definitions common to mystics of all ages from
Valentinus and Basilides to Eckhart.   In some of the
mystics this 'nothingness' became a morbid quietism
which mistook for spiritual perfection a pathological indifference, where all consciousness both of self and of the
world is reduced to zero, after the manner of the Eastern
fakir.   The root of such quietism is the false conception,
so common in all medieval speculation, that God, as the
transcendent, Perfect Being, must necessarily be without
attributes.   As the author of the *Theologia Germanica*
puts it : 'To God as Godhead appertains neither will,
nor knowledge, nor manifestation, nor anything that we
can name, or say, or conceive.'   But this is to confuse the
Infinite with the Indefinite, or rather with zero raised to
the infinite—if we may adopt a mathematical expression.
The historic source of this teaching would appear to be
found in the works of the Neoplatonist Proclus.

To the above characteristics of Mysticism we would add
another of great importance for our present investigation.
We refer to what, for want of a better word, we must call
its immortality.   "To-day," says Maeterlinck finely, " you
may pass through the infirmaries of the human soul, where
all thoughts come day by day to die, and you will not find
there a single mystic thought." [1]   There is nothing more
remarkable in the wide range of the visible Church than
the persistence across the centuries of the mystic sense, and
of the spacious joy and expansive freedom which it brings.
Mysticism, though at times it may sleep, is never dead.   A
corollary of this is also true.   There is in Mysticism a
certain timelessness, which is the despair of the historian,
especially if he be possessed with the thought of progress.
This timelessness manifests itself in the absence of local
marks, whether national or ecclesiastical.   Mystics of
every age are akin.   There is no speech or language where
their voice is not heard.   When, therefore, Harnack [2]

[1] Maeterlinck, *Ruysbroec*, p. 23.   [2] *H.D.* vi. p. 101 *n*.

refuses to discuss the German medieval mystics because he would " like to avoid even seeming to countenance the error that they expressed anything one cannot read in Origen, Plotinus, the Areopagite, Augustine, Erigena, Bernard, and Thomas," he points in a perverse sort of way to a great truth. The mystics are in reality a timeless brotherhood, who repeat with but slight variations of form or language certain eternal principles. Nevertheless, in the very repetition there is progress.

In certain of its aspects it was inevitable that in un-balanced minds Mysticism should pass into unorthodoxy. One of the dangers of Mysticism is Antinomianism. This it was that in the eighteenth century gave Wesley his dislike, more fancied, however, than real, to all forms of Mysticism.[1] How great was the danger in the Middle Ages we see in the protests of the mystic John of Ruysbroek against those who ' like to call themselves " theopaths." They take every impulse to be divine, and repudiate all responsibility.' That Mysticism was also ofttimes semi-Pelagian in char-acter was the outcome of certain fundamental positions. When Juliana of Norwich (fl. 1373) says that ' in every soul that shall be saved there is a goodly will that never assented to sin, nor ever shall,' she but puts into clear English the basis of the condemnation of Eckhart that he had main-tained, that there is in the soul ' something uncreated ' of a divine, and, therefore, of an untainted character :

—the spark
He gave us from His fire of fires, and bade
Remember whence it sprang, nor be afraid
While that burns on, though all the rest grow dark.

The doctrine of the ' uncreated ground ' was fatal to the strict Augustinian conception of total depravity. But not less fatal was the general position of Mysticism, that God may be found, not by deliverance from without, but by

[1] See my remarks in *New History of Methodism*, i. p. 58 ff.

sinking into the depths of our own consciousness : ' If thou desirest,' says Richard of St. Victor, ' to search out the deep things of God, search out the depths of thine own spirit.' On its philosophical side such a view sprang from the conception of man as a microcosm.

Another danger of Mysticism was pantheism. The source of the danger was twofold. The doctrine of the ' uncreated ground ' in the soul could easily be pushed into the heretical conclusion that man was ὁμοούσιος with God, in the same sense as Christ. At the other end was the danger which came from looking upon absorption with the Deity as the aim of the soul's experiences. But pantheism is a loose charge, and, on that account, a favourite missile. Strictly speaking, pantheism is the identification of every- thing with God. But a faith which looks upon everything as equally real, good, and divine is incompatible with any belief in personality, will, purpose, or morality. Now, however much the Christian mystics might play with pantheistic phrases, there are few of them—certainly not Eckhart—who do not seek to conserve personality. For the mystics were conscious that the originality of Chris- tianity consists in its revelation through the person of Christ of the depth and inexhaustibleness of human person- ality. Accordingly, in the Christian mystics, dangerous as their language with reference to absorption may be at times, there is always an emphasis of purpose; in the later mystics, for instance, much is made of the will—and this in itself is fatal to pantheism.

In his subtle survey of Christian Mysticism, Professor Inge has pointed out certain tendencies, loosely labelled pantheistic, which should be carefully distinguished. The first he calls *Acosmism*, the denial of reality to the visible world, the only existence being the ' intelligible world of ideas ' in the mind of God. Of this system the most thorough modern representative is Spinoza ; of the older philosophers we may take the Neoplatonists or Eckhart.

A second belief is *Panentheism*, the belief in the immanence of a God who is also transcendent. " In its true form it is an integral part of Christian philosophy, and indeed of all rational theology. But in proportion as the indwelling of God, or of Christ, or of the Holy Spirit in the heart of man, is regarded as an *opus operatum* or as a complete substitution of the Divine for the human, we are in danger of a self-deception which resembles the maddest phase of Pantheism." [1] An example may be found in Catherine of Genoa's claim : ' I find no more *me* ; there is no longer any other *I* but God.'

Of these dangers of Mysticism we give an illustration. At the commencement of the thirteenth century we note the rediscovery of John Scotus Erigena. The result was seen in the rise at Paris of a school of mystics who exaggerated the inward experience of God into a pantheistic independence of all external means of grace, and thus " launched, without sufficient store of charts and compasses, on the dangerous sea of Spiritual Freedom." [2] The leader of these, Amalrich or Amaury of Bena, taught that ' every one ought to believe as an article of faith that each one of us is a member of Christ ' ; words of innocent evangelical ring, which, however, were used by Amalrich in the sense that anything in the universe in the last analysis is God, and that the purified soul becomes God Himself. In 1205 Amalrich's doctrines were condemned ; but the seed he had sown bore fruit in the formation of a vigorous society, whose central tenet was the Antinomian doctrine that one who finds himself ' free in God ' is thereby raised above rules and forms and rites, which are merely of use for those on a lower spiritual level. The members of this society (according to the contemporary account of Caesarius of Heisterbach) taught ' that there is neither heaven nor hell, as places, but he who knows God possesses heaven, and he who commits mortal sin carries hell within himself.' They

---

[1] Inge, *op. cit.* p. 121.   [2] R. Jones, *Mystical Religion*, p. 195.

claimed (and in this we detect the influence of the teaching of Joachim di Fiori) that they lived in the third age. The age of the Father had been succeeded by that of the Son ; this again was followed by the dispensation of the Spirit, Who had become incarnate in them, and Whose direct work brings salvation without any exterior act, whether baptism or eucharist. The society was broken up, and its more important members burnt at the stake at Paris in 1209 ; but the doctrines took refuge among the Albigensians, and were only extirpated by a deluge of blood and the counter-reaction of the friars. In Rhineland the teaching issued in the formation of a widespread Antinomian sect known as Brethren of the Free Spirit. In Strassburg in 1215 we read of the burning of eighty heretics, whose leader Ortlieb had taught that ' a man ought to give up all externals and follow the promptings of the Spirit within himself,' inasmuch as every man is really of the same substance as God, and, if he put forth the will, can become divine. For the man in such a state sin is impossible, for all that he does is the act of God.

II

On its historical or genealogical side Mysticism in the Church was of Eastern or Platonic origin. With the mystical elements in the Early Church, especially in the Alexandrian school, we have already dealt. But Eastern Mysticism, in which the stress was laid upon emanation, had little attraction for the ruder West. Such Eastern Mysticism as entered into Western theology came in chiefly under false pretences. Dionysius the Areopagite was *in* but not *of* the Western Church. His work, while widely reverenced, was really alien in spirit to the genius of Latin Christianity, while the Mysticism of his interpreter, Erigena, had been without abiding influence either on his own or later generations. Nevertheless, if only because of the Platonic Realism underlying Latin theology up to the rise

o

of Scholasticism, there was never a time when a certain element of Mysticism was not to be found in some of its writers, apart altogether from the quotations from Dionysius with which all medieval commonplace books were filled. Two Latin writers, in especial, had introduced Mysticism into theology : Victorinus, the first Christian Neoplatonist who wrote in Latin,[1] who was converted to Christianity in his old age (about 360) ; and a greater than Victorinus, though he owed much to him—St. Augustine. In Victorinus, who had received as a tutor the rare honour of a statue in the Roman Forum, there is one original conception which afterwards, through Augustine, became common in the Church. In his treatment of the doctrine of the Trinity he speaks of the Holy Ghost as the bond (*copula*) who joins in perfect love the Father and the Son.

The mystical elements in St. Augustine are of supreme importance. It is true that Mysticism only touched him on one side of his nature ; it formed one only of the many contradictory forces the synthesis of which in one system gave to St. Augustine his unique position. St. Augustine's hold upon the Western world was, however, too profound for such Mysticism as he had incorporated not to be far-reaching. But perhaps his chief influence as a mystic was that in the doctrines of Austin we find the great offset to the rationalism into which the predominant Aristotelianism was ever tending to degenerate. At the same time, in his orthodoxy we find the preservative against mystic pantheism.

The mystic elements in St. Augustine became most conspicuous when thrown against the background of the current Scholasticism. When Aristotle conquered the schools, and logic became supreme in theology, Mysticism was forced to become articulate, if only because otherwise Mysticism would have been lost. Such attempts at sys-

[1] For Victorinus and his importance, see Bishop Gore in *D.C.B.* iv. s.v., or Harnack, *H.D.* v. p. 35 ff.

tematisation were twofold.   Some of the writers, anxious
above all for the conservation of authority, attempted to
combine Scholasticism and Mysticism ; others, on the
contrary, were indifferent to, and independent of, the
schools.   The gulf between the two classes is not slight,
and grew with the increasing formalism of the schools.
St. Bernard, who lived before the schoolman had become
supreme, is naturally less sharply marked off as a mystic
than Eckhart or Tauler or others, who were driven into
independence or even revolt.   In the first class, Mysticism,
following Augustine, is more psychological : the emphasis
of self-knowledge is the key to divine knowledge.   Union
with God is achieved through the faculties of the soul.   In
the second class it is ontological : the capacity for union
with God is inherent in the essence of the soul.   In the
mystics of the second school there is a tendency to dis-
parage reason in comparison with ' ecstasy.'   By the
writers of the first school ' contemplation,' ' intuition,' or
' ecstasy ' is regarded as an additional faculty, which
supplements but not invalidates reason ; reason deals with
the natural, ' contemplation ' with the supernatural.   This
distinction was soon pushed into an " intractable dualism,"[1]
and has led to the identification, in the modern Roman
Church, of Mysticism with " the science which treats of
supernatural phenomena," including witchcraft and the
like.   On the other hand, the alliance of Scholasticism with
Mysticism issued in Gerson's attempted reduction of
Mysticism to an exact science, in which all mystical
experiences are carefully tabulated and classified.   In such
an atmosphere Mysticism was inevitably asphyxiated.
In the consequent reaction, orthodox mysticism, after
Gerson, took refuge in devotion without troubling itself
much about its logical basis.   Mysticism became a mode
of piety and life, a substitute for reasoning rather than a
form of the schools.

[1] Inge, *op. cit.* i. p. 43.

Of the scholastic mystics—leaving out Bernard, who was scarcely a schoolman—the chief were Hugo and Richard of St. Victor, Bonaventura, Albert the Great, and Gerson. Of these Hugo of St. Victor (†1141) is the most important, if only because of his development of the sharp opposition between the natural and the supernatural. In the scholastic mystics, as we might expect from the influence of Aristotle, with whom God is the transcendent One beyond the All, the method of reaching Him is either the *via negativa*, the rising above all the marks which give definition and reality to our world of experience, or else it is a supernatural communication from the transcendent which we gain by esctasy. Of this ' negative way,' so beloved by medieval orthodoxy, the language is always that of the cloister. Thus in the *De adhaerendo Deo* of Albert the Great (1193-1280), and in Bonaventura (1221-1274), all the emphasis is on the nakedness and passivity of soul which is necessary if we would enter into the ' Divine Darkness.' Only by the ' darkness of the mind,' *i.e.* a mind in which ' the doors of the senses are kept barred and bolted aganist all phantasms and images,' ' as if the soul were already separated from the body,' can the soul arise to the vision of God and ' view the world from afar off.' In this respect the language of these orthodox mystics does not differ from that of Tauler or Ruysbroek. But in Bonaventura we find a departure from the Dionysian tradition in the teaching that God is both immanent and transcendent.

III

Of the mystics in whom we find independence of the scholastic tradition, the greatest is Meister Heinrich Eckhart, ' from whom,' as one of his pupils proudly proclaims, ' God kept nothing hid.' Eckhart was born, probably, at Hockheim in Thuringia, shortly before 1260. In his fifteenth year he entered the Dominican convent of

Erfurt, and thence passed to Cologne, where Albert the Great's teaching, with its emphasis on scholastic or orthodox mysticism, was still reverenced, though slowly giving place to that of his greater pupil, Thomas Aquinas. In addition to Albert and Aquinas, and, of course, Dionysius, Eckhart seems to have known Erigena and, possibly, Averroes also. Eckhart's election as prior of Erfurt was followed by a course of study at Paris (about 1302), which he finally left in 1312 for Strassburg, at that time the foremost religious centre in Germany. About 1320 he returned to Cologne, where he preached, with astonishing results, Mysticism in German to the common people, and in Latin to the theologians. For some time he seems to have been sheltered from attack by his eminently practical and saintly life. In the year before he died (1327) complaint of heterodoxy was for the first time brought against him, the chief charge being that he had maintained ' that there is something uncreated in the soul.' In answer to his appeal to Rome, Eckhart was condemned two years after his death : ' He had wished to know more than he should.' Seventeen propositions were classed as ' heretical,' and eleven as having an ' ill-sound,' and ' very rash.' While Rome thus condemned, Henry Suso had a vision of the ' blessed master, in exceeding glory, his soul quite transformed and deified in God.'

In comparing the Mysticism of Eckhart with that of his predecessors from Dionysius downwards, and of the scholastics down to Gerson, we find an obvious change in the disappearance of the long ladders of ascent, the graduated scales of virtues, faculties, and states of mind, which fill so large a place in those systems. These lists are the natural product of the imagination when it plays upon the theory of *emanation*. But with Eckhart the fundamental truth is the *immanence* of God Himself, not in the faculties, but in the ground of the soul.[1]

[1] Inge, *Christian Mysticism*, p. 162.

In the teaching of Eckhart we find constant insistence upon ' the Divine Spirit ' within the soul whereby we may rise into union with the Godhead in an ' Eternal Now,' and become ' transformed totally into God, even as in the sacrament the bread is converted into the body of Christ.' It is, however, of importance that we should remember that Eckhart always distinguishes between ' God ' and the ' Godhead.' Behind ' God,' *i.e.* ' natured Nature,' or the Divine revealed in Personal Form, there is the Godhead who is the Revealer or ' non-natured Nature,' *i.e.* unoriginated Reality, the ' Ground ' of the revelation, just as behind the *me* and its conscious processes of thought there is a deeper *ego* which is ever unknown, but none the less real. This Godhead or Ground ever transcends knowledge, and therefore is a ' nameless,' ' naked ' ' Nothing,' for nothing can ever be predicated of ' the impenetrable Darkness of the eternal Godhead.' Such Ground is an ' Eternal Now,' the self-consciousness of which is the differentiation within Himself of subject and object, *i.e.* of Father and Son. This self-consciousness is not temporal, but eternal ; the Son, therefore, is eternally begotten. ' God ' or the revelation of the ' Godhead ' must therefore of necessity be the Father and the Son. The Trinity—for the Holy Spirit is regarded as the personalisation of this bond of love—is thus the eternal process of the Divine Self-consciousness, and no mere emanation or appearance of the Absolute.

" The reader who finds himself somewhat dazed in this height of speculation would run up into the same difficulty himself if he should undertake strenuously to think out what is involved in the word *Infinite*, which he, without giving it much thought, applies to God. Few of us, like Eckhart, have either the desire or the intellectual power to think our thoughts through to the bottom." [1] We may take, as an instance of " thinking our thoughts through to the bottom," the origin of our belief in the eternal genera-

[1] R. Jones, *Mystical Religion*, p. 226.

tion of the Son, one of the phrases found in all theological text-books. In its ultimate philosophic analysis this is but the logical consequence of saying that God is Love. But love must have some object, and if the Love is eternal the object must be eternal. Nor can that object be outside the ' Godhead,' for, as Eckhart would have phrased it, that would involve that ' something ' could be eternally predicated of the ' nameless Nothing.' The ' other,' whose existence is essential if the Godhead is conscious Love, must therefore be within the Deity.

Eckhart, following the Neoplatonists, regards creation as an eternal process also, the self-consciousness of God beholding within Himself the Ideas of the universe, the projection of which into space and time becomes the world of creatures. Creation is thus the eternal thought of ' God,' *i.e.* of ' natured Nature,' just as the Son is the expression of the Eternal Love of the Godhead or ' unnatured Nature.' Of such creation the only reality consists in the Divine Ideas, which necessarily exist in an ' eternal Now.'

The Neoplatonists were fond of making a distinction between the higher and lower self, of which the former was untainted by the sins of the latter. In Eckhart the distinction is drawn with great sharpness. Just as in God there is a Ground or Essence, so also in man ' there is something which is above the soul, divine, simple, nameless rather than named.' This ' something ' Eckhart calls ' the Spark,' ' the Ground of the Soul,' or ' the Soul's Eye.' The soul deals with phenomena in time, it gives us the empirical self—our phraseology is modern, but would seem to express Eckhart's meaning. The ego or ground is the super-temporal presupposition of experience, and can escape beyond the particular and finite, and dwell in ' the ever-present Now.' [1] In such escape lies ' the blessed-

[1] The non-philosophic reader may find this easier to understand if he compares the current conception of Conscience as something distinct from, and independent of, the empirical moral contents of his life.

ness of the poor in spirit,' when the soul has withdrawn from all sense experience, and 'wills nothing, knows nothing, desires nothing.' Whether this Ground or Spark of the soul is in God, the point in common between the soul and the Divine Ground, or whether it is, as Aquinas had taught, a created faculty, supplementary to the other faculties, and transcending reason, Eckhart is not always decided. In his earlier days he taught the latter, in his later the former doctrine. A similar indecision is seen in another matter. If in one place he teaches that ' the eye with which I see God is the same eye with which He sees me,' elsewhere he maintains the separate individuality of the human and Divine Grounds. The soul is a mirror which when placed in the sunlight sends back a reflection ; only in this sense are ' sun and reflection the same thing.' But whatever the nature of the ' Ground,' it is by rising into this ' Ground ' that the soul becomes one with the Godhead in an Eternal Now. As a rule, Eckhart's language in describing this union becomes little less than pantheistic. ' Where I am,' he tells us, ' there God is ; and where God is, there am I.' Nevertheless, it may be urged that he just saves himself, more by his balanced Christian instinct than by his logic. He insists that however much the soul ' may sink and sink in the eternity of the Divine essence,' yet it never loses its identity. Personality, in fact, belongs to the very nature of the soul ; for Eckhart it is the eternal ground-form of all true being.

Eckhart does not find it easy to fit into his scheme the historical Atonement. With Eckhart, as with most mystics, the Incarnation, rather than the Cross, is the central fact of Christianity. Christ is the Ideal Man, in whom all men have their unity and reality, inasmuch as in the ' Ground ' of this ideal they rise to their own ' Ground.' The Incarnation, or self-revelation of God, was thus a real necessity, and would have been even if Adam had never sinned. This view of the Incarnation, which fits in so well with the modern teleological view of the universe and the familiar idea of the ascent of man, was a favourite with medieval writers of many different schools. It would appear to be first found in Rupert of Deutz (†1135).[1]

In his doctrine of sin Eckhart makes everything turn on the will. In this, perhaps, we may detect the influence of Duns Scotus, whom he may have met at Cologne. In his view sin is self-will. Love itself ' resides in the will ; the more will, the more love.' But he does not reconcile his doctrine with his belief that it is the nature of all phenomenal things to return to God, from whom they proceeded. The effect of his teaching is often the identification of perfection with ἀπάθεια, and this in spite of his strong insistence upon the value of the life of service—' better to feed the hungry than to see the visions of St. Paul.' But such insistence was rather due to his heart than his logic, for, since the right will is everything—' if your will is right, you cannot go wrong '—Eckhart, in opposition to all medieval thought, necessarily attaches no value to good works.

IV

The influence of Eckhart was not exhausted with his life. A succession of German mystics carried on his teaching. If on the speculative side they added nothing of value to ' the Master,' the spiritual beauty of their lives, their constant pursuit ' of the eternal, uncreated truth,' and the intense earnestness with which they emphasised the fact of experience, and the necessity of spiritual communion with God, give to these mystics of the Rhine an important place in Christian thought. It is because of the want of this personal experience that in a well-known incident (1346), in the *Book of the Master*, the ' Friend of God from the Oberland ' is reported as rebuking ' a great doctor, a master

---

[1] On this doctrine see Westcott, *Gospel of Creation*, in his *Ep. John.* Cf Ottley, *op. cit.* ii. p. 202 ff.

of the Holy Scripture,' who, on somewhat slender historical grounds, has been identified with Tauler. The primary teaching of all those writers may be expressed in the words of John Ruysbroek (1293-1381) : ' The soul finds God in its own depths.' In the history of their inner lives we mark the revolt of the individual, especially of the layman—this point is of great importance—against a Church life which tended to his suppression. Their Mysticism has for the reader much the same interest as St. Augustine's *Confessions.* He finds himself transplanted, especially in the *Theologia Germanica* and in the *Imitatio Christi,* into the inner sanctuary of the soul. A study of their writings belongs rather to the history of Christian piety than to that of Christian thought. Their story is conditioned so much by struggle and suffering as to belong more to the psychology than the philosophy of Mysticism. There are, however, a few matters in connection with these mystics that demand attention.

In the first place, these mystics, whether under the name of Friends of God, Beghards, Beguins, or Brethren of the Common Life, were all part of the same general revolt against a materialised church as produced Wyclif and Hus. But where Wyclif was active, they were passive. With political and ecclesiastical movements they had no concern. Nor were they anxious to reconstruct either the Church or its theology. But on the side of spiritual life and experience theirs was a silent, unorganised protest against an age of which the chief event for the Church was the disgraceful " Babylonish captivity " of the papacy at Avignon (1309-1377). The student, anxious to understand the contrast, cannot do better than take up any treatise of Wyclif, whether in English or Latin, and compare it with Rulman Merswin's remarkable literary creation of ' the Friend of God from the Oberland,' that strange being whose mythical existence has misled centuries, but who was really " the ' Christian ' of a fourteenth-century Pilgrim's Progress,

illustrating how God does His work for the world and for
the Church through a divinely trained and spiritually
illuminated layman." [1]

We have referred to the psychological or psychic rather
than the philosophical character of their Mysticism. We
see this, in one direction, in their excessive expectation of
ecstasy or supernatural incorporation, and their extreme
asceticism—Suso gives us a dreadful picture of his self-
scourgings—in all ages the fruitful cause of such halluci-
nations. We see it also in the apocalyptic strain of their
utterances, though in this they were at one with the contemporary canonised prophetesses, St. Bridget, St. Hilde-
gard, and St. Elizabeth of Schoenau. It is also apparent
in their writings. The *Book of the Nine Rocks* (1351), the
chief work of the Friends of God, is in reality a series of
visions. Apart from ecstasy, personal life is made the
constant subject of observation and delineatiou. Merswin
(†1382) and his friend Nicholas von Löwen have left us
some twenty treatises, the historical elements in which, if
real at all, are altogether secondary to their value as
' tendency-literature,' or the analysis of the ideals and
inspirations of the Friends of God. Henry Suso (b. 1285)
of Swabia, with extraordinary minuteness and much literary skill, in a remarkable autobiography exposes to us his
inmost soul, as he unfolds his struggles ' to divest himself of himself, pass into God, and become wholly one with
Him, as a drop of water mingled with a cask of wine.'
The psychological character of this human document is
heightened by being written throughout in the third person,
as if Suso had attained his heart's desire and stood apart
from himself.

As with mystics of all ages, so with these medieval
Germans ; they especially served the Church by the emphasis they laid upon the doctrine of the Holy Spirit, and
that at a time when His work and place were almost totally

[1] R. Jones, *op. cit.* p. 251.

ignored. In their insistence upon the reality of present
inspiration for all who receive ' the luminous grace of the
Holy Spirit,' and have entered into His ' upper school,'
they remind us of George Fox and the later Friends.   ' The
Holy Spirit,' says ' the Friend of God from the Oberland '
in the *Book of the Master*, ' has the same power to-day as
ever.'   In the *Book of the Nine Rocks* this becomes the
claim that ' God can still write a book ' ; the Bible is not
the exhaustion of His thoughts.   In publishing his wonderful autobiography, Suso believed that the Divine Wisdom
was making use of his pen.   Says Thomas à Kempis :
' Some place their religion in books, some in images, some
in the pomp and splendour of external worship.   But some,
with illuminated understandings, hear what the Holy
Spirit speaketh in their hearts.'   The practical bearing
of the doctrine is best seen in the oft-quoted passage in
which Tauler claims this gift as the basis of a consecrated
life : ' One man can spin, another can make shoes, and all
these are gifts of the Holy Spirit.   I tell you if I were not
a priest I should esteem it a great gift that I was able to
make shoes, and I would try to make them so well as to be
a pattern to all.'

Of the Friends of God the best known is John Tauler of
Strassburg (1300-1361).   He was the preacher of the movement, and the great theme of his sermons is the need of the
inner light and of the indwelling of God in the soul.   In
most points his doctrine is the same as Eckhart's, but " his
sense of sin is too deep for him to be satisfied with the Neoplatonic doctrine of its negativity " ; [1] nor does he look
upon creation as necessary to the nature of God, though he
owns that the ' ideas ' of the world exist in the Son ' from
all eternity.'   In the *Theologia Germanica* " a golden little
treatise," the influence of which upon Luther was so profound, we find a constant cry against self-will : ' Put off
thy own will and there will be no hell.   If there were any

[1] Inge, *Christian Mysticism*. p. 181.

person in hell who should get quit of his self-will and call nothing his own, he would come out of hell into heaven.' The result of such loss of self-will will be the fulfilment of the author's great prayer : 'I would fain be to the Eternal Goodness what His own hand is to a man.' In one matter the *Theologia Germanica* breaks away from the traditional standpoint, especially from the hard legalism of Anselm. In his doctrine of the Atonement he dwells upon the anguish of God because of sin, in a manner that reminds us of much modern thought. Sin is so hateful to God that He would willingly suffer agony and death to purge away one man's sin. Wherever there is grief for sin there we find the presence of God. For the accusation sometimes brought against the *Theologia Germanica* of pantheism there seems little justification.[1] The 'dreaming oneself into God' is one of the extravagances of the 'false light' against which he warns his readers.

In the fifteenth century Mysticism passed into common life. But it was no longer the Mysticism of Dionysius and Erigena, or of the Schoolmen, or even of Eckhart and Tauler. It was a mysticism which abandoned speculation for practice. Its keynote was the positive 'imitation' of Christ, and the reality of inward religion. In Catherine of Siena, Walter Hilton, and the nun Juliana of Norwich ; in the great mystical brotherhood of Holland, the Brethren of the Common Life, with Gerard Groote (b. 1340), the Wesley of the fourteenth century, at their head, we mark the rise of this new Mysticism in every country in Europe. The outcome of the whole movement on its intellectual side is seen in the most influential mystic writing the world has ever known, the *Imitation of Christ*.

The life of Thomas Haemerlein of Kempen covers nearly a century, but it is characteristic that his work belongs to no age, and scarcely reflects at all the long days through which he lived. After resuming his education at the

[1] See Inge, *op. cit.* p. 184, also p. 365,

schools of the Brethren of the Common Life at Deventer, Thomas entered in 1400 the community at Mount St. Agnes, and there in 1471 he died. But in this " silent, motionless centre of a whirling and incomprehensible world," [1] neither sound of trumpet nor voice of words disturbed those whose only thought was of Christ and of His imitation. There, somewhere between 1400 and 1425, Thomas wrote his book. " It was written down by a hand that waited for the heart's prompting ; it is the chronicle of a solitary, hidden anguish, struggle, trust, and triumph—not written on velvet cushions to teach endurance to those who are treading with bleeding feet on the stones. And so it remains to all time a lasting record of human needs and human consolations, the voice of a brother : who, ages ago, felt and suffered and renounced." [2]

From the standpoint of Christian thought the value or Thomas's work is twofold. Historically it is the last, as it is the best, expression and defence of the ideals of a monastic world ; it is the swan-like song of a system whose effective work in the world was in reality finished, and whose days, therefore, were numbered. Of more importance is it to note its abandonment of the mere negative side of self-renunciation. The negative side, it is true, is there ; for that matter, there can be no spiritual life where it is not found. At times also this negative side appears in a mischievous form, illustrations of which will readily occur to every reader of the *Imitation*. But in the very title of the work we find a protest against negation. The insistence on the negative road had so often ended with medieval mystics in the futile quest of the Absolute, ' the Divine Darkness,' and the like. For this dangerous tendency Thomas substitutes the imitation of Christ ; in place of the ' immeasurable ' he holds before us, imperfectly perhaps, but with marvellous power, the measure of the stature of Christ. Hence the

[1] de Montmorency, *Thomas à Kempis* p. 89.
[2] George Eliot, *Mill on the Floss*, book IV. chap. iii.

core of the message of Thomas is that no mere abandonment, self-mortification, self-crucifixion, without a holy passion of love can bring us to our goal. 'Without contending,' he tells us, 'there can be no conquest.' Such a belief is fatal to all quietism, its logical issue is the advice of Thomas : ' Never be idle or vacant. Be always reading or writing or praying or meditating or employed in some useful labour for the common good.'

The effect of this positive side of Thomas is seen in his disciple, John Wesel Gansfoort (1419-1481), who worked unceasingly for the spiritual reformation of the Church. But with John Wesel we begin the Reformation. ' If I had read Wesel sooner,' said Luther, ' my adversaries would have said that I had borrowed my whole doctrine from him. Our minds are so consonant.' Unfortunately Luther, in spite of the mysticism that underlies his cardinal doctrine of justification by faith, never really understood the mystics. Owing to this and other causes, the work which the speculative mystics performed for medieval thought has since the Reformation been taken over by philosophy, though, alas ! without the association with religion invariable in the Middle Ages.

CHAPTER IX

THE SCHOOLMEN

Argument

I

THE student would do well to understand the new forces
in life and thought which differentiate the early from the
later Schoolmen. In the main they were three in number :
the rise of the secular universities as the centres of learning
and thought, in place of the monasteries or cathedral
schools ; the coming of the friars ; and the adoption by
the Church of Aristotle as her pilot in the search for truth.
Judged by permanent effect, the greatest of these three
was the growth of the new universities. But for our
present purpose this was secondary in importance to the
influence of the ' new logic.' For the new universities,
though destined to become the homes of culture and science,
were at first completely dominated by the prevailing passion
for dialectics. The few who, like Roger Bacon, pleaded for
a larger outlook were ' unheard, forgotten, buried '—to
quote Bacon's own sad verdict on his life.

The later Scholasticism was powerfully assisted by the
revival of religion in the thirteenth century, under the
lead of Francis of Assisi (†1226) and Dominic (†1221). On
the side of practical piety the coming of the friars was,
perhaps, the greatest popular movement recorded in history.
But the influence of the revival upon religious thought
should not be overlooked. Francis himself had dreaded
the effects of learning. He was not willing even that the
friars should become men of one book ; his ideal rather
was men of one life. ' When you have a psalter,' he
said to one of the novices, ' you will want a breviary,
and when you have a breviary you will seat yourself in a
pulpit like a great prelate.' Then taking up some ashes,

Francis scattered them over the head of the novice, saying :
' There is your breviary, there is your breviary.' Francis
was right in so far as he saw that logic and canon law
monopolised the thought of the secular clergy. But Francis
failed to see that, by laying the foundations of life in
love, knowledge would become a true handmaid to work.
Nevertheless, to Francis Europe owes, indirectly, the rise
of science. He taught men, though he knew it not, to
turn from verbal quibblings to the study of nature; for
instance, the care of the friars for men's bodies soon developed the physical studies for which the Order became
celebrated. But, owing to the dominance of dialectics,
the return to nature found its chief field in the rise of a
new art, under the lead of Giotto, Fra Angelico, and other
Italians. From art the transition was easily made in
Italy to the rediscovery of the humanities and the commencement of the Renaissance. Once more Hellas claimed
her own.

Within a few years of the death of St. Francis the friars
became the intellectual leaders of Europe. They learned
the great truth repeated in every revival, that no Church
can be built upon mere experience, or by descending to
the social condition of the outcast. They set out to win
the towns for Christ; they found the towns in a ferment
of unbelief. To maintain a hold they must enter into the
intellectual as well as the moral difficulties of their flocks.
The Dominicans perceived this from the first, and eagerly
sought out the centres of learning. Their headquarters
were at Paris and Bologna; in England their first convent
was at Oxford. The Franciscans were not slow to follow.
Their first English provincial ' built a school in the fratry
of Oxford and persuaded Master Robert Grosseteste, of holy
memory, to read lectures there to the brethren.' The six
great doctors of later Scholasticism all belonged to the
Mendicants. Alexander of Hales, Albert the Great, and
Thomas Aquinas were followers of Dominic; Bonaventura,

Duns Scotus, and William of Ockham, of Francis. To
these we must add Adam Marsh, Raymond Lull, Roger
Bacon, and a long list of distinguished names.

The effect upon thought of the great revival was many-
sided. It infused new energy into every form of life,
religious, ecclesiastical, political, and heretical. In the
schools the movement happened to coincide with the discovery of Aristotle. From the first the friars, especially
the Dominicans, flung themselves into the adaptation of
the Greek philosopher to the needs of orthodoxy. Not
less important was the part that two Dominicans, Eckhart
and Tauler, played in the setting forth of the philosophic
grounds of Mysticism. On the ecclesiastical-political side
we have in William of Ockham and Michael of Cesena two
of the leaders of revolt. They were Franciscans, for it
was ever among the Brothers Minor that we find an intellectual and moral ferment that drove them either into
new dogmas of orthodoxy, or into the most daring heresies
of religion and philosophy.

In the Eastern Church the great struggle of the fourth
and fifth centuries had raged over the definitions of the
nature of Christ. It is equally characteristic of the Western
world that in the thirteenth and fourteenth centuries there
should be passionate controversy concerning the meaning
and obligations of ' poverty,' the extent to which the
' poverty ' of Jesus and the apostles was absolute, and
so forth. The controversy, though in its developments
associated with the Franciscans, by no means began with
them. The dispute was " in the air " ; it formed the
motive of the movements before St. Francis associated
with Waldo, the Poor Men of Lyons, and the Catholic Poor
of Durand of Huesca ; it was part of the general revolt
against a Church which had forgotten the precepts of its
Founder. Far be it from us to enter into the dreary conflicts of the Spiritual Franciscans. The quarrels between
the ' Zealots ' and ' Moderates ' have long since burnt them-

selves out into ashes which we would not lightly disturb.
Suffice that we note the part played by the Spiritual
Franciscans in the revival of apocalyptic prophecy. For
in their indignation against the attempts of Rome to whittle
away the obligation of absolute poverty, the Spiritual
Franciscans began to circulate writings ascribed to Joachim
di Fiori (1145-1202). In these Rome was described as the
great whore and the barren fig-tree; the Empire as the instrument of God which should overthrow a corrupt Church.
Joachim had prophesied that in 1260 the dominion of
the Holy Ghost, the third age of the Church, would suc-
ceed the exhausted dispensations of the Father and the
Son. A terrible persecution would separate the wheat
from the chaff, and the elect would enter into peace, with
the incoming of the reign of love or ' age of lilies.'

For sixty years these speculations of Joachim had been
prized by the Church. Popes and theologians had failed
to discern their dangerous tendencies. But in 1254 the
' Spirituals '—who had, in fact, appropriated this name
to themselves from Joachim's prophecy—forced them
into fatal prominence by their publication at Paris of the
famous treatise, *The Introduction to the Eternal Gospel*, the
work of the learned enthusiast Gherardo da Borgo San
Donnino. This book, now lost, met among all classes with
unbounded success; yet nothing more revolutionary of
the whole order of the Church had ever been penned.
Gherardo sweeps away the whole sacerdotal system; love
would replace all the sacraments of the Church; contemplation take the place of active life.

The great part played by these apocalyptic visions and
ideals in the thought of the fourteenth and fifteenth centuries has hardly been sufficiently appreciated as yet by
scholars, possibly because they have kept too much to the
highways of thought instead of diverging into its by-paths.
Many of the Lollard writings, some of the works attributed
to Wyclif, many of those attributed to Hus, are saturated

with these ideas. By diverse subterranean channels we
find the prophetic spirit influencing life far and wide, ever
and anon rising to the surface in open revolt or dangerous
heresy.

We should do well to note that when the Spiritual Franciscans launched on Europe the question of the ' poverty of
Christ,' the thoughtful realised that beneath this academic
issue there were involved two principles of importance.
The first struck at the worldliness of the representatives of
the apostles, and at the existence of vast Church endow-
ments. As a political issue we see how large a part this
played in the life and writings of Wyclif, and even of some
who would have had little sympathy with his advanced
ideas. The second was a direct challenge to the papal
claim to be the dictator of right and wrong, with powers of
binding and loosing at will, and of dispensing from the
obligations of vow or rule. The leaders in this crusade
were Michael of Cesena and William of Ockham. In his
Contra Errores Papae Michael denounced the utterances of
Pope John XXII. as heresies, and appealed ' to the universal
Church and to a General Council which in faith and morals
is superior to the pope. For a pope can err in faith and
morals, as many human popes have fallen from the faith.
But the universal Church cannot err, and a council re-
presenting the universal Church is also free from error.'
In a flood of scholastic subtleties William of Ockham
pursued the same theme to further conclusions. The pope
may err, a general council may err, the doctors of the
Church may err ; only Holy Scripture and the beliefs of the
Church are of universal validity, and with these to guide
him the meanest peasant may know the truth. The drift
of such arguments needs no explanation. The thoughtful
realised that Europe had awakened to the criticism of an
institution whose claims had been accepted for generations
as divine. Henceforth the more conservative looked for
reformation to a general council, the upshot of which was

Constance; the more revolutionary to the working out of the plans of Marsiglio and Ockham. In the next generation the work of these two was taken up by an even greater iconoclast. In many respects John Wyclif (†1384) sums up in himself the movements and forces, many of them contradictory, which in the previous century had gathered for the overthrow of their common foe.

We have referred to Marsiglio of Padua, one of the most interesting if impracticable of medieval thinkers. In 1324, with the help of his friend, John of Jandun—' the two beasts,' as the Pope called them, ' from the abyss of Satan ' —he wrote his great work, *Defensor Pacis*, the most original political treatise of the Middle Ages. In the second book of this work Marsiglio examines the nature of the priesthood and its relation to the State. He begins by defining the Church as the entire body of Christian men. The sole business of the priest is to preach the faith and administer the sacraments. To this duty his rights and claims should be limited. Excommunication, for instance, can only be decreed by the congregation to which the believer belongs ; while the clergy, in all but their strictly spiritual functions, must be treated exactly the same as all other members of the civil society, save only that their crimes should be punished with greater strictness, because they cannot plead the same excuse of ignorance. Marsiglio follows Jerome in maintaining that bishop and priest are convertible terms. More original is his claim that heresy must be unpunished except in so far as it may prove dangerous to society. Even in this case the penalty should only be inflicted by the civil courts. Errors of opinion, ' howsoever great they may be,' must on no account be punished.' Of these Jesus alone is the judge in the world to come.

Marsiglio reduced Church government to a question of expediency. Though in theory all priests are equal, the papacy, he held, is convenient as a symbol of the unity of the Church, and as providing a needed president for its councils. None the less, Marsiglio sweeps aside all the fictions, ancient and modern, of papal historians. He even doubts whether Peter was ever bishop of Rome at all; he disbelieves in his superiority over the other apostles, and questions his power to hand on his gift to his successors. The *Decretals* he brushes aside as not necessary to salvation. With rare historical insight Marsiglio traces the origin of the papacy to the influence of the Roman Empire, and to the donation of Constantine, the genuineness of which he does not dispute. The power of the keys, he holds, is but of limited extent. The keys open and close the door of forgiveness, but the turnkey is not the judge. Without the penitence of the sinner priestly absolution is of no avail, for it is God alone who cleanses the man inwardly. The argument of the "two swords" he sweeps aside by the text, "My kingdom is not of this world." Thus the papacy can have no temporal sovereignty or jurisdiction— 'what have priests to do with meddling of secular coactive judgments?' With Marsiglio the State is absolutely supreme; 'neither bishop nor pope have any co-active jurisdiction in this world, neither upon any priest, neither upon any other person being no priest, unless such jurisdiction be granted to them by the human power, in whose power it is always to remove and call again the same authority from them for any reasonable cause.' Ecclesiastics, even the Pope himself, must be subject to the tribunals of the State; their number is limited by its pleasure. To the State also belongs all patronage, which should, as a rule, be exercised by the free election of the parish itself. With the parish also should rest the power of dismissal. Ecclesiastical property must be vested in the State, which can at any time secularise superfluities to other uses.

Perhaps the most fruitful of Marsiglio's contentions was his defence of a general council, formed of clergy and laity alike, as the supreme power in the Church. Such a council

would voice the Church Universal, and be a parliament of
the nations, both in matters temporal and spiritual. The
Catholic creed is determined by its interpretations, though
these must in all cases be based on Scripture alone, for the
Bible is the foundation of faith and of the authority of
the Church. To the decisions of the council the Pope
would of necessity be subject, and it alone could pronounce
excommunication upon peoples and their rulers.

Of necessity Marsiglio was before his age. The Church
preferred to listen to such champions of papal infallibility
as Augustine Triompho and Alvaro Pelayo. But no seer
had a clearer vision of the new order towards which the
world was moving ; no prophet ever glanced deeper into
the future. The works of Marsiglio give us in clear outline the ideals which now regulate the progress of Europe.
In his emphasis of Scripture we have the voice of Luther ;
in his call to the laity he foreshadowed Wesley ; in his
view as to the rights of separate congregations he was
the forerunner of the Independents. But " in the clear
definition of the limits of ecclesiastical authority, and
in his assertion of the dignity of the individual believer,
Marsiglio's ideas still remain unrealised." In these speculations he remains alone among medieval writers so far
above his age in the breadth of his outlook " that the
truths which he brought to light had to be rediscovered,
without even the knowledge that he had found them
out beforehand, by the political philosophers of modern
times." [1]

Before we pass away from the dreamers and seers of the
thirteenth century a word should be added with reference
to a revolutionist of another kind, though the seed that he
sowed was not destined to bring forth immediate fruit : we
refer to Roger Bacon (d. 1292 ?). Bacon's influence was
twofold. As a man of science his achievements have,
perhaps, been exaggerated ; certainly his antagonism to

[1] Poole, *Illustrations of Medieval Thought*, p. 277.

speculative thought. But it is impossible to exaggerate the zeal with which this martyr of science pursued his way amid difficulties that would have baffled or crushed others. Both in science and philosophy his principle was one, that truth cannot be attained by syllogisms built up on *a priori* premises, to the neglect of experiment and observation. He did not despise authority, but the authority, if we may so put it, must not rest, like the world in the Hindoo cosmogony, on the back of a tortoise. The effort he made to obtain texts of Aristotle and Seneca shows the value he attached to those great writers ; it shows also his anxiety to get behind the *ipse dixit* of Schoolmen to the actual thoughts of their authorities. We see the same spirit in his insistence that the study of Greek was the key to the real meaning of Aristotle. With equal daring he carried this principle into theology. He insisted that a knowledge of the Bible in the original was the one foundation upon which the Queen of Sciences could rest. As a Schoolman, Bacon was the predecessor of Scotus and Ockham. Though he founded no school he powerfully assisted the revolt, whose head-centre was in Oxford, against Aquinas and the great Dominican doctors.

II

The great object of the later Schoolmen was the adjustment of the theology of the Church—a determined quantity assumed to be absolutely true—to human consciousness, no longer, as Anselm, by *a priori* speculations, or, as the mystics, by ' contemplation,' but by a scientific, logical system (' *summa* ') in which all the forces of the mind should do homage to the Church. For centuries she had been slowly departing from the most valuable doctrines of Augustine, while his philosophy could contribute nothing to the scholastic disputes. A change was necessary. With her customary intuition the Latin Church discerned in

Aristotle the instrument she now needed. She felt that, if reason and authority are to be made one, there must be a pope in philosophy as well as in theology. Of the monastic principles on the basis of which Hildebrand had reorganised the Church, " poverty " was played out or troublesome, but " obedience " still remained, and had become almost synonymous with religion, vital for theology.

For this end Rome went contrary to her former judgments. In 1210 the use of Aristotle had been officially condemned by the synod of Paris. In 1228 Gregory ix. warned the masters regent of theology in Paris against mundane science, and the adulteration of the word of God with the figments of the philosophers. ' Theologians,' he said, ' ought to expound theology according to the approved traditions of the saints,' and refuse the aid of ' carnal weapons.' But the current was too strong even for Gregory ix. The condemnation, renewed in 1231, against students using the Aristotelian natural philosophy was coupled with the significant addition, ' until it shall have been examined and purged from all suspicion of error.' A commission of three was appointed by Gregory for this purpose. They were bidden to cut out ' doctrines either erroneous or productive of scandal or error,' so that ' with the removal of the suspicious matters the rest might be studied harmlessly.' The commission was not long in bringing in its report, the result of which was the setting aside of the restriction, and the issue of a decree for the absolution of the masters and students who had been reading the condemned books. Rome could not do otherwise ; for Aristotle, his physical works included, had become the text-book of the Church, his authority final in almost every branch of knowledge. On 19th March 1255 the books of the ' new logic ' were formally adopted by Paris as the text-books of the university. Oxford, the second university of Europe, followed suit in 1267 ; the new universities, as they were established, copied the example. Kings and

potentates may boast of their conquests, but Aristotle
from his tomb ruled for centuries over the intellect of
almost universal man, Christian and Muslim alike. Even
to-day " the legend " of his dialectics " though worn is not
effaced from the current coin of our philosophy and our
theology." [1]

There is nothing in the history of thought more remarkable than the rapidity with which in the thirteenth century
Aristotle captured the Church. One illustration must
suffice. The name of Aristotle, it would appear, only
occurs in one incidental reference in the great medieval
text-book of theology, Peter Lombard's *Sentences*. A
century later the name of the Stagirite is more familiar
than that of St. Augustine. At the beginning of the
thirteenth century the whole of Aristotle's works, previously
only known in fragments, and held secondary to Plato, were
gradually making their way into the Western world, in
part through the orthodox channel of the translation of
the *Organon* made about 1128 by James of Venice, in part
through intercourse with the Moors in Spain, in part
through the Crusades, especially through the Latin conquest of Constantinople (1204). Of these channels the
most important was the Arabian. In the middle of the
twelfth century portions of Aristotle were translated into
Latin from the Arabic commentaries of Avicenna by a
band of workers in the employ of Archbishop Raymund
of Seville. Shortly before 1230 the physical books of
Aristotle, translated from the Arabic of Averroes in part
by the famous Michael Scot of Toledo, made their appearance in Northern Europe. But the Aristotle thus translated was overlaid with Averroistic glosses. With the
new rendering from the Greek made in 1273 by the Dominican friar William of Brabant, the Arabic glosses ceased
to be so prominent. The need of a new translation will
be evident, if it be true that, as Renan tells us, some of

[1] Hampden, *Scholastic Philosophy*, p. 76.

the current translations were really "Latin translations from a Hebrew translation of a commentary of Averroes made on an Arabic translation of a Syriac translation of a Greek text."[1]

The new Aristotle, especially in his Eastern dress, was at first regarded by the Church with suspicion and dread. His introduction led to an outburst of scepticism ; his Arab interpreters threatened to sweep men away from their moorings into vasty deeps of pantheism. The anti-Christian elements in Aristotle, or rather in Averroes, were emphasised to the full. In 1210, for instance, David of Dinant was condemned at Paris for teaching that ' God, intelligence, and matter are a single thing, one and the same.' The intellects of men seemed intoxicated with the new powers which the method of Aristotle had revealed. Reality became secondary to syllogistic smartness. We read of a certain Parisian master, Simon of Tournai, who defended the doctrine of the Trinity ' so eloquently, so lucidly, so catholicly ' that thunders of applause greeted his performance. At once he announced that he could demolish with equal plausibility the faith that he had that day maintained. Matthew of Paris tells us of the stroke of paralysis which punished his blasphemies, and how ' with difficulty the famous doctor relearned from his own child the *Credo* and *Paternoster*.' Nevertheless, in spite of all dangers Aristotle conquered. Until the Reformation his sway over the Church was almost undisputed.

As a result of this adoption of Aristotle by the Church, the great Arabic and Jewish commentators of the master were no longer treated as atheists and heretics. Their theories were examined, their arguments discussed, oftentimes with a strange sympathy. The celebrated Jewish theologian, Moses Maimonides (†1204), ascribed to Aristotle unconditioned authority in sublunary science ; and the influence of Maimonides on Aquinas was considerable.

[1] Renan, *Averroes*, p. 52.

At Paris in 1347 every Master of Arts was required to swear that he would teach no doctrine inconsistent ' with that of Aristotle, and his commentator Averroes.' Dante, the faithful exponent of Aquinas, even places Averroes and Avicenna in the circle of those who only needed baptism in order to be saved.

The influence of these two Arabs upon Christian thought forms one of the most astonishing chapters in the history of the Church. Of the two men Avicenna (a Latinised form of the Arabic Abu 'Ibn Sīnā) was the more purely Eastern. The greater part of his life (980-1036) was spent at the court of Bokhara, where his skill as a physician procured him great favour. He was one of the leaders in a ' school of philosophers '—al falāsifa, as the Arabs transliterated it—who made a special study of the Greek works introduced to the Arabs by Syrian Monophysites and Nestorians. Though not the founder of Arabic Scholasticism, he first gave it clear, systematic expression. His knowledge of Aristotle's logical works was sound, but of his other philosophical treatises more superficial. Averroes (a corruption of the Arabic name Abu 'Ibn Rashd) was born at Cordova, of which city his grandfather had been kadi, in 1126. He died at Marrakesh in 1198, a few years before the great battle of Las Navas de Tolosa (1212) broke for ever the dominion of the Moors in Spain. Many of his extensive and careful commentaries upon Aristotle, whom he regarded with the highest reverence, were translated into Latin and Hebrew, though it is by no means certain that these Latin translations give us a true idea of his doctrine. But, whether faulty or not, it is to these Latin translations that Averroes owes his influence upon Christian thought.

There was much in the philosophy of Averroes, as presented by his Latin interpreters, that naturally gave rise to suspicion. His doctrine has a strongly marked evolutionary character, in which the eternalness of matter, the evolution of the germ by its own latent power, the impersonality of intelligence, absolute determinism, and the reabsorption of the individual, constitute essential points. It is possible that on some points his views have been exaggerated and misrepresented by opponents. For instance Averroes, though claiming that the world is eternal, carefully distinguishes between an eternity without agent or cause, which can be ascribed to God alone, and the eternity with cause of a continuous and incessant creation. But while the student of the original philosophy of Averroes may see reasons for suspension of judgment, for the student of Christian thought the charges in the main are true. The Averroes known to the West was interpreted almost universally to hold these doctrines.

For Averroes, as indeed for the whole Arabic school, with its constant insistence that God is one, the great difficulty is to explain the origin of individuality. In his efforts to account for the individual he seems at times to claim that God is ignorant of His own creation. To the same cause we can trace his insistence that there is but one soul, or active reason, in the universe, as there is but one light, a conclusion that led to the accusation of his opponents that he denied immortality, or rather denied that the soul could remain individualised after the death of the body. This dogma of Averroes was the consequence of his interpretations of Aristotle's doctrine of the νοῦς ποιητικός, or Creative Reason immanent both in mind and in the external world, whereby it is possible for the mind to know things. Alexander of Aphrodisias (fl. 200 A.D.) explained this Creative Reason as no faculty or part of the soul itself, but something working from without upon the passive intellect (νοῦς παθητικός) ; thus identifying it with the Spirit of God working in us. As death was the cessation of the passive intellect, this involved the denial of immortality. From an Arabic translation of Alexander the idea had been taken up by Averroes.

In spite of the services of Averroes in the introduction of Aristotle to the West, it was impossible that his teaching should go unchallenged in the Church. Monopsychism, the belief that there is only one active intellect in the world, or naturalistic pantheism in any form are fatal to Christianity. The triumph of Averroes would have been the reintroduction of Gnosticism. But the excitement of the new ideas soon passed away ; the vigilance of the authorities repressed dangerous heresy. Above all, the Church itself developed a body of orthodox Aristotelian doctrine under the lead of its great scholastic doctors.

III

In her exaltation of Aristotle into the new dictator of reason the Latin Church not only went back on her own decisions, but cut herself off from the philosophic drift of the Early Church. To the early fathers Aristotle, with his dualistic outlook, with his insistence upon clear thinking as the one cure for all the evils of the individual or of society, seemed " a profane intruder, bringing the noisy jargon of the world into a sanctuary where every thought and feeling should be hushed in holy contemplation." [1] Aristotle, therefore, was neglected by all the orthodox, with the exception of the school of Antioch, until Augustine gave to the theology of the West that bent which, to some degree, it still retains. The thought of the Church —especially in the East, where the influence of Clement and Origen was supreme—had been moulded, broadly considered, on the idealism or monism of Plato, with a leaven of Stoic influence. Augustine too, considered philosophically, was a disciple of Plato, and that, too, in spite of the fact that the tendency of Plato was to modify, if not supersede, Christian dogma. But with the

[1] Hampden, *Scholastic Philosophy*, p. 62.

suppression by Justinian in 529 of Neoplatonism, the Aristotelian philosophy gained in authority. The Aristotle whom the East had neglected became in due course the great doctor of the Latin Church. At the same time, though for the theologian this is a minor matter, the Church inverted the position which Plato and Aristotle had held in the development of philosophy.

For this change from Plato to Aristotle there were other reasons than the accident of his new discovery. In every age the study of Plato has tended in a twofold direction. His doctrine of the immanence of God is the basis of all mysticism and of all pantheism, while his dreams of ideal beauty and perfection lead to dissatisfaction with things as they are. Aristotle, on the contrary, has been called " the high priest of common-sense." " Even in its classical form Aristotelianism is a morality without religion." [1] As a justification of this stern verdict we may instance the Aristotelian position that a complete provision of external goods is an indispensable condition of well-living. The last charge that could be brought against Aristotle is mysticism, for his " final appeal is always to man's natural reason." [2] The deeper sources of dispeace, of pain of soul, of unfulfilled wants of the heart, remain dark in his investigation. He is only interested in the life of the soul in so far as it turns outward to a great practical world. Thus while Plato points the way to a world where things correspond to the perfection of their original Divine Idea, the tendency of Aristotle, with his doctrine of the mean, is to concentrate thought on the exact definition of existing species and institutions.

This it was that commended him to the busy spirit of the Latin Churchmen. For the medieval Church was profoundly satisfied that her institution was part of the eternal order of the universe. She did not seek ideal

[1] Harnack, *H.D.* v. p. 109 *n.*
[2] Brewer, *Monumenta Franciscana*, i. p. liii.

reconstruction, but the reasoned defence of a set of dogmas
in the form in which they were already established.   For
the speculations of the East she cared nothing ; the centre
of her theology was not so much God as man, his state,
relations, and duties.   And in this theology of man the
central idea was the *Civitas Dei*, that spiritualised empire
and organisation which " named the name of Christ, but
whose form was the form of Caesar."   Its continuous and
comprehensive existence was the first axiom of truth.   By
this she demonstrated her correspondence with the Divine
Ideal ; nor was she disturbed in this self-complacency by
her own shortcomings, by the ideal yearning of the mystics,
or the angry outbursts of the discontented.

Of this clerical self-satisfaction, which demanded adjustment not progress, dialectics not metaphysics, Aristotle
was the natural prophet.   His system provided means for
accomplishing the impossible, " of uniting immanence and
transcendence, history and miracle, the immutability of
God and mutability, Idealism and Realism, reason and
authority." [1]   In the development of the conception of the
Church as a monarchy his influence was invaluable.   " If
churches always canonised their benefactors, he would
long ago have been at the head of the Roman calendar.
There were many schoolmen, but they all had one master,
and they built by his help, and to his honour, systems
that even he would have acknowledged to be encyclopaedic
and marvels of architectonic craft." [2]   Their aim was to
exhibit the unity in thought of reason and authority, of
the papal Church and its sacerdotal theology.   Thus the
Papacy and Scholasticism grew strong and decayed together.   The forces that dissolved the one disintegrated the
other, leaving behind the ponderous tomes in our libraries
which, like the tombstones of our cemeteries, speak of
departed reputations.

[1] Harnack, *H.D.* vi. p. 43.
[2] Fairbairn, *Christ in Modern Theology*, p. 119.

Q

Yet one reputation can never die. For the student of Church history it is all-important that he realise the vast significance of the teaching of the greatest of all Schoolmen— Thomas Aquinas (1225-1274), the glory of the Dominicans. The work of Albert the Great we can pass by. All that was valuable in it was given form and grace by his greatest pupil, who built carefully upon the foundations he had laid. The world-historical importance of Thomas Aquinas lies in his synthesis of Aristotle, Augustine, and the pseudo-Dionysius with the creed and practice of papal Rome. In Augustine, Rome had ever recognised the champion of her faith, though careful to crush those who, like Gottschalk, should exaggerate his predestinarian errors. But the formulae of Augustine were full of contradictions, and in the nine centuries since his death the Western Church had drifted away from some of his main tenets. A new synthesis was needed if the reasonableness of the current faith and practice should be maintained. In the pseudo-Dionysius the Western Church recognised the chief source of its mysticism, and in Thomas there is full emphasis of the value of a sane mysticism based upon communion with God. The extent of the mysticism of Thomas is seen in the exaggerated attempt of Denifle to show that Meister Eckhart owes everything to him. In Aristotle, as we have seen, we have the opponent of mysticism, the exponent of cold reason and formal logic. But the Aristotle of Aquinas is probably coloured by the Neoplatonism that had been introduced into it from the days of Alexander of Aphrodisias. Nor must we in this connection entirely overlook the influence of Maimonides and the Arabs.

In seventeen folio volumes Thomas undertook to eliminate difficulties and obtain a homogeneous creed. The result is " one of the most magnificent monuments of the human intellect, dwarfing all other bodies of theology into insignificance. Apart from its importance as the authoritative code of Latin Christianity, it is great as a work of

art." [1]   Harnack puts his finger on the cause of the success.
" Just as the perfect Gothic cathedral, from its exhibiting
what is really an organic style, expresses a single architectural thought, and subordinates all to this, so this
structure of thought, although all ecclesiastical doctrines
are faithfully taken account of, still proclaims the one
thought, that the soul has had its origin in God, and
returns to Him through Christ." [2]   Yet from the nature of
the case the new Augustine was not able to create a satisfactory unity ; the elements were too contradictory. But
one thing Aquinas did which needs no reversal. Hitherto
there had been no formal distinction between the domain
of philosophy and that of theology. Thomas laid down
a clear line between theology and philosophy, between
natural and revealed religion, and the province of reason
as regards both, which has remained in force among
thinkers of all creeds ever since. Philosophy passes from
the consideration of the creatures to God ; theology from
God to the creature.

Thomism has become the standard theology of the
Roman Church. The question, therefore, whether as a
system it is still valid brings in large considerations to
which we can here attempt no answer. But one thing is
clear : Thomism and Evolution are absolutely incompatible. Aquinas' future reputation cannot therefore but
be regarded as uncertain. To own this is only to emphasise
the real nature of his task. " The work which Aquinas
did for the Church of his day—the fusion of the highest
speculative thought of the time with its profoundest
spiritual convictions, the reconciliation of the new truths
of the present with the kernel of truth embodied in the
traditional creed—is a task which will have to be done again
and again so long as the human mind continues progressive,
and religion remains a vital force with it. It will have to

be done in a different spirit, by different methods, and with very different results from those of the *Summa*. But in one respect the work of Aquinas is built on the solid foundation upon which all such efforts must repose—the grand conviction that religion is rational and that reason is divine, and that all knowledge and all truth must be capable of harmonious adjustment." [1] It is characteristic both of the man and his work that when doubts and difficulties arose while he was writing, he laid all aside to seek enlightenment in prayer.

The theology of Thomas marks the hour of Rome's greatest triumph. After overcoming all other powers she annexed the human reason itself. With the death of Thomas we begin a new era in the history of thought. Henceforth in every movement there lurks, or seems to lurk, the struggle of reason and faith. The triumph of Thomas had been the triumph of a moderate Realism. Nominalism seemed silenced, but in the next generation it recovered its strength. But more important than the victory of a philosophical creed was the powerful dissolvent of all faith, or rather of the Thomist conceptions of faith, which the leaders in this reaction introduced into the schools. For Nominalism, by denying objective reality to general notions, leads, directly or indirectly, to the introduction of the experience of the senses, *i.e.* of inductive science, as the test of reality. But the full consequences of this tendency were not felt until after the discredit of Scholasticism in general. A prior result was an outburst of philosophic scepticism, the leader of which was the opponent of Thomas, the famous Franciscan John Duns Scotus.[2]

The fates have dealt hardly with the writings of this marvellous Scot. His interminable length and spider-like

[1] Rashdall, *Univs. in Middle Ages*, i. p. 367 ; cf. *supra*, p. 44.
[2] Born (?1274) probably at Duns in Berwick, died at Cologne 7th November 1308. In 1300 we find him at Oxford in a list of Franciscan friars presented for ordination. That he was ever at Merton is an impossible legend.

logic concentrated upon him the wrath of the New
Learning. Luther, who was brought up at a German
university where Nominalism reigned supreme, arrayed
against him the hatred of the Reformers. Tyndale and
others used his name as the synonym for a stupid, a meaning
which still cleaves to it. Colet could not speak of him with
patience, and caused Erasmus, who had been nurtured
on his subtleties in Paris, to abhor him also.[1] In 1535
Layton wrote to Thomas Cromwell : ' We have set Dunce
in Bocardo and have utterly banished him Oxford for ever.
He is now made a common servant to every man, fast nailed
upon posts in all houses of common easement.' The New
Learning had no sympathy with the fallen Schoolmen.
With the cry of *Vae Victis* it overwhelmed them all with
contempt, indifferent alike to their superhuman diligence,
their manifest desire to get at the bottom of things, their
high ideals—however inadequate the accomplishment—
of a science which should embrace all in one grand whole
within the fold of the Church.

Of the influence of Duns and the acuteness of his intellect
there can be no doubt. Though not himself a Nominalist,
no one did more to secure for Nominalism the triumph
which it won in the fifteenth century. The drift of his
teaching is also clear. In twelve volumes this remarkable
Scot destroyed by his criticism of Thomas the rational
grounds of faith, and therefore the validity of the whole
scholastic method. Reason, he held, relates solely to the
realm of the worldly and sensible ; Belief is a mere matter
of obedience to the unconditional will of God, or rather
of subjection to the authority of the Church. Thus he
shook confidence in the Augustinian conceptions of grace.
The Augustinian doctrine of sin was equally destroyed by
his reduction of morals to the arbitrary and unintelligent,
as we see in his statement that murder would be right if
commanded by God. The ease with which such arbitrary

---

[1] Seebohm, *Oxford Reformers*, pp. 102-112.

ethics could be changed into the doctrine that the end justifies the means, and that the Church's power of binding and loosing is equivalent to ' the good,' has probably led to the favour with which Duns has always been regarded by the Jesuits. Nor did Duns see that such unreality in sin could only result in the unreality of redemption, and of love. Though himself an ardent champion of the Roman creed, even in the extremer forms—Duns defended as a Franciscan the dogma of the Immaculate Conception, which Thomas the Dominican had refused to recognise—his criticism of the validity of the arguments put forward in defence of faith prepared the way for the coming rupture of the alliance between philosophy and theology. We see this rupture also in his emphasis of the independence of all secular sciences —a necessary step, we may remark, for their true development—and the independence of the world as over against God. He will not allow any place for reason in such a doctrine as immortality. His appeal to the sacred and inviolable authority of the Roman Church—he would not believe, he said, even the Gospels save on the witness of the Church—was a mere personal conviction, full use of which, however, was made by his later disciples in the development of papal autocracy. His destructive criticism bore fruit after he had passed away. In some minds it led to scepticism. With Duns we mark for Scholasticism the beginning of the end. In others we see its results in " the emotional prostration before authority, popularly called faith." [1] It is this last that gives him his prominence in the life and thought of the medieval world.

IV

As yet we have kept clear of the great struggle between Nominalists and Realists. But the later theological bearings of the controversy, especially in their connection with

[1] Rashdall, *Univs.* ii. p. 534 ; cf. Harnack, *H.D.* vi. p. 164.

the medieval doctrine of Transubstantiation, demand some notice. For in the fourteenth century there came about a curious inversion of the relations between Realism and Orthodoxy. Hitherto Nominalism had been branded by the Church as heretical. Its dangerous tendencies had become manifest, first in Roscelin, who, starting with the assumption that the individual alone is real, had driven the theologians to choose between an absolute unitarianism and a tritheistic explanation of the Trinity. This early outcome rather than any prescient discernment that, if the individual is the only real, Nominalism must end in the sensationalistic scepticism of Hume, had alarmed, not without reason, the fathers of the Church. For long years Realism and Orthodoxy were looked upon as almost synonymous. But when William of Ockham refounded Nominalism, its fortunes became curiously altered.

In many respects the Nominalism of Ockham is a philosophy of centuries later. Some of it might have come from the pen of Hobbes. Realism, he argued, in whatever form it may be expressed, was bound to lead to absurdities ; the universal exists only in the thinking mind, and is thus essentially a relation. Even in the mind of God universals do not exist, but are simply God's knowledge of singulars, which alone have reality. This modern doctrine of Conceptualism was followed up, as it is often followed up to-day, by the relegation of all knowledge which transcends mere experience to the sphere of faith. In this point, especially, we see the essential oneness, though for different causes, of Duns and Ockham. Thus Ockham, as Duns before him, heralds the dissolution of Scholasticism. The Thomist doctrine of the unity of reason and faith is giving place to a growing consciousness of their discrepancy.

The Nominalism of Ockham swept all before it. Four times between 1339 and 1347 were his writings proscribed by the university of Paris, and his doctrines condemned. At Avignon, as the catalogue of the papal library shows, Nominalist writers were not admitted. But from the first the condemnation was vain. By the time of the council of Constance, Nominalism was in the ascendant in Germany, and, though to a lesser extent, in France also. At Paris the great chancellor of the university, the celebrated John Gerson, was its open advocate. The effect of this revival of Nominalism was felt most disastrously, strange to say, by the Reformers of the day. Nominalism had become the ally of the extreme materialistic conceptions of Transubstantiation which the fifteenth century did so much to develop, and against which the Reformers protested.

To understand the growth of this alliance and its consequence we must glance at the later history of the doctrine of Transubstantiation. In the dispute of Lanfranc and Berengar, as in the previous discussion of the dogma, we see the union of Realism and Orthodoxy. For Lanfranc and others had tried to save the doctrine from its grosser forms by falling back upon the distinction of Realism between the substance—that impalpable but real universal which was held to be present in every particular included under it—and the accidents or sensible qualities which come into existence when the pure universal *clothes* itself with matter. The bread and wine, at the touch of that glorious Substance which takes possession of them, pass out of existence and are lost, leaving behind them nothing but shadowy appearances of themselves—accidents— though the underlying reality is something totally different.

But this explanation, though at first it seems to have satisfied the medieval Church, was soon discovered to be itself a mystery requiring explanation; for how can appearances possibly exist without anything that appears, how can the *noumenon* alone be changed while the *phenomena* remain? The subtle intellect of Thomas Aquinas answered the question by his conception of 'quantity,' or as we should now term it, *subsistence*, as distinct from *substance*. 'Quantity' remains in the

Eucharist " as the subject of form, colour, movement, taste, and all other phenomena observed in the visible and tangible Host. The reader will, of course, ask : ' Can ' quantity ' exist without anything that has quantity ? ' But the very question shows that he has not sufficiently understood the hypothesis. ' Quantity ' is not a mere abstraction, not a mere mode of being : it is quite different from extension, for it is that which makes extension, and may be defined as a force that extends material substance. . . . Thus after the words of consecration the substance of bread is no longer there, but quantity takes its place and upholds the other accidents naturally." [1] When asked what becomes of the bread after consecration, St. Thomas is in a difficulty ; he admits that the bread is nowhere, but denies that it is annihilated, since it is changed into Christ's body. According to Wyclif, opinions differed considerably as to what remained ; in the province of Canterbury the favourite idea was weight ; in the diocese of Lincoln, which then included Oxford, ' quantity ' ; in Wales and Ireland, quality.

The theology of Aquinas is hard to understand, and is not, we believe, an article *de fide*. There are, in fact, three other explanations of the dogma, all of which are allowed by the Roman Church, and between which a cautious infallibility takes care not to decide. The first of these is the theory of the great rival of Aquinas, John Duns Scotus.[2] Scotus takes refuge in his treatment of Transubstantiation, as he had done in his doctrine of Creation, of Incarnation, and of Atonement, in the omnipotence of God's arbitrary will. The miracle which the acute scepticism of Duns and Ockham destroyed must be accepted on the authority of the Church, or on the fiat of a Will above proof or reason. Duns held, therefore, that though the substance of the elements is absolutely annihilated, the accidents of the

---

[1] Dziewicke's Introduction to Wyclif's *De Apostasia*, p. xv.
[2] The other two theories fall without our period ; they are the Cartesian theory of the conservation of ' *surface*,' and the theory of purely subjective accidents.

bread and wine remain, maintained as verities by the unconditional will of God.

At this point we come across the alliance between Nominalism and the Church. In defence of its great central dogma of Transubstantiation the Church was prepared to abandon reason and fall back upon authority, the arbitrary fiat of God or of His vicar. Now the Nominalists who held that the universal was a mere *flatus vocis* found it easy to believe in the annihilation of the substance of the elements, a dogma that for the Realist was full of difficulties ; in fact, for the Realist, inasmuch as material essence is absolutely identical in all things, the destruction of the smallest substance implies the destruction of all the substance. So a strong party in the Church abandoned its ancient antagonism and embraced Nominalism. The consequences were remarkable. Hence arose, in fact, the strong opposition which Wyclif, the Realist, encountered at Oxford from Nominalists and Scotists, chiefly of the ' Southern nation,' who had set aside the cautious Thomist doctrine and substituted their arbitrary annihilations and recreations. For Wyclif was a Realist who held that even space and time had objective reality, to whom, also, the Scotist idea of the annihilation of anything real was absolutely inconceivable, ' the abomination of desolation,' a departure from early tradition and especially from that of St. Augustine ' not known before Lanfranc,' by means of which ' Antichrist subverts grammar, logic, and natural science.' But Wyclif's moral nature was too earnest to be content with these subtleties, and he soon passed to larger issues and controversies, into which, however, we cannot now follow him.[1]

From Oxford the struggle surged elsewhere, with consequences writ large in history. The modern man who looks upon all philosophy as the harmless, if useless, occupation

----

For Wyclif I may be allowed to refer to my work, *The Dawn of the Reformation*, vol. i., Wyclif.

or leisure of a few dreamers out of touch with a world of facts, can form little conception of the fury with which the rival schools attacked each other. In Prague the *odium philosophicum* descended into the streets. In the confused faction fights that raged there before the great migration of five hundred Germans in 1409 to found a new university at Leipzig, it would be difficult to say which hatred was uppermost, that of Czech against Teuton, of heretic against orthodox, or of Realist against Nominalist. The Germans had embraced Nominalism ; of itself a sufficient reason for the Czechs to become uncompromising Realists, and to welcome the works of so thorough-going a Realist as Wyclif. As a matter of fact, John Hus was condemned almost as much for being a Realist in philosophy, as his master Wyclif before him, as for being a heretic in theology ; his most bitter enemies were men who had at one time been Realists, but who to his disgust became what he calls ' Terminists,' *i.e.* Nominalists.[1] At Constance his opponents were the two leading Nominalists of Paris, both of them reformers in their way, Peter d'Ailli and John Gerson.

One result of the development of Nominalism must not be overlooked. Nominalism, as we have seen, tends to deny the rationality of the objects of faith, and so to lay the stress on the will of God. For both reasons, in their doctrine of salvation the Scotists laid stress upon the will of man : it is by the will and by its union with the will of God that man attains to eternal life. To the influence of this Scotist doctrine of the primacy of the undetermined will, with its distrust of reason, upon the Mysticism of the fifteenth century, we have already alluded. Insistence upon will is incompatible with the old Areopagite pantheism which had so long been the ban of Mysticism. A further development was reached when the question was asked how the will can

---

[1] For Hus and the bearings of the struggle I may refer to my *Dawn of the Reformation*, vol. ii., Age of Hus ; or to the *Letters of Hus*, ed. Workman and Pope. (London, 1904.)

be so influenced as to lead us to God. Such a question found its answer at the Reformation in the revival of the doctrine of grace. Strange to say, the return to Augustinian doctrine in the Middle Ages generally issued in the subordination of reason to the will, for Augustine had so presented the relation of the two " that no inner state, and no activity of thought, existed apart from the will." [1] The Scotist conception of the absolute arbitrariness of the Divine Will thus prepared the way for Calvin.

V

In many respects, both philosophical and theological, Aquinas had departed from the teaching of St. Augustine, in this following the Church of his day and the general drift of Scholasticism. The recognition of this gives us the key to later developments other than the scepticism of Duns. Even in St. Thomas's life there was a conservative reaction to the undiluted Augustinian doctrine. Bradwardine, Wyclif, Hus, followed by the Dutch thinkers Wesel, Wessel, and Pupper of Goch, began that return to Augustine and to the neglected Pauline side of his teaching which the Reformers of the sixteenth century completed in their different ways, not always, be it remarked, to the advantage of a spiritual Christianity. With Bradwardine (†1349) and Wyclif the belief in predestination is absolute. No man, not even a pope, ' wots whether he be of the Church, or whether he be a limb of the fiend.' Of this predestination the remorseless logic of Wyclif was not slow in drawing the conclusion. The Church, as the mystical body of the predestinated, is a unity that knows nothing of papal primacies and hierarchies, or of the ' sects ' of monks, friars, and priests ; nor can the salvation of the elect be conditioned by masses, indulgences, penance, or other devices of sacerdotalism.

[1] Harnack, *H.D.* v. p. 123 n

With Wyclif Scholasticism became played out. "The Aristotelian form refused to fit a matter for which it was never intended ; the matter of Christian theology refused to be forced into an alien form." [1] In its earlier years this great movement had brought a measure of deliverance to the human mind. Her energies were now exhausted, her vital force spent. If in common repute Scholasticism stands damned for ever, the cause must be found in the worse than uselessness of her latter days. Her services have been forgotten in the abiding memory of her servile follies and parrot repetitions. As an intellectual movement her work finished with Ockham, for Wyclif as a Schoolman does little more than gyrate on a well-beaten path, oftentimes concealing his track with clouds of dust. Great as is his importance as a politician and popular controversialist, his philosophical works, as modern research has shown, contain little that can claim to be original, with the partial exception of his political doctrine of ' dominion.' Theology, too, in the fourteenth century had become utterly sterile. No manuscript of the fathers dates from the century, with the exception of a few brief tracts. What the age knew of the past it was content to obtain from well-known Commonplace books, arranged alphabetically.

Scholasticism, in fact, with the work of Ockham became unreal. We see this unreality in the favourite idea of the later Schoolmen that there is a double truth. The result of such teaching is seen in the list, condemned at Paris in 1277, of two hundred and nineteen propositions, which Siger of Brabant and others maintained might be true in philosophy though false in theology. In these theses— some of which were revivals of Averroism—we find denials of the doctrines of the Trinity, the divinity of Christ, the immortality of the soul, and the resurrection of the dead, besides assertions of the eternity of matter, the uselessness of prayer, and the existence of fables in the Gospels. There

[1] Prof. Seth, "Scholasticism," in *Enc. Brit.* (9), xxi. p. 418.

was, in fact, nothing which the later Schoolmen were not prepared to fling into their syllogistic machine, as they mistook an endless output of wind for reality and truth. They held that it was open to debate whether continence was a virtue, or voluntary fornication a sin. Wyclif himself was real, especially in the width of his social sympathies ; his bitterest foes could not label him otherwise. Unfortunately in his philosophical outlook he was no prophet. He did not see that the soil that he ploughed was exhausted, and that neither his religious zeal nor his genius could produce from it any further harvest.

Thus the labours of the later Schoolmen are mere mental gymnastics without bearing on life ; researches which result in no discovery ; the worship of logic for logic's own sake ; elaboration of distinctions without difference ; endless conflicts in which the foes lose sight of each other in a more than Egyptian darkness and in labyrinths without issue. Whether the Schoolmen debated, as is popularly supposed, how many angels could dance on the point of a needle, we know not. But other questions of equal absurdity were common subjects of dispute. In 1614 Christopher Binder published at Tübingen his *Scholastica Theologia.* Its controversy with the Jesuits we may pass by. But the collection in his second chapter of the absurdities which formed the diet of the schools is still of value, provided always that the student remember that such absurdities were not the whole work of Scholasticism. We find among other matters of debate such questions as these : Whether the Angel of the Annunciation appeared as a serpent, as a deer, or in human form ; whether the body of Mary was exposed to the influence of the stars ; whether if man had not fallen all would have been males ; whether a dumb priest is able to consecrate ; or whether a baptism would be valid ' if you inverted the syllables and read Trispa, Liisfi, and Ctisan Tus Spiri,' or ' said Buff, Baff.'

We could pardon the failure of Scholasticism to discover

a primary law governing the whole realm of mind and matter, for in the nature of things success was impossible. We could pardon the self-assurance of her sons, for as yet there was no consciousness of the infinite range of science to impress humility on all but the ignorant. But the flippancy and unreality of the later Schoolmen are sins unto death, which brought the inevitable penalty in the overthrow of Scholasticism itself. We need not wonder at the enthusiasm with which, when the opportunity arose, Europe turned away from these barren puerilities to the New Learning with its revelation of the forgotten treasures of Hellas. With the incoming of a new intellectual method and outlook there came also of necessity a complete revolution in theological conceptions. But the consideration of these and of other later developments of Christian Thought lies outside our limits.

SELECT BIBLIOGRAPHY

[To give an adequate Bibliography of a subject that covers fifteen centuries of the history of Philosophy, Theology, and of the Church would demand a volume in itself. In the following pages a few only of the more accessible works are indicated. In all cases where good English authorities exist only slight reference is made to French or German writers. But in many matters we are still dependent on the guidance of foreign scholars.]

GENERAL AUTHORITIES

A. HARNACK, *Hist. of Dogma* (Eng. Tr. from 3rd German ed., 7 vols., 1905), a vast storehouse which can never be neglected. Harnack's *Outlines of the Hist. of Dogma* (1 vol., 1893) may be specially commended to the busy general reader.

The works of C. R. HAGENBACH (Eng. Tr., 1846-47, 1850); J. A. W. NEANDER (Eng. Tr., in 12 vols.); G. P. FISHER, *Hist. of Christian Doctrine* (2nd ed., 1897); W. G. T. SHEDD (2 vols., 1865); F. LOOFS, *Leitfaden z. Studium d. Dogmengeschichte* (Halle, 4th ed., 1906); A. V. G. ALLEN, *Continuity of Christian Thought* (new ed., 1895); J. F. BETHUNE-BAKER, *Introd. to Early Hist. of Christian Doctrine* (1903, four centuries only), all deserve study.

For the Middle Ages the following works should be added :—

R. L. POOLE, *Illustrations of the Hist. of Medieval Thought* (1884).

J. B. HAURÉAU, *Hist. de la Philosophie Scolastique* (2 vols., Paris, 1872-80).

C. V. PRANTL, *Gesch. d. Logik im Abendlande* (4 vols., Leipzig, 1855-70).

H. RASHDALL, *Universities of Europe in the Middle Ages* (3 vols., 1895).

R. D. HAMPDEN, *Scholastic Philosophy* (1837, 1848).

A. H. RITTER, *Christl. Philos.* (2 vols., Göttingen, 1858-59).

W. J. TOWNSEND, *Great Schoolmen* (1881). (A popular work.)

V. COUSIN, *Philosoph. Scolastique* (Paris, 1840).

M. DE WULF, *Hist. de la Philos. Médiévale* (2nd ed., Paris, 1905).

H. F. Reuter, *Gesch. d. relig. Aufklärung im Mittelalter* (2 vols., Berlin, 1875-77).

C. Werner, *Die Scholastik d. späteren Mittelalters* (4 vols., Vienna, 1881-87).

Reference should also be made to the many excellent articles in—

Smith-Wace, *Dictionary of Christian Biography* (4 vols.), and

H. Hastings, *Encyc. of Religion and Ethics* [3 vols. as yet (1911) published].

Special features are also treated at length in the following :—

R. L. Ottley, *The Doctrine of the Incarnation* (2 vols., 1896).

C. E. Luthardt, *Hist. of Christian Ethics* (1888).

W. E. H. Lecky, *Hist. of European Morals from Augustus to Charlemagne* (1869, many eds.).

J. A. Dorner, *Person of Christ* (Eng. Tr. by D. W. Simon, in 5 vols., 1861).

A. Harnack, *Chronologie der Altchrist. Litteratur* (2 vols., Leipzig, 1897, 1904).

F. Ueberweg, *Hist. of Philosophy* (Eng. Tr. by G. S. Morris, 2 vols., 1872).

CHAPTER I

§ I. F. J. A. Hort, *Clementine Recognitions* (1901), and *Judaistic Christianity* (1894).

H. Waitz, *Die Pseudoklementinen* (1904).

§ II. H. Kihn, *Theodore von Mopsuestia und Junilius Africanus als Exegeten* (Freiburg, 1880).

F. W. Farrar, *Hist. of Interpretation* (1886).

L. Diestel, *Gesch. des Alt. Test. in der Christl. Kirche* (Jena, 1869).

§ III. On the difficult subject of Apocalyptic and Eschatological Literature the student may be referred to the works of R. H. Charles, *Enoch* (1893), *Baruch* (1896), *Jubilees* (1895).

For the chaotic wilderness of the *Sibylline Oracles*, see the editions of C. Alexandre (Paris, 1841-56 ; 2nd ed., 1869, with excursuses omitted) ; or J. H. Friedlieb (1852) ; or, best of all, the new edition by F. Geffcken (Leipzig, 1902). See also E. Schürer, *Jewish People in the Time of Christ* (Eng. Tr., Edin. 1890, 5 vols.), vol. iii. (2), 271-92 ; R. A. Lipsius and M. Bonnet, *Acta Apostol. Apocrypha* (Leipzig, 1891, 3 vols.) ; W. Bousset, *Jüd. Apokalyptik* (1903) ; W. Wright, *Apocryphal Acts of Apostles* (2 vols., 1871).

The problem stated by A. Schweitzer, *Von Reimarus zu Wrede* (1906, Eng. Tr., 'The Quest of the Historical Jesus,' 1910), as to the Eschatological teaching of Christ, cannot be neglected.

Reference may also be made to H. N. Oxenham, *Catholic Eschatology and Universalism* (1876); R. H. Charles, *A Critical Hist. of the Doctrine of a Future Life in Israel and Christianity* (1879).

For the 'prophets' of the Church, see T. M. Lindsay, *Church and Ministry*, p. 90 ff.; A. V. G. Allen, *Christian Institutions* (1898), p. 54 ff.; E. C. Selwyn, *Christian Prophets* (1900).

§ IV. A. F. Gfrörer, *Philo u. d. Alexandrinische Theosophie* (Stuttgart, 1831, 1835).

A. F. Dähne, *Gesch. Darstellung d. jüdisch-alexand. Religions-Philosophie* (Halle, 1834).

E. Schürer, *Jewish People in the Time of Christ*, espec. v. 3.

J. Drummond, *Philo Judaeus* (2 vols., 1888).

T. Mozley, *The Word* (1889).

C. Siegfried, *Philo v. Alexandria* (Jena, 1875).

Also article s.v. in *Jewish Encyc.*, vol. x.

CHAPTER II

§§ I. and II. Good general works are the following:—

E. Caird, *Evolution of Theology in Greek Philosophers* (2 vols., 1904).

E. Hatch, *The Influence of Greek Ideas and Usages upon the Christian Church* (1888).

E. Zeller, *Stoics, Epicureans, and Sceptics* (tr. O. J. Reichel, 1880, 1892).

J. E. Erdmann, *Hist. of Philosophy* (Eng. Tr., S. F. Alleyne, 1883, 1890).

J. F. D. Maurice, *Moral and Metaphysical Philosophy* (1873).

T. R. Glover, *The Conflict of Religions in the Early Roman Empire* (3rd ed., 1909).

S. Dill, *Roman Soc. from Nero to Marcus Aurelius* (1904).

§ I. T. Whittaker, *Apollonius of Tyana* (1906).

G. R. S. Mead, *Apollonius of Tyana* (1901).

§ III. Of the older works on Gnosticism reference may be made to—

H. L. Mansel, *Gnostic Heresies* (1875, ed. Bishop Lightfoot).

R. A. Lipsius, *Der Gnosticismus* (Leipzig, 1860), and the series of articles by Lipsius in *D.C.B.*

A. Merx, *Bardesanes v. Edessa* (Halle, 1863).

F. C. Baur, *Die Christl. Gnosis* (Tübingen, 1835), and *Das Manichäische Religionssystem* (1831).

Of recent critical works—J. Kunze, *de hist. Gnostic. fontibus* (1894).

A. Harnack, *Altchrist. Lit.* i. 171 ff. ; ii. 533 ff.

G. R. S. Mead, *Fragments of a Faith Forgotten* (1900).

W. Bousset, *Hauptprobleme der Gnosis* (Göttingen, 1907).

The fragments of Gnostic writings have been edited in—

A. Hilgenfeld's *Ketzerges. d. Urchristentums* (Leipzig, 1884).

For the *Pistis-Sophia*, see *Texte u. Untersuch.* vii. 2, and viii. 1, 2 ; and the Eng. Tr. by G. R. S. Mead (1896).

§ IV. The most useful edition of the Apologists is that of J. C. Otto, *Corpus Apologetarum* (2nd ed., Jena, 1876).

§ V. F. J. A. Hort, *Six Lectures on the Ante-Nicene Fathers.*

B. F. Westcott, s.v. in *D.C.B.*, and in his *Religious Thought in the West* (1891), c. 5.

C. Bigg, *Christian Platonists of Alexandria.*

E. de Faye, *Clém. d'Alexandrie* (Paris, 1898).

J. Patrick, *The Apology of Origen in Reply to Celsus* (1892).

The standard edition of Clement is by O. Stählin (Leipzig, 1905 f.) ; of Origen by C. H. Lommatzsch (Berlin, 1831-48) ; Eng. Tr. by F. Crombie (1869-72).

§ VI. The works of Plotinus have been edited—Oxford, 1855 ; Leipzig, 1856.   There is an Eng. Tr. of select works by T. Taylor (1794), edited, with Notes, by G. R. S. Mead (1895).

CHAPTER III

§ III. H. M. Gwatkin, *Studies of Arianism* (1882, 1900) ; *Arian Controversy* (1896).

J. H. Newman, *Arians of Fourth Century* (1871), chiefly of controversial interest.

W. Bright, *The Age of the Fathers* (2 vols., 1903).

A. Robertson, *Selected Works of Athanasius translated into English* (Oxford, 1892).

E. C. S. Gibson, *Three Creeds* (1908).

C. A. Swainson, *Nicene and Apostles' Creed* (1875).

F. J. A. Hort, *Two Dissertations* (1876).

§ **IV.** G. W. Ommanney, *A Critical Dissertation on the Athanasian Creed* (1897).

 A. E. Burn, *The Athanasian Creed* (1896); *Introduction to the Creeds* (1890).

 J. A. Robinson, *The Athanasian Creed* (1905).

 J. Dräseke, *Apollinarios von Laodicea* (Leipzig, 1892), with appendix of remains.

 G. Voisin, *L'Apollinarisme* (Louvain, 1901).

 J. F. Bethune-Baker, *Nestorius and his Teachings* (1908).

 A. Thierry, *Nestorius and Eutychès* (Paris, 1878).

 F. Loofs, *Nestoriana, die Fragmente des Nestorius* (Halle, 1905).

 Nestorius, *Le Livre d'Héraclide de Damas, traduit en Français par F. Nau,* etc. (Paris, 1910).

CHAPTER IV

§ **II.** C. P. Caspari, *Quellen z. Gesch. des Taufsymbols* (Christiania, 1866-9, 1879).

 F. Kattenbusch, *Das Apostolische Symbol* (2 vols., 1894, 1900).

 A. C. McGiffert, *The Apostles' Creed* (1902).

 H. B. Swete, *The Apostles' Creed* (1894, 1899).

 T. Zahn, *Das Apostolische Symbolum* (1893).

§ **III.** G. N. Bonwetsch, *Gesch. d. Montanismus* (Erlangen, 1881; with full sources).

 A. Ritschl, *Die Entstehung d. altkathol. Kirche* (2nd ed., Bonn, 1857).

§ **IV.** For Tertullian, the most useful edition is that by F. Oehler (3 vols., Leipzig, 1854); best text by Reifferscheid, Wissowa, and Kroymann in *C.S.E.L.* (Vienna, 1890, 1906).

 J. A. Neander, *Antignosticus or Spirit of Tertullian* (tr. by Ryland, London, 1851).

 For Cyprian, best text by G. Hartel, *C.S.E.L.* (3 vols., Vienna, 1868-71).

 E. W. Benson, *Life and Times of Cyprian* (1898).

CHAPTER V

From the vast literature on St. Augustine we select :—

W. Cunningham, *St. Austin and his Place in the Hist. of Christian Thought* (1886).

C. Bindemann, *Der heil. Augustinus* (Greifswald, 1844-61, 3 vols.).

P. Schaff, *Life and Labours of St. Augustine* (1851).

H. A. Naville, *St. Augustin, étude sur le développement de sa pensée* (Geneva, 1872).

G. von Hertling, *Augustin* (Mainz, 1902).

H. F. REUTER, *Augustinische Studien* (Gotha, 1887).

F. RIBBECK, *Donatus and Augustinus* (Elberfeld, 1858).

A. HATZFELD, *St. Augustin* (6th ed., Paris, 1902).

S. ANGUS, *The Sources of the First Ten Books of Augustine's de Civitate Dei* (Princeton, 1906).

J. F. NOURRISSON, *Philos. de S. August.* (2 vols., Paris, 1866).

A. DORNER, *Augustinus* (Berlin, 1873).

For St. Augustine's writings the best edition is the new critical Vienna Corpus (*C.S.E.L.*), of which about 14 vols. have been published. There is an extensive Eng. Tr. in the Select Library of the Nicene Fathers. Of older editions, the best is the Benedictine (Paris, 1679-1700), reprinted in Migne, *P.L.* vols. xxxii.-xlvii., or by Gaume, 11 vols. (Paris, 1838).

The Anti-Pelagian treatises have been edited separately by Dr. Bright (Oxford, 1880).

CHAPTER VI

§ I. F. H. DUDDEN, *Gregory the Great: His Place in Hist. and Thought* (2 vols., 1905).

'J. BARMBY, *Gregory the Great* (1892).

§ II. H. C. LEA, *Hist. of Auricular Confession and Indulgences* (3 vols., Philadelphia, 1896).

(See also "Canon Law" in *Encyc. Brit.*, 11th ed.)

§ V. ALICE GARDNER, *Studies in John the Scot* (1900).

W. KAULICH, *Entwicklung der scholastischen Philosophie von J. Scotus Erigena bis Abälard* (Prag, 1863).

B. F. WESTCOTT in *Essays in Hist. of Christian Thought in the West* (1891).

J. HAVET, *Les Origines de S. Denis* (Paris, 1896).

H. O. TAYLOR, *Classical Heritage of the Middle Ages* (1903), for his later influence.

F. SEEBOHM, *Oxford Reformers* (3rd ed., 1896, pp. 60-78).

A. L. FROTHINGHAM, *Stephen bar Sudaili* (Leyden, 1886).

There is a complete edition of Erigena's works in Migne, *P.L.* cxxii.; of Dionysius in *P.G.* iii.-iv. There is an English version by J. Parker (London, 1894 and 1897).

CHAPTER VII

§ I. A. F. VISCHER, *Berengar. Turon. de sacra coena adv. Lanfranc.* (Berlin, 1834), and Lanfranc's works in Migne, *P.L.* vol. cl.

D. STONE, *Hist. of Doctrine of Holy Eucharist* (1909).

C. GORE, *Dissertations on Subjects connected with the Incarnation*, pp. 248-64 (1895).

§ III. J. M. Rigg, *Anselm of Canterbury* (1896).
G. C. Foley, *Anselm's Theory of the Atonement* (1909).
Ch. de Rémusat, *St. Anselme* (2nd ed., Paris, 1868).
Anselm's works are in Migne, *P.L.* clviii. and clix.

§ IV. E. Vacandard, *Vie de S. Bernard* (2 vols., Paris, 1895).
J. C. Morison, *St. Bernard* (1868 ; many later editions).
Bernard's works are in Migne, *P.L.* clxxxii.-v.

§ V. S. M. Deutsch, *Peter Abälard* (Leipzig, 1883).
Ch. de Rémusat, *Abélard* (2 vols., Paris, 1845).
E. Vacandard, *Abélard, sa lutte avec S. Bernard* (Paris, 1881).

Abailard's works are in Migne, *P.L.* clxxviii. (1855), but without the *Tractatus de Unitate et Trinitate,* first ed. by R. Stölzle (Freiburg, 1891).

CHAPTER VIII

For the Mystics in general see :—

W. R. Inge, *Christian Mysticism* (1899).
R. M. Jones, *Mystical Religion* (1909).
A. Jundt, *Hist. du panthéisme populaire au moyen âge* (Paris, 1875).
W. Preger, *Gesch. d. deutschen Mystik* (3 vols., Leipzig, 1874-93). F. Pfeiffer, *Deutsche Mystiker d. xiv. Jahrhund.* (New edition, 2 vols., Göttingen, 1906-7).
H. Joly, *Psychology of Saints* (Eng. Tr., 1898).
R. A. Vaughan, *Hours with the Mystics* (2 vols., 1856).
F. R. v. Hügel, *Mystical Element of Religion* (2 vols., 1909).
W. R. Inge, *Life, Light, and Love* (1904).
E. Gebhardt, *L'Italie Mystique* (3rd ed., 1899).

§ III. A. Lasson, *Meister Eckhart der Mystiker* (Berlin, 1868).
H. Delacroix, *Le Mysticisme spéculatif en Allemagne au xive siècle* (Paris, 1900).
K. Pearson in *Mind* (1886).
Josiah Royce, *Studies of Good and Evil* (New York, 1898).
A. Jundt, *Essai sur le mysticisme spéculatif de Eckhart* (Strassburg, 1871).

For Eckhart's German writings, see F. Pfeiffer, *Deutscher Mystiker,* vol. 2 (Leipzig, 1857), and for his Latin, H. Denifle in *Archiv. f. Litt. u. Kirchengesch.* (1886 and 1889).

§ IV. H. Denifle, *Der Gottesfreund im Oberland u. Nikolaus v. Basel* (Munich, 1870).
Charles Schmidt, *Nicolaus v. Basel* (Strassburg, 1875).
K. Rieder, *Der Gottesfreund vom Oberland* (Innsbruck, 1905).

A. Jundt, *Rulman Merswin et l'ami de Dieu de l'Oberland* (Paris, 1890).

H. Suso, *Life of the Blessed Henry Suso* (tr. by T. F. Knox, 1865).

S. Winkworth, *John Tauler* (1857).

A. W. Hutton, *The Inner Way, being Tauler's Sermons for Festivals* (n.d.).

J. P. Arthur, *The Founders of the New Devotion* (London, 1905) ; *Chronicle of Mount St. Agnes* (London, 1906).

S. Kettlewell, *Thomas à Kempis and the Brothers of the Common Life* (2 vols., 1882).

S. H. Gem, *Hidden Saints* (1907).

F. Cruise, *Thomas à Kempis* (1887).

M. Maeterlinck, *Ruysbroeck and the Mystics* (Eng. Tr., 1894).

CHAPTER IX

§ I. S. Riezler, *Die literarischen Widersacher der Päpste zur Zeit Ludwig des Baiers* (Leipzig, 1874).

The works of Marsiglio and Ockham are in Goldast, vol. 2 (Ed. Hanover, 1611 ; but vol. 3 in ed. 1621).

§ II. For Aristotle's conquest of the Schools the best source is—

H. Denifle, *Chartularium Univ. Paris.*, espec. vols. 2 and 3.

For Averroism, etc.—

P. F. Mandonnet, *Siger de Brabant et l'averroïsme latin* (Fribourg, 1899).

J. Müller, *Philos. and Theol. of Averroës* (Munich, 1859).

E. Renan, *Averroès et l'Averroïsme* (3rd ed., Paris, 1869).

T. J. de Boer, *The Hist. of Philos. in Islam* (1903).

Carra de Vaux, *Avicenne* (Paris, 1900) ; "Arabian Philosophy" in *Encyc. Brit.*, 11th ed.

§ III. E. Zeller, *Aristotle and the Earlier Peripatetics* (Eng. Tr., 2 vols., 1897).

C. Jourdain, *Philos. de Thomas d'Aquin* (2 vols., Paris, 1858).

J. Kleutgen, *Die Philos. der Vorzeit vertheidigt* (1878), and *Die Theol. der Vorzeit vertheidigt* (6 vols., Münster, 1867) ; *La Philos. scolastique exposée et défendue* (tr. C. Sierp, 4 vols., Paris, 1868-70).

C. Werner, *Thomas v. Aquino* (3 vols., 1858, 1889).

M. Liberatore, *On Universals* (tr. 1889).

INDEX